D0595722

The aim of the *Earth Quest* series is to examine and explain how shamanic principles can be applied in the journey towards self-discovery
– and beyond.

Each person's Earth quest is the search for meaning and purpose in their
life – it is the establishment of identity and the realization of inner potentials and individual responsibility.

Each book in the series examines aspects of a life science that is in harmony with the Earth and shows how each person can attune themselves to nature. Each book imparts knowledge of the Craft of Life.

Where Eagles Fly

For more than thirty years, **Kenneth Meadows** sought answers to some of life's most perplexing mysteries: Who am I? What am I? Why am I here? Where am I going? What is life's *purpose*? He explored the world's great religions and was offered *beliefs*. He considered the philosophies of great thinkers and gathered *opinions*. He examined the theories of materialistic science to find that most were based upon *assumptions*. His persistence brought him in touch with the simplicity of indigenous peoples whose wisdom had been passed on through oral traditions. He was directed to look not in the archives of learned institutions, but into the Book of Nature which reveals how the Universe *is* and that we humans are part of it and it is part of us. He found that by reconnecting with Nature we can make contact with our own Source and thereby find the answers we seek.

Kenneth, a Leeds University qualified teacher and former college lecturer and journalist, is the author of three books on contemporary shamanism – *Earth Medicine*, *The Medicine Way*, and *Shamanic Experience*.

E A R T H QUEST

Where
Eagles Fly

*A Shamanic Way
to Inner Wisdom*

KENNETH MEADOWS

ELEMENT

Shaftesbury, Dorset ● Rockport, Massachusetts
Brisbane, Queensland

First published in Great Britain in 1995 by
Element Books Ltd
Shaftesbury, Dorset

Published in the USA in 1995 by
Element, Inc.
42 Broadway, Rockport, MA 01966

Published in Australia in 1995 by
Element Books Ltd
for Jacaranda Wiley Ltd
33 Park Road, Milton, Brisbane, 4064

Cover illustration by Robert Hall
Cover design by Max Fairbrother
Design by Roger Lightfoot
Illustrations by David Woodroffe
Typeset by Footnote Graphics, Warminster, Wilts
Printed and bound in Great Britain by
Redwood Books Ltd, Trowbridge, Wiltshire

British Library Cataloguing in Publication
data available

Library of Congress Cataloging in Publication
data available

ISBN 1–85230–620–3

Contents

Experiences

Undertaken with respect, the Experiences presented in this book can only be beneficial. The author and publisher, however, can accept no responsibility for any undesirable effect that may result from the reader's own application of them without supervision.

This book is dedicated to the Great Being that is the Universe, and to all who seek the truth of their *own* being.

Through the Eagle's ability to fly higher than any other creature, and therefore closer to the Sun, it has been recognized throughout history as a symbol of spiritual insight and mental illumination. Among indigenous peoples, the Eagle has represented an ability to perceive realities other than the material and, from a higher perspective, understand the true nature of things. In ancient times, Greeks and Romans considered the Eagle to be the only bird that could reach beyond the temporal to find the Source of Light and Life – in the place *Where Eagles Fly*.

Kenneth Meadows

Acknowledgements

My grateful and abundant thanks to all who have contributed in some way to my preparation in the undertaking of writing this book, and without whom it could not have been completed.

To my Native American teachers who set me on a shamanic path to self-discovery.

To three Taoist monks who opened the way for me to obtain insight and understanding of the ancient Tao wisdom.

To Rod Nicholson who travelled halfway round the world to 're-mind' me of what I needed to know and to recognize the true nature of that which prevents us all from perceiving the real.

To Australian Gaye Wright for enabling me to bridge the divide between East and West, experience the relevance of Chi Dynamics, and allowing me to share its fundamental truths with others.

To Inoha, whose Polynesian spirituality parallels my path in many ways, for the 'confirmations' his insights brought.

To my principal mentor, Silver Bear, and Kili, whose Hawaiian name means 'Gentle Rain', for revealing to me the Water of Life.

To those of my Anglo-Saxon and European heritage who have taught me about my roots.

To my students of many nationalities who have shared in the extraordinary teachings and experiences which are related in this book, and who in so doing have taught me so much as I have watched their lives change and the beauty of their individual spirits come shining through.

To my helpers and guides in the Spiritual Ecology – the living beings in the Animal, Plant and Mineral Kingdoms – who share the wonders of this Earth environment with us yet are exploited so cruelly by humankind, still ignorant that they are our 'relatives' too.

And not least, to my wife, Beryl, my partner and companion along the way, and such a wonderful mentor.

How This Book Came to be Written

Words are tools that help us to convey our thoughts, ideas and concepts to others, and to describe what has been learned and experienced. In this very action of writing is sometimes conveyed an essence that is not of the mind, for it is not an activity of the intellect or of the imagination. That essence comes from the Spirit and is conveyed to the Spirit of the one who reads the words with an open heart.

That is how this book came to be written.

*Every experience in your life is an
opportunity to learn something new and to
make a change for your ultimate benefit.*

Preface

SHAMANICS IS ABOUT EXPERIENCING the extraordinary whilst living an ordinary life. Shamanics is a word I have coined to describe a way to extend your awareness to new and exciting levels of perception and enhance your life in many ways. Its application will improve your vitality, balance your emotions, release your hidden potentials, and stimulate your creativity. It will develop your inner powers by bringing you into harmony with the beneficent energies of Nature and the Cosmic forces of the Universe.

Shamanics is a modern-day expression of an ancient wisdom and is the essence of the understandings of benevolent shamans – the visionaries and 'Wise Ones' of all races and cultures – who guarded their knowledge of life's 'mysteries' within their own oral traditions until the time for their revealing, which is now. Shamanics lifts the veil from these 'hidden' truths and expresses them in the language of today so they may be readily understood, and it adapts them for modern times so that whoever responds to them in a positive way has an effective means of coming into balance with Nature and establishing harmony within themselves.

Shamanics is not a religion or a philosophy. There are no doctrines to be believed, no concepts to be argued, no spiritual leaders requiring allegiance, no hierarchy demanding obedience, no guru to be followed. It goes beyond the boundaries of belief, for it is a process of attaining a knowingness through the experience of doing. For the answers to some of life's most perplexing mysteries lie beyond the constraints imposed by historical, social and political conditioning every culture has

imposed upon itself. Shamanics identifies an essence that runs through them all, and by releasing it from a cultural, religious and racial context brings this essence to the threshold of the twenty-first century and makes it available for universal use and for the benefit of all. Nor is there any similarity with mind-training systems that are conditioned by method and require adherence to a strict disciplinary code in order to be effective. Shamanics is not an exercise of mind over matter, but a natural process that will enable you to take control of your own life through the Spirit and find meaning, purpose and fulfilment in it.

Shamanics is a way of connecting with Nature and what is inherent in your life, so it is not only the most natural but also the most practical of all metaphysical systems. Although Nature-based, it advocates not a *worshipping* but an *honouring* of Nature.

The true challenge of our time is to discover our own inner-most Self; to uncover who and what we truly are – a *Spirit* – and as a result make real sense of our lives. Shamanics helps us to a new understanding of what it is to be truly 'spiritual' – which is not the same as being religious. Being spiritual is an *ordinary* activity concerned with down-to-earth practicality and has nothing to do with belief! It is effective even in the midst of intense activity, so even a mundane chore like preparing a meal or washing up, shopping at a supermarket or fixing some-thing, can hold more spiritual value than repeating a prayer in a church, meditating in a home sanctuary, chanting a mantra in isolation, or performing a mystical ritual! For being spiritual is coming into harmony with our *natural* Self, which is com-posed of Spirit.

Shamanics is a bringing of the mind into unity with the heart and the Spirit. It is a way of life-enhancement in which Body, Mind, Soul and Spirit are all cultivated so they may function together in a dynamic and harmonious relationship to bring about a realization of our own *multi-dimensional* nature. It is a process that is *confirmable* through practical experience and *verifiable* by our own perceptions. Shamanics might, therefore, be regarded as a Science of the Spirit.

The revival of shamanism in recent years indicates a re-emergence of mankind's need to find attunement with Nature and the dormant powers that lie within, and to make sense of

our existence. But a regurgitation of the customs, rituals and traditions of indigenous peoples serves only to replace one conditioning with another and foster yet another cult. We cannot progress by endeavouring to live in the Past, but by learning from the Past we can ensure a better Future through the choices and decisions we make in the Present. A progression is required that goes beyond the limitations of tribal shamanism and cultural traditions if we are to be freed from the conditioning that has isolated us from Nature and prevents us from attaining a state in which a shift in awareness can take place and raise our nature to higher levels of consciousness.

Our civilization has developed in accordance with the principle that progress can be made only by the manipulation and exploitation of both natural forces and other beings. It is at the heart of political, economic, scientific and medical thinking – and, yes, religious attitudes, too. We have all been conditioned into supposing that we humans are essentially *thinking* beings, that we have a superiority over all other creatures and an ability to change our environment to suit ourselves through the power of *thought*. Yet it is not our *thoughts* that have brought about the difficulties we encounter personally and collectively, but our *choices*! Shamanics encourages a different approach – choosing to put our *hearts* into what we are doing. Making our choices in accordance with the promptings of the *Spirit* – and choices that work towards harmony rather than seeking to satisfy the *Ego* and its sense of self-interest. Self-interest is being concerned primarily with our own wants and desires. It indulges the Ego and is reflected in selfishness, inconsideration, indifference, ignorance, intolerance, greed, dogmatism and domination.

It is not, therefore, the ability to entertain thoughts and to create ideas that has the effect of bringing about changes in our lives and the lives of others. It is the ability to make *choices*. That is where the real power lies. Our own personal world as well as the 'greater' world around us is a direct result of choices that have been made. We are each and all experiencing the consequences of our individual and collective choices. And that is partly what life as a human being is about – learning through the experiences created by our own choices and those of others.

The turmoil and disharmony in the world 'out there' is a

consequence of choices that have been made with the mind to the exclusion of the Spirit. If we consider that the world is in a mess and the Earth is suffering from the pollution and exploitation inflicted upon it, that is because we *inside* are polluted and exploited by the conditioning imposed upon *us*. The world 'out there' is but a projection of the world within each and all of us. If we crave for a better world, we need to make the world *within* us a better place for our spiritual 'Self'. Transformation can only take place *outside* if we first change the *inside*. Changes 'out there' begin 'in here' – *within* ourselves. In Shamanics the changes we make are first with ourselves, for that is the natural way – the way of Nature. Change comes first from *within*. The natural state is towards harmony. Harmony may be defined as a combination of qualities that create beauty. When a native American shaman urged his people to 'Walk in Beauty' he was encouraging them to express their energies in natural ways that would bring beauty. Whatever word, thought, feeling, sound, sight, object or action creates harmony produces beauty, for harmony is what *creates* beauty. Beauty comes from within that which is intrinsically beautiful. Ugliness, disharmony and chaos derive from that which ignores what is natural and imposes its own conditioned beliefs, which work from the outside in.

The majority of us go through life not knowing what we want, but being entirely certain that whatever it is, we don't have it. Our appetite for material things has become insatiable, stimulated by a wasteful, throw-away society and encouraged by a consumer-oriented system that sublimely conditions us to get, get, get, whilst keeping us in a state of want, want, want. Those who have educated us, governed us and led us spiritually, have actually conditioned us into this state! The living Earth is now choked with pollution, ravaged by exploitation, racked with pain, shamed by mankind's folly, ignorance, greed and lust, and, unrecognized as the Mother she is, regarded only as an inanimate object to be 'used'.

A restoration of balance and a healing of the Earth can take place only by freeing ourselves from this conditioning and refusing to allow manipulators to have power over us, allowing our search for Truth to come from the *heart* in response to a cry from the *Soul*. The truth about our own spiritual nature is so valuable that no price can be put upon it. Offered free, it might

be discarded for appearing to have no value at all. Yet if a price were put upon it, no one would have the means to afford it. But what that light of truth reveals has to be applied in order that it may be understood. So it is not the truth itself that is so important, but its *understanding*. Understanding is the priceless treasure. **Only when Truth is understood can it be truly valued**.

You hold in your hands a distillation of an ancient wisdom that works towards harmony and beauty. It has been gathered from esoteric sources of the West, from Taoist teachings of the East, from mystical traditions of the Northern peoples, from the spirituality of American Indians and the understandings of Hawaiian kahunas, from Aborigine naturalism of the South, and from channellings from the inner planes of existence. Its purpose is to help to restore a missing dimension in human understanding – a knowledge of our true identity which, once 'lost', is now being regained to make possible a leap forward to a higher level of human consciousness.

The veil of secrecy that once shrouded such knowledge so that it was kept for the exclusive use of an élite few, is now being lifted, through the enlightenment of numbers of seemingly unconnected individuals and groups of all races and nationalities, so that it may be available to the many whose hearts and minds are open enough to receive it. This is an apparent fulfilment of an American Indian prophecy that a *Revealing* Time would come when the Sacred Fires, to which the Teachings were symbolically committed by tribal Elders before a holocaust overtook their peoples, would be rekindled in other lands, by peoples of different races and tongues, and by descendants of their oppressors. The story goes that the Revealing Time would come when the Earth itself was in torment and when greed and selfishness were rampant. That time of spiritual *revealing* is now!

Spiritual truth is so elusive that you cannot set out to prove it before applying it, as you would in conducting an experiment to test a scientific theory. The reason is that the truth you are setting out to 'prove' is not separate from you. It is not that you are an observer examining an experiment objectively from the *outside*. The truth is part of you and you are part of it. It is *inside*. You confirm the validity of a spiritual truth by the simple act of *doing* it!

So this book is laced not with tedious exercises but with exciting opportunities to discover your own truth through *Experiences*. All of these Experiences have been tried and tested by many others and found to be powerful, enlightening and effective. Shamanics, then, gets you off the never-ending track of *seeking* and onto a way that enables you to experience the joy of *finding*.

Finding harmony with Nature and with yourself.

Finding that the Earth is a living being who nurtures and sustains you, and by so doing experiencing a relationship with all living creatures that share the Earth's environment with you.

Finding ways of coming nearer to your Soul and integrating all aspects of yourself which are functioning at different levels of your existence.

Finding your original 'self', who is your True Self, and coming into an awareness of the composite 'You'.

Finding that Shamanics is not a 'system' or a 'method' but simply a *process* – a process of transformation that changes your perception of life so that each day can be entered into with the kind of joyful anticipation you perhaps once had as a child, when life was a great adventure of discovery.

Indeed, the application of Shamanics will turn every day of your life from now on into an exciting and wonder-full adventure; it will transform your awareness and extend the understanding you have of yourself!

Change itself is not painful. It is resistance to change that causes us pain.

1. Wonderful You

WE ARE EMBARKING, YOU AND I, on an exciting and fascinating adventure. An adventure of true discovery. An adventure whose mission is to find the purpose of our being and to discover *who* we are and *what* we are and *why* we are as we are. But before we begin, let us consider for a few minutes the *wonder* of our being. The wonder of being *You*!

You are alive and aware. You can see and hear and feel and taste and smell the reality around you. You can see sky and clouds, trees and grass and flowers. You can feel the wind in your hair and the gentle splash of rain on your face. You can hear the singing of birds and the rumble of traffic. You can reach out to touch a flower and feel the texture of its leaves and smell the sweet aroma of its petals. You can pick up a book and read words and sentences which have been written by someone you have never met, and by so doing can share that person's innermost thoughts. You can move to wherever you want to go because your body will respond automatically to that desire. Your body is a living miracle-machine that has only to be fuelled and watered and valeted in order to maintain itself. It is self-repairing – continually renewing itself.

THE PHYSICAL BODY

Your physical body is a complex structure populated by some 100 million million (100,000,000,000,000) individual cells. Cells, like individual people, have differences as well as similarities. They live together in 'families', and work in groups and

1

communities towards the well-being of the whole – just as human beings undertake work and family responsibilities and contribute to the good of the society in which they live.

Every microscopic cell is 'complete' in itself. It has its own fluidic 'body' contained within a porous 'skin'. It even experiences its own individual identity and is aware of its own individual function; yet with the myriad of other cells it is part of a greater body that houses *You*! Through the nucleus at its very centre, its functions are intelligently directed and controlled. This nucleus stores a vast amount of information through the DNA substance (deoxyribonucleic acid – a double helix of sugar-phosphate molecules that are cross-linked with nucleic acids), which carries with it a wave pattern containing the master plan for building your human form. Indeed, the nucleus of each cell contains enough information to replace your entire human body! Yet whatever its own purpose and specialist function may be, each cell acts only on the instructions contained within it to enable it to fulfil this purpose and to reproduce itself.

The soft tissues and flesh of the body are supported in their rightful place by a skeleton of bones which also protects the vital organs that constitute the body's control centres and support systems. All movement of the body is performed by muscles. Each one of these fibrous structures – there are more than 600 of them – is responsible for a specific function. Basically, there are two types. Voluntary muscles are those whose activity is instigated by the conscious and subconscious aspects of the mind, and these contract and relax in accordance with messages received from the central nervous system, the body's communications network. Involuntary muscles are those which perform their functions automatically at unconscious levels and are regulated by their own impulses. An involuntary muscle never rests. The monitoring system is the glands which work together with the nerves to ensure the harmonious functioning of the entire body.

Every cell is fuelled with nutrients and life-maintaining oxygen through a circulatory system of veins, arteries and capillaries which carry these substances in the bloodstream. Blood is pumped through this circulatory system by the pulsations of the heart – a muscular organ whose pumping action also ensures a return flow which carries waste products: carbon dioxide is distributed to the lungs where it can be expelled on

the outbreath, and toxics are conveyed to other organs that comprise the body's waste disposal system. The liver is the body's purification plant, and the kidneys and intestines deal with the disposal of waste products. The digestive system operates like a dis-assembly line. Foods taken into the mouth are broken down into their chemical components and the absorbable nutrients are extracted to keep the entire body functioning efficiently.

The body's sensory equipment is the means by which information about external surroundings can be conveyed to the brain for processing and analysing. Information about the physical world is carried on vibrations of light-energy to the retina of the eyes, which then send responses to the brain by means of electrical impulses. These messages are unscrambled and decoded instantly.

The skin is equipped with special sense receptors that register heat, cold, pain, pressure and touch, and these form another source of information about the physical realm as well as indicating likely danger.

The ears are organs for locating sounds: vibrations are deflected into a channel that leads to the eardrum and from here the impulses are transmitted to the brain. The human ear hears sounds with wave frequencies ranging from 16 to as many as 20,000 cycles a second.

A sense of smell enables the physical body to discern the aroma of physical substances that it encounters. This is performed through a chemical reaction between mucous and sensory receptors in the noise, which then sends nerve impulses to the brain for analysis. Receptors we call taste buds are located on different parts of the tongue and enable us to experience sensations of sweetness, bitterness, sourness and saltiness, and to gain pleasure from consuming the food we need for converting into energy. The tongue also conveys information about the temperature and texture of substances that enter the mouth, and saliva is a liquid that is produced to dissolve each mouthful of solid food.

A principal means of communication with other life forms is speech. The mouth channels the sounds produced by the movement of the vocal cords, located in the respiratory tract in the throat and activated by the breath, and by impulses its muscles receive from the brain.

The physical body has an automatic life-saving mechanism. Should danger threaten, a fuel-injection system squirts adrenalin into the bloodstream to 'supercharge' the muscles so they can move the body more speedily out of the path of danger, or strengthen them to face a possible threat to survival. At the same time the heart is triggered to beat more rapidly, and an automatic emotional response is activated, arousing anger or fear, so awareness is intensified to enable you to cope with the emergency.

The body not only constructs and maintains itself, regulates its own activities and repairs itself, but it has an inbuilt facility to reproduce itself and so ensure the continuation of its specification.

So take care of your body. Give it at least the same amount of attention that you devote to your car. Enjoy it. But don't become so 'attached' to it that you become possessed by it. Listen to what it has to tell you about itself, but don't confuse its messages with the mind's cravings, for then your Ego will take control and turn valeting into vanity. Respect your body. It is a bridge between your Soul and your mind. It is what enables you to be grounded and rooted. It is your friend and companion on your Earth Walk. Nurture it. Care for it. It is a friend, not an adversary, so why cause it distress?

THE MIND

As a piece of equipment for you to use, your physical body has certain similarities with the personal computer on which I am writing this book, though it is far more sophisticated and wonderful. The computer is personal because it belongs to me – its operator. In computer terminology, my physical body is the 'hardware' of my personal computer system. Before that hardware can function, it requires 'software' to tell it what to do. The software that is built into the personal computer that is your physical body is your mind, which programs the computer and enables it to function effectively as a physical entity. The software contains your thoughts and words and the imagery that enables your body to function in various ways.

So the 'you' that does the 'operating' and the looking, listening, feeling and responding, is not the physical body, in spite

of its many fine qualities and its multitude of functions. It is something else. Something that is not the physical body.

What, then, of the mind which provides you with the capacity to have control over your body's movements and to have thoughts that can analyse and make sense of the happenings taking place around you and help you to fashion your own perception of reality? Your mind enables you to retain a memory of what you experience and, through a bio-computer that is your brain, store it for instant recall when needed. The mind, then, is a functional centre of the physical body even though it is 'apart' from it.

The brain is a physical organ that is used to regulate and control all the voluntary and involuntary functions of the body. By electro-chemical impulses it both receives and transmits messages through the body's communications network and has the capacity to store, retrieve and process information. But unlike a man-made computer it can reprogram itself should you re-orient yourself on a new direction in life and dispose of certain past conditioning. It is the mind that enables you to devise plans for new things to do – and bring them into manifestation. The thoughts, ideas and beliefs you have are yours, but they are no more 'You' than your physical body. So 'You' are not your mind either. The mind is something 'You' use.

THE SOUL

So if you are not your body and you are not your mind, what are you? A Soul, perhaps? You may have been taught that you have a Soul, but you may not have been told what the Soul *is*! The reason may be that whoever told you about the Soul did not themselves understand what it is. The Soul, after all, is usually regarded as something to be *believed* rather than *known*, for physical science cannot describe, define or discover it because it is non-material, and mental science cannot relate to it either because it is not of the mind. It is regarded as being somehow 'spiritual' and therefore the province of the theologian. But even a theological description is vague, for the Soul is projected as a nebulous, spiritual 'something' that somehow embodies your moral, ethical and behavioural qualities, and

can even be in danger of becoming 'lost'. Since the majority of people, even those with strong religious convictions, are unaware of their own Soul, it would appear to have gone missing for the vast majority of humanity!

Shamanic understanding is much clearer. The Soul is a body of *light*. It is an inner light that is within you and within us all. Light is a form of energy and your Soul is your body of Light-energy and a centre of Life-energy. Although your Soul is integral to you and exists in approximately the same spatial location as your body, and interpenetrates it, it is not in the same 'place'; it exists in another plane or level of being-ness – in what we might call the Dimension of the Soul. In other words, your Soul, like your mind, is a non-physical aspect of your total Self, but with an entirely different function and purpose. It is not that your Soul is an extension of your physical being, but that your physical body is an emanation of your Soul. One reason why your Soul is not part of your conscious, everyday life is that you have confined it to the uncertainty of *belief* rather than experiencing it as a part of your ordinary *reality*. This is a pity, because the Soul is as *real* as the physical body. More 'real', in fact, because it has greater permanence.

We shall examine the nature of the Soul in some detail later, but for the moment let us regard it as something you have, like your body and your mind. It is still not 'You', but is closely identified with 'You'. So if 'You' are not your body and you are not your mind and you are not your Soul, what are you?

THE SPIRIT

You are a Spirit! Not a body with a Spirit, but the very opposite of what you may have been led to suppose – a Spirit with a physical body. A Spirit with a mind. A Spirit with a Soul. A composite being comprising body, mind, Soul and Spirit, yet 'disconnected' from this totality when the body and mind have no conscious contact with the Soul and Spirit, and when one or more is out of synchronization with the others.

What is the difference between the Soul and the Spirit? The Soul may be regarded as the 'Light' of the individual, whereas the Spirit is the 'Life' – the essential being. The Spirit is the

original being before the manifestation of form. The Soul is its functional centre – Mission Control. Each individual spirit has the gift of *freedom*. Freedom to *choose* to dedicate and generate its Life-energies towards harmony in mutual interdependence with other beings through respecting and perfecting individuality, or to direct energies for the purpose of expanding itself through the deprivation and control of others. Freedom to choose a direction of Harmony or one of Self-will. Harmony is a foundation that balances the evolution of the Whole with the development of the individual: as individual growth develops others are helped to grow also. Self-will is what disconnects a being from the rest, for it seeks self-enlargement at the expense of others and by so doing generates destructive energies such as greed, envy, jealousy, hatred, revenge, malice, lust, despair and confusion.

So the Real You is spiritual, with physical and mental outlets. That which is spiritual cannot be seen, but its presence can be felt and it is aware of its own existence. You, then, are a Spirit – aware of your own existence, of your own individual identity, of your own unique being-ness here on the Earth. A Spirit with a physical body through which it can experience the consequences of its own choices and actions and those of others, both individually and collectively. Life on Earth is thus a journey made by the Spirit through the 'slower' vibrations of physical reality in order to express itself through physical world experiences and so shape and fashion its own future – its own *destiny*.

Your Spirit is the essence of *you* and it is ageless. That is why, as you get older in Earth years, you feel no difference 'inside'. Although your physical body is in a constant state of change – from birth through infancy and childhood to adolescence, adulthood and maturity – and your appearance changes, you remain 'you'. You are aware of the same 'you' throughout all those years. So although your body changes, as do your thoughts and opinions, your identity remains the same. Age does not diminish 'you'. At sixty you are the same 'you' as you were at sixteen. You are always 'you' and always will be because the purpose of Life is to thrive and endure – that is, to grow *naturally* (organically) – in a continuous process of educating, cultivating and perfecting the Spirit.

Your life thus has purpose. There is purpose in your be-ing.

You are in existence not through an 'accident' of birth but to fulfil that purpose – a reason for being *you*. Wonderful, wonder-ful *you*!

We are each like a frog on a lily pond with the freedom to move in any direction. By choosing which lily leaf to land on next, we determine our own destiny.

2. The Energic Body

YOUR PHYSICAL BODY IS SURROUNDED by and immersed in a force field of energy that follows the contours of the body and, although it might be likened to a shadow, is like a 'twin'. This twin body, although invisible, may be perceived by someone who is sensitive and whose vision extends beyond the vibratory range of normal eyesight, as a bluish, vapour-like luminescence which some psychic people call 'etheric'. I prefer to call it the *Energic* Body because it energizes and 'moulds' the physical. It is the densest of our subtle bodies for it is the one closest to the physical, extending just beyond the surface of the skin, and comprises the first band or layer of an auric cocoon which surrounds us. This Energic Body, though approximately the same shape as the physical, is not only an extension but also a 'mould', for it enables the physical body to maintain its shape and form. It energizes the physical body by distributing vitalizing power that charges it with a dynamism and without which it would simply wither and die. We will examine the nature of this dynamic power in Chapter 7.

The Energic Body may be regarded as an intermediate body between physical and non-physical realities. Its purpose is to serve as a transformer of finer and more subtle non-physical energies. Although it cannot ordinarily be seen with the physical eyes it can be experienced through sensation, just as sensation is a means by which we experience our physical body.

As we have gathered in Chapter 1, the physical body is a physiological system whose functions of maintenance are carried out largely instinctively. Each part interacts with and supports all the others in a delicately-balanced holistic structure.

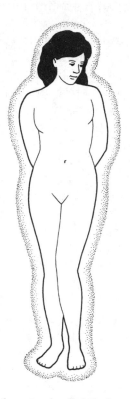

Figure 1. The Energic Body extends slightly beyond the physical body and interpenetrates it. It moulds and shapes the physical body and retains its approximate form.

The digestive system, for instance, absorbs and breaks down the food we eat and eliminates what is not needed. The circulatory system transports the nourishment that is obtained to all areas of the body where it can be used as energy to perform work. The nerves are the body's communications network which relays messages and co-ordinates information. And so on. The Energic Body provides the physical body with access to higher-frequency energies, and in serving as a transformer, absorbs and converts these higher energies into slower-frequency levels that enable them to be compatible with physical energies and, like the digestive system, it eliminates and expels what is not assimilated.

Knowledge of the Energic Body is vitally important because

it is the means by which illumination becomes possible through the circulation of 'inner' Light, and personal empowerment becomes enhanced through nourishment of the inner nature. 'Illumination' is that which enables us to 'see' more clearly with 'inner' eyes, and is a process that affects the intellect also.

The condition of the Energic Body has a powerful effect, therefore, on the physical body, and any intrusion, disharmony, congestion or malfunctioning in any area of its energy-field will manifest sooner or later in an associated part of the physical body. Similarly, any ailment or injury suffered by the physical body will cause an associated leak of energy from the Energic Body. Preventative medicine is mostly a treatment of the Energic Body.

THE CHAKRAS

Subtle higher energies are drawn into the Energic Body through a system of whirling, wheel-like vortexes arranged in a vertical column down its centre. These spinning, spiralling discs have become more generally known as 'chakras'. In the Sanskrit language of ancient India, the word *chakrum* meant 'spiralling wheel', although a chakra's in-pulling movement is more akin to a whirlpool than a revolving disc. Chakras, however, are more than energy-centres; they are also openings to levels of awareness. The initiation rites which marked a neophyte's passage through a 'gateway' in Western esoteric 'mystery' school traditions were, indeed, attempts to gain access through the chakras to other levels of awareness that might ultimately lead to attainment as Seer or Adept.

There are seven major chakras listed in the teachings of both the Hindu Hatha Yoga system and Buddhist tradition, from which Western understanding of them has been derived. There are seven because the chakras were originally related astrologically to the energies of seven known planets to which they are in attunement – Saturn, Jupiter, Mars, Venus, Mercury, the Sun (which is really a star) and the Moon (which is really a satellite). Although 'true', these traditional systems are incomplete today for, with the discovery of Uranus, Neptune, and Pluto, three more chakras were activated as human beings became exposed to a wider range of cosmic energies which had

not previously been available. For instance, an 'additional' chakra, situated between the ankles, is related to movement, and rapid movement is very much a feature of modern living. Similarly, a primary function of a chakra at the base of the brain is related to power, and today the average person has awesome power at his or her fingertips with the availability of computer technology; instant communication through television, radio and telecommunications; and sophisticated household gadgetry powered by energies beyond the imagination of people living even a century ago. The root chakra beneath the feet is primarily concerned with nurturing. People of modern industrialized nations are more compassionate and considerate of human life than was the populace of ancient cultures under Chaldean influence, as is evidenced by responses to famine and other human tragedies in less advanced countries.

These three 'new' chakras had once functioned in human beings during the legendary civilizations of Atlantis and Mu, but became dormant following a shift in the Earth's orbit of the Sun and a change in the Earth's polar axis; this had a catastrophic effect on the ecology and brought about changes in land formations as whole continents disappeared under tidal floods and new mountain ranges were pushed up. Nothing of the technology of these prehistoric civilizations survived, but some of the knowledge was encapsulated by the comparatively few survivors, in myths and legends and rituals and ceremonies which they passed down to succeeding generations through the oral teachings of shamans and which became incorporated also in religious concepts and mystical traditions. It is only during the last hundred years or so that the three 'dormant' chakras have begun to function again in human beings in general.

In understanding the function of all ten chakras it is important to realize that they are not situated in the physical body, and this is why they cannot be discovered by dissection or removed by surgery. They are located in the Energic Body and may be considered as vital 'organs' of that body. Their placing in areas of the physical body is only an *indication* of their location in relation to the physical body, though some take this indication as a literal fact. They are in that spatial *location* but not in that physical *place*!

Two of the ten chakras – one located just above the head and the other beneath the soles of the feet – serve also as

polarities, for they are the 'terminals' that connect the cosmic with the material, 'Heaven' with 'Earth'. The one above the head is widely known as the Crown chakra because, like a crown, it is 'worn' *on* the head. The one beneath the feet I prefer to call the Root chakra because it is the one that actually *roots* us to the Earth and provides a sense of 'grounding'. The other eight chakras are positioned in an octave – the structure of cycles of eight – in accordance with a universal Law of Harmonics which is fundamental to Medicine Wheel teachings of American Indians and the eight-spoked mandala of Eastern and Western mystical traditions.

Currents of energy from the Cosmos – from the Sun, and also from the Moon, stars and planets – are drawn into the chakras in wave patterns through vertical strands in the Energic Body. These fine columns are sometimes referred to by the name they were known by in ancient India – *nadis*. The main nadi connects the chakra at the base of the spine with the one at the brow, and also with the one beneath the soles of the feet. The two other nadi channels – one carrying a positive, the other a negative current – entwine the main nadi and cross and re-cross in figure of eight patterns around the rotating chakras.

In this way the currents of energy alternate and each of the power centres from the Base to the Brow rotates in the opposite direction to the one immediately above or below it. The chakras supply subtle energies to the physical body and its vital organs. Indeed, the endocrine system may be considered the physical extension of the chakras, and the parasympathetic nervous system an extension of the nadis.

The chakras are positioned in the Energic Body where different levels of your Total Self meet or merge, so they are indicators, too, of different layers of your being. An understanding of each chakra's nature and purpose will thus help you to better understand its functioning in regard to these different 'layers'. Let us now examine briefly the nature and purpose of each major chakra and how it relates to physical reality.

Root Chakra

The Root chakra is located beneath the soles of the feet. Its purpose is to connect and root you to the Earth. It is a reminder that you are a child of the Earth, nourished and nurtured by

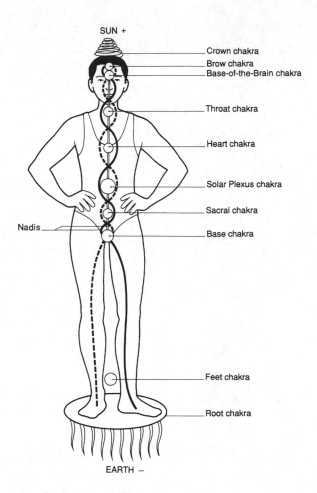

SUN +
Crown chakra
Brow chakra
Base-of-the-Brain chakra
Throat chakra
Heart chakra
Solar Plexus chakra
Sacral chakra
Nadis
Base chakra
Feet chakra
Root chakra
EARTH −

Figure 2. An indication of the wave pattern of energy flow through the nadi channels or pathways, and the alternation of the currents. The positive charge or Yang polarity is from above (Sun), and the negative charge or Yin polarity is from below (Earth).

Mother Earth and by the heritage of your primal past. It keeps you 'grounded' in practical reality, for that is where your 'spirituality' is expressed – through your physicality, your mortality. It is thus concerned with the qualities of stability and support, with growing and developing in an organic way – that is, naturally, *Nature's* way. Without the effective functioning of the Root chakra we are impractical, unstable and lacking

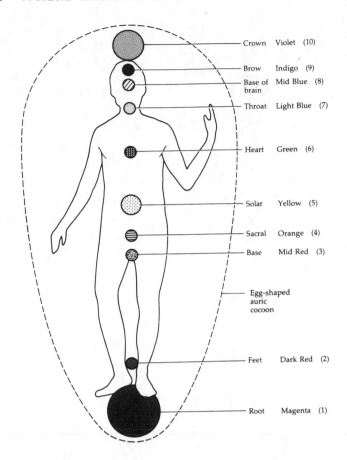

Figure 3. The location of the ten chakras in relation to the physical body

in a firm foundation. The colloquialism about 'not having our feet on the ground' is a way of indicating that we are not allowing our Root chakra to anchor us to the Earth adequately. We become unbalanced by living our lives too much in the mind. There is much truth in another colloquialism that says one can be very spiritual, very religious, but of no Earthly good! The functional significance of the Root chakra is rooting, grounding and nurturing.

Feet Chakra

The Feet chakra is located in the area of the ankles. Its primary function is mobility – balanced movement – so you are enabled

to explore the physical 'layer' of your being with freedom whilst being 'connected' to the Earth. It enables your life to be not just an Earth 'Walk' but more of a 'Dance' – a choreography of energy-movement to bring you joyfulness.

Base Chakra

The Base chakra, located at the bottom of the spine between the anus and the genitals, is associated with the downward force of gravity and with solidity. It is supportive because, in relation to the physical body, it is situated in the area that supports and upholds the structure above it when we are seated. The Base chakra is associated with the bones and the densest flesh, such as the muscles, and the large intestine through which pass the solids the body is in the process of eliminating. It manifests in the physical body as the adrenal glands which cap the kidneys and pump adrenalin into the bloodstream when the physical body is in need of a super-charge of energy to face a particular challenge or a threat to its survival. So this chakra is very much concerned with tangible existence, with material needs, and with the survival instinct. It energizes the sciatic nerve, the largest nerve in the body, which runs down each thigh and into the foot and so connects the whole nervous system with the Earth. The functional significance of the Base chakra is foundation and elimination. Obesity, constipation, spinal problems, and illnesses such as anorexia nervosa and sciatica, are indications of a malfunctioning of this chakra.

Sacral Chakra

The Sacral chakra is located in the abdomen area just below the navel and externalizes as the gonads – the ovaries or testicles. It is thus a centre of reproduction and motivation. The Sacral chakra affects the liquid functions of the physical body – circulation, urination and reproduction – and is associated with the emotions and especially the desires, passions, pleasures and 'gut' feelings. Our desires put us in touch with our needs and generate the motivation that enables change and expansion to

take place. Passion is an intensity of expression, and pleasure is a joyful experience of one's aliveness. Strange, isn't it, that many of us have been subject to a religious conditioning that relates pleasure with evil, that for centuries has denigrated women as temptresses, regards desire as an impulse that should be repressed and physical life as an existence that should be suffered and endured rather than enjoyed? It is conditioning of this kind that has denied so many human beings the experience of their most subtle and delicate energies, cut them off from access to their wholeness, and alienated them from Nature and the Earth. The functional significance of the Sacral chakra is motivation and re-creation. Impotence, frigidity, circulatory problems, and kidney and bladder troubles are indications of a malfunctioning of this chakra.

Solar Plexus Chakra

The Solar Plexus chakra is situated between the navel and the division of the ribs, and externalizes in the pancreas. It regulates the metabolism of the physical body. Its functional significance relates to control and proper growth and development. It is sometimes referred to as the 'fiery' chakra because it is regarded as the Sun centre of the physical body. It is associated with a fiery power that ignites action, generates personal empowerment and that feeling of wanting to 'get up and go'. It thus radiates transmutation. The Solar Plexus chakra is concerned with the direction and use of energies, for that is what power is – the direction and employment of energy. Action demands responsibility – responsibility for the consequences of what is initiated. Digestive disorders, ulcers and diabetes are physical results of a malfunctioning of the Solar Plexus chakra.

Heart Chakra

The Heart chakra is located in the centre of the chest and externalizes as the thymus gland. It is associated with love and compassion because the Heart chakra is where the Binding Force is at its strongest. The Binding Force is one of the Four Great Powers of the Universe – the other three are Life, Light

and Law. The Binding Force is the power that merges, harmonizes and bonds. It is also a power that seeks to combine the qualities of the Spirit descending from Above with those of matter ascending from Below. I must emphasize that the qualities of the Force are of a bonding nature that is without limitation or constraint. And that is what Love is. A merging of energies. A being in harmony with whatever or whoever is being loved. True Love is unconditional for it makes no demands; it seeks not to possess or control but rather to come into harmony with others.

The Heart chakra is concerned with relationships and with equilibrium – balancing input with output; activating, refreshing and nurturing every part lovingly. So the functional significance of the Heart chakra is love and compassion. Lung problems, asthma, high blood pressure and heart conditions are indications of a malfunctioning of this chakra.

Throat Chakra

The Throat chakra is positioned at the centre of the neck and externalizes as the thyroid gland. It is concerned with communication – the transmission and receiving of information. Information comes to you as bundles of energy-patterns which require to be interpreted and given meaning by the mind. The Throat chakra is a sound centre – sending and receiving vibrations – so it is concerned with extending your connectedness. It is associated with the neck, shoulders, arms, hands and ears – all parts of the physical body involved in communication and expression, which is this chakra's functional significance. Sore throats, colds, stiff necks and poor hearing are indicators of a malfunctioning.

Base-of-the-Brain Chakra

The Base-of-the-Brain chakra is situated in the centre of the head roughly in line with the bridge of the nose. It externalizes as the pineal gland – the body 'clock' – which is situated at the base of the brain and approximately level with the bridge of the nose. The Base-of-the-Brain chakra might be regarded as

the Chakra of Light because it regulates the function that enables the mind to 'see'. In other words, it activates the mind's 'eye'. Although most of the information that comes to you from the outside world is through the visual sense of sight, it is not the eyes that do the 'see-ing'. They discern only vibrating impulses emitted by light rays reflected by objects, and the spaces around and between them. These are impressed upon the retina of the eyes which, through the optic nerves, convey those impulses to the brain which then decodes them into meaningful patterns. The Base-of-the-Brain chakra governs access to internal information retrieval systems. It 'stores' shapes and patterns which have previously been experienced and enables patterns of what is wilfully image-d to be projected onto the screen of the mind as image-ination. So it may be regarded as the chakra of the imagination and a seat of empowerment that enables the 'not possible' to become possible. Eye troubles indicate a malfunctioning of this chakra.

Brow Chakra

The Brow chakra, situated just behind the forehead and on a level with the eyebrows, externalizes as the pituitary gland – the conductor of the glandular system – which indicates why this chakra was sometimes referred to as the 'Controller'. This gland is situated in the brain just above the roof of the mouth near the soft palate. The Brow chakra might be described as an 'organ' of intuitiveness and perception; but whereas the Base-of-the-Brain chakra is related to insight, the Brow chakra is related to *intention*, which is what transmits subtle energies and controls activity, and to perception, which is an ability to obtain meaning from what is observed. Uncertainty, confusion and indecisiveness are indications that this chakra is not functioning adequately.

Crown Chakra

The chakra that 'crowns' the entire chakra system and is situated on top of the head influences the pituitary gland because it is concerned with the 'higher' purpose and direction of life –

the *Soul's* purpose – the imprint of which is gained from the Soul with which it is connected. This chakra is sometimes referred to as 'the Thousand-petalled Lotus' because it appears to rise up as if from the 'mud' of matter to blossom out to the dimensions 'Above', thus opening up infinite possibilities. Depression, boredom and apathy are indications that the Crown chakra is malfunctioning.

The 'Third Eye'

When the Crown chakra at the top of the head and the Brow and Base-of-the-Brain chakras begin to function in unison, the vortex of energy that is formed develops as another organ of perception – the so-called 'Third Eye' – which was symbolized anciently as an eye in a triangle.

Although it is associated with the pineal and pituitary glands as well as these three chakras, the Third Eye is none of these. It is an organ of the Energic Body that is activated when the physical body comes into harmony with the subtle bodies and a level of integration takes place between them. Some people call this 'spiritual development', but it is more of a holistic development because it involves the physical, mental, emotional and spiritual aspects of the total being. Once activated, the Third Eye empowers us with a sense of 'super' sight, enabling us to 'see' into dimensions of awareness other than 'ordinary' physical reality and the mental ecology of our own mind.

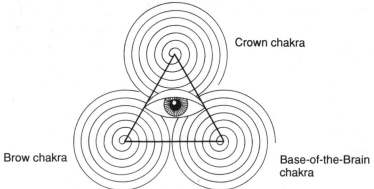

Figure 4. The Third Eye is in the vortex created by the interplay of the Crown, Brow and Base-of-the-Brain chakras when the physical body comes into harmony with the subtle bodies of the human being and a level of integration takes place that enables this organ of perception to develop.

Be wary of anyone who offers to 'adjust' your Third Eye. The Third Eye develops naturally in accordance with the integration that is taking place within at multi-dimensional levels. Whilst its development may be encouraged in many ways, it should by no means be forced. External 'adjustment', however well-meaning, can have the effect of obscuring the developing inner vision and, indeed, distorting it or preventing further development. In certain cases it can be a means of aligning the perception with that of the manipulator – in other words, of exerting control or influence!

Chakra Malfunction

The chakras are flexible power-centres which function like valves and pulsate as they open and close to draw in energy and eliminate what is not wanted. A chakra malfunctions if it becomes congested – perhaps as the result of a shock or trauma suffered by the individual, by some adverse life experience, or simply by emotional stress. In this case the energy-flow is diminished and there is a consequent loss of vitality to the corresponding area of the physical body. A chakra can also malfunction if its valve-like function is impeded in any way. If the chakra remains open the individual becomes vulnerable to all sorts of external influences and to manipulation by others. Today, drug and alcohol abuse are the principal causes of a chakra remaining open after it has been unnaturally opened up, with, as a consequence, the individual suffering loss of control.

A congested chakra can be cleared through simple breathing techniques combined with dynamic movements which serve to normalize the flow of subtle energies. These will be explained in later chapters. A resolving of the crisis or trauma at the root of the malfunctioning, or an ending of an abuse, will enable the chakra to regain its normal function naturally. There are a number of therapies which can help to restore harmony to the chakras gently and naturally.

Colours Associated with the Chakras

The chakra system of the Hindu and Buddhist traditions and the meridian system of the Chinese Taoists are not, however,

different perceptions of the same thing. The meridians are essentially the distributors of *Life*-energy, and the chakras of *Light*-energy. This is why colours are associated with the chakras. A current of pure Light is drawn into the human energy-system through the Crown chakra and the pineal gland and, as it descends to the Brow chakra, the pituitary gland with which that chakra is associated, acts as a prism and refracts the Light into a spectrum of colours, or qualities, which are distributed down through the other chakras to be utilized. The colours become progressively more dense in the descent. So what was white as it entered the Crown above the head becomes black at the Root beneath the feet. This current of Light might be likened to the main power source of an electricity generating station, with the chakras as the distribution centres. The current, which is then absorbent, returns upwards, and the output of energy as it does so is extended outwards into the energy-field that is commonly referred to as the Aura.

The chakras also indicate levels of awareness and these are also associated with Light; the colours at the brighter end of the spectrum expressing movement to a higher state of awareness and of greater illumination and enlightenment. The colour associated with a chakra is not necessarily a 'pure' colour, but one colour predominates at that particular level, giving an indication of the energy-frequency that is being transmitted and the quality of consciousness seeking expression. Thus consciousness itself is a quality of energy, and different states of awareness are associated with different energy-levels. The basic colours associated with the chakras, according to this understanding, are:

Crown	White
Brow	Violet
Base-of-the-Brain	Indigo
Throat	Blue
Heart	Green
Solar Plexus	Yellow
Sacral	Orange
Base	Red
Feet	Magenta
Root	Black

Meridians

The meridians to which I have referred are thread-like routes along which flows the vitalizing essence of the Life Force that sustains and operates all the life functions of the physical body. According to Taoist understanding, there are twelve pairs of primary meridians, each of which connects and flows through a vital organ, supplying it with vital essence. Depletion of this essence through the meridians, and of Light through the chakras, can be caused by stress and anxiety, by destructive emotions such as hatred, jealousy and envy, by continuous frustration

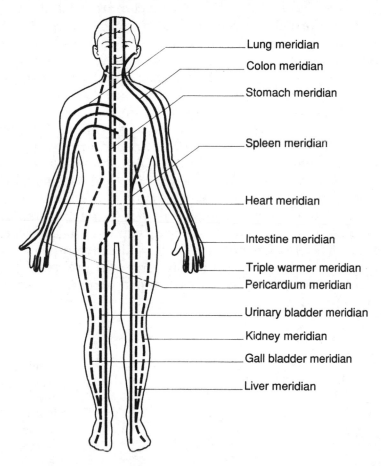

Figure 5. The twelve primary meridians, each of which flows through a vital organ of the physical body, supplying it with the essence of the Life Force

and feelings that are suppressed, and by a negative attitude or conditioning.

WORKING WITH THE ENERGIC BODY

The explanation of the chakras I have given here differs to some extent from the 'traditional' sources on which most past teaching has been based. But this does not imply that it is contrary – it is merely a different facet of a fundamental truth. In the past much of the teaching that was imparted was incomplete. An inner core was withheld and kept secret, given only to a select few who had to demonstrate by persistent effort and the fruits of their endeavours that they were ready to receive it.

Traditional teachings have usually contained three principal methods of working with the chakras for the purpose of spiritual development and life-enhancement – breath control, visualization and meditation. Breath-control techniques are a means of wilfully directing a rhythmic flow of subtle energy through the chakras. A 'hidden' purpose was to clarify and discipline the intent – which shamanically is the means by which subtle energy can be directed and controlled. Visualization was taught as a means of 'thinking' in pictures and of purposefully guiding the flow of thoughts. The underlying purpose was to acquire a way of functioning at subconscious levels whilst remaining fully alert and in control of the Will, for at this level of awareness the 'language' is not one of words but of images and impressions. Meditation techniques were taught as a means of controlling the flow of thoughts in order to attain a state of tranquil attentiveness in which one could be aware of every thought and feeling in an attitude of objective detachment – that is, selflessly. It was a way of becoming self-aware without the selfish regard of the Ego. Its 'hidden' purpose was a mind-oriented means of being oneself – of experiencing being *Spirit*! Of enjoying oneself! The *pleasure* of you being you and me being me!

The mind thus has an influence on the Energic Body. Positive thoughts have a generally beneficial effect because they uphold the harmonics within the Energic Body, whereas negative thoughts make disharmonious chords in the wave pattern

of energies. So there are internal factors that contribute to illness and disease as well as external causes such as toxins, pollutants, germs and viruses. The Energic Body serves also as a shield to protect the physical body from harmful intrusions, much as the Earth's atmosphere protects the planet from debris entering its orbit from Outer Space. Some intrusions, however, are able to get through, and they are then dealt with by the body's internal defence mechanism.

The subtle energy of the Energic Body can be experienced in the following simple exercise with the hands. For this you will need a partner or friend who is willing to allow you to scan their Energic Body. Your helper should be encouraged to stand relaxed, just beyond touching distance.

Experience 1: Scanning the Energic Body

It is first necessary to activate your hands so they become more sensitive to the finer energies of the Energic Body. They need to be washed so they are cleansed of any dirt or grime, and they should be dried thoroughly. Then stand relaxed, arms to the sides, feet slightly apart. Raise your arms to chest level and about 25 centimetres (12 inches) in front of you, with the palms facing, about 10–12 centimetres (6 inches) apart. Focus your attention on the palms, breathing and exhaling slowly and rhythmically as you do so, but there must be no straining or discomfort. Everything must be done in a relaxed manner. Keep this up for a few minutes until you feel a sensation in the palms or in the fingertips. It may be a warm glow or a tingling sensation. Then very slowly bring the palms closer together and become aware of any sensation of gentle pressure, as if you are holding a small balloon between them. Move the palms closer and then apart in gentle pressing and relaxing motions, and continue this a number of times. Don't be discouraged if you do not experience slight pressure between the palms at this first attempt. You may need to practise several times before you experience a soft and gentle sensation.

Now approach your helper. Stretch out your arms with the palms facing outwards, and with your attention firmly focused in your palms, walk slowly towards him or her.

Stop immediately you feel any slight pressure against your hands, or any warmth or coolness, or experience a tingling in your fingers or palms. This may occur as far as a metre or so away from your helper, or as close as 20 centimetres or so (10–12 inches). What you are sensing is the outer membrane of the auric cocoon.

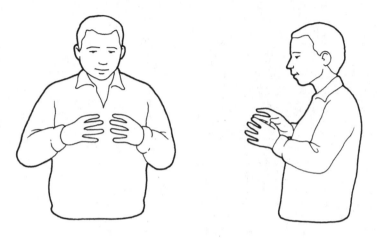

Figure 6. Sensing the Energic Body by feeling a gentle pressure between the palms of the hands

Very slowly move closer to your helper until the sensation gets a little more intense. Keep your attention concentrated on your hands. You don't have to think. Just be aware of any sensations you are experiencing, or impressions that spring into the mind, or any feeling in the abdomen – gut feeling! When your palms are just a few centimetres from your helper, scan the left side of the body with your right hand, moving it slowly upwards to above the head and then gently downwards – stooping as you reach the waist and thighs – and down towards the feet. During this scanning you may notice undulations in the movement of your hands as they respond to the pressure. Now do the same with the right side of the body, this time using your left hand. Again, confirm any undulations. Then move behind your helper, or ask him or her to turn around if the space in the room is limited, and repeat the procedure on the back, first using your right hand and then the left until you have scanned the entire body.

Figure 7. You may sense the outer membrane of a person's auric cocoon by moving slowly forward, with palms extended and facing your helper, until you feel a gentle pressure, warmth or coolness on your hands

When you have finished, shake your hands as if you were shaking off water after a wash and had no towel. Then rub your hands together vigorously, massaging the palms and backs.

We need to understand that there are these subtle non-physical energies in the Universe which are more powerful than physical energies, and that they are also an integral part of our own being. Indeed, it is possible to flood our physical body with a subtle energy that has instant transformational powers. It can nourish the whole body with a secretion that will unblock energy channels, release stress and refresh the vital organs. Practise it yourself and your perception of the outside world will undergo a change, for your response to what is happening in your ordinary reality is conditioned by what is happening

to you within. By transforming the inner reality of your own energy-system you will be changing the world also. That sounds a very difficult thing to do. A tremendous accomplishment to achieve. Yet it is simple. So simple that it has escaped the notice of the vast majority of mankind. So natural that like all natural things it requires very little effort. All you have to 'do' to release this powerful transformational force is to activate a smile within you.

The technique of the Smile Within is derived from the shamanic origins of Taoist yoga of China and Tibet. It spreads harmonizing energy through the Energic Body and the entire physical structure and creates a happy condition. A smile is an expression of pleasure, so by developing an inner smile and directing it to every part of the body the vital organs and the glands, muscles, nerves and cells can be brought into a pleasurable condition. Life is intended to be a pleasurable experience, so let us begin to make our own life more pleasurable by practising the inner smile.

Experience 2: The Smile Within

Sit upright, either in a straight-backed chair or on the floor, whichever you prefer. The important thing is to be able to stay relaxed yet alert without the distraction of bodily discomfort.

Close your eyes to screen out any visual distractions and breathe normally. Relax your mouth and allow it to form into a smile. It may help to recall to mind a pleasant experience you recently enjoyed, or being with a person whose company is pleasurable, or being in a place which generates a feeling of well-being. Your smile will then be more than a facial expression for it will be empowered by a pleasurable healing energy which you have generated.

Now take a slow, deep breath and experience inhaling the soft, warm flow of energy that is contained in your smile. Without strain, pause and hold the breath for a few moments to experience the *glow* of that smile. Then exhale gently and wallow in the sensation of the flow of energy coursing through your body. Repeat this entire sequence several times.

Now direct that warm, sunny smile to each part of your body in turn. Smile at your brain and the Third Eye behind the centre of your forehead. Smile at your ears and nose. Smile at your eyes. Smile at the thyroid gland in your throat. Smile at your heart and lungs. Smile at your stomach and your liver and kidneys. Smile at your spleen and

your bladder. At your sex organs. At your thighs and knees and legs and feet. In this way you will be acknowledging every part of your body and sending loving thoughts to it.

By smiling loving thoughts into your body you are expressing love to the body you have neglected for so long. *Love* your body. It belongs to *you*. It is *yours*. It is a wonderful, beautiful body that enables you to experience physical reality in ways that are in your eventual best interests. So *recognize* it. *Respect* it. *Appreciate* it. *Esteem* it. *Love* it. For when you express love you are experiencing a quality of life. Be in love with your body. Being *in* love is experiencing the movement of life-energy that is fundamental to your very nature. You *need* love, and that love can be generated from the core of your being and activated by a simple *smile*!

Don't hurry this Experience. Take it slowly and gently. When you have finished, take a few deep breaths and stretch your arms and legs and walk around for a few minutes before resuming your normal activities.

Practise this Experience regularly and you will not only come more into tune with your physical and Energic bodies, but you will also be revitalizing every organ, every chakra, every cell, with the radiance of love-energy which you have generated. The more love-energy you generate, the more love will become manifest in your life. It will help you also to recognize your self-worth and value as a self-aware being, and through engendering self-esteem you will be honouring your own unique qualities with their potential for furthering goodness on the Earth.

A loving smile is half a circle activated by the Soul to generate a response that will complete it and so generate joy and harmony.

3. Different Realities

THE WONDER OF *YOU* IS that you actually exist in several realities, all at the same time. This is possible because you have 'bodies' other than the physical and Energic ones we have examined in the first two chapters. Your physical and Energic bodies enable you to experience life through *sensation*. In addition, you have a Mental Body which enables you to function in the reality of the mind, where you can shape thoughts, initiate ideas, consider and compare, evaluate and make judgements, exercise the imagination, and enjoy your dreams and visions. This mental body experiences life through *impression*. You have also a Soul Body which functions in the reality of the Soul and experiences existence through *expression*. And you have a Spirit which experiences life through *be*-ing – through being *aware*. Through *self-awareness*.

AWARENESS

Different bodies. Different vehicles. Different realities. But before we examine these different realities, let us consider this matter of awareness because it is a key to Shamanics' understanding. Awareness is essentially an activity of the Spirit, because it is an act of effortless attention – an experience of *be*-ing rather than *do*-ing. It is a mode of not-doing, which is not a mode of inactivity but rather one of receptive and dynamic *alertness*. Awareness is a receiving of sensations, impressions and feelings, in an attitude of objective neutrality. It is an approach to what is to be experienced with a willingness to

experience – a willing *openness*. It is being watchful and attentive. It is a *letting go* and a *letting be*.

The simplicity of Shamanics is what makes it 'difficult' for
some of us, because our conditioning has caused us to believe
that a skill can be acquired only through long and persistent
effort. Awareness, however, requires no effort, because it is
neither a physical nor a mental activity. It is simply being *alert*
to what is happening and being *sensitive* to that activity. It is not
an ability to form clear mental images in the mind. Nor is it an
attempt to slow the thoughts. It requires no skill in analysing or
categorizing. All such endeavours entail a process of thought
and exercise the intellect. A state of awareness requires none of
these attributes. Further, because shamanic work is primarily
spiritual or metaphysical, the mind and the intellect are not
engaged as they are in other kinds of endeavour. In shamanic
work it is awareness that is activated, not the mind, and the
mind is regarded as a servant of the Spirit, not the Spirit the
servant of the mind.

Experience this for yourself. Choose a time when you are
unlikely to be disturbed, and a room where you can be alone
and sit comfortably and relaxed. You will need to have a notebook and pen handy.

Experience 3: Experiencing Awareness

Hold out your right hand, palm upwards, with your elbow resting
on the arm of a chair or into your side so there is no tension in your
arm.

Close your eyes and focus your attention on your hand. What kind
of sensation are you experiencing there? Examine that sensation.
How would you describe it?

Open your eyes and write a description of that sensation in your
notebook whilst it is still fresh in your mind.

Then hold out your hand again and close your eyes. Now relate
the sensation you are experiencing in your hand with how you feel
about it inside. Not an emotion, but a feeling. Is it pleasant? Invigorating? Uncomfortable? Examine any feeling you are having as you
hold out your hand. Then open your eyes and write a brief description in your notebook. If you did not feel anything, that is perfectly
all right. Note that, too.

Again, hold out your hand and close your eyes, but this time as you
focus attention on your hand, be aware of any mental impressions

that come into your mind – visual images, colours, shapes, symbols. Carefully watch those visual images in the mind's eye. Examine the detail, but don't attempt to analyse them or interpret their meaning in any way. Just observe. Then open your eyes and write a description of any mental impressions you experienced as you held out your hand.

What you have just experienced is a registering of your awareness, unhampered by your mind. Your mind was put into a receptive mode. It was not directed in any way. You were simply registering what activity was taking place at different levels and noting the nature of that activity. It was gentle and effortless. And you have experienced for yourself how to shift your awareness – in this case from your head to your hand.

Through this simple Experience you have attained a state of being that an entire range of mental exercises might aim to reach. And you have learned a key secret of how to enter what some people call 'an altered state of consciousness' by simply *disengaging* the mind while staying fully alert and in control. The mind is still *there*, but it is at rest. We might liken it to having the gear lever of an automobile in neutral with the engine running. You can engage it at any moment, but in that mode the engine is just quietly ticking over. The Spirit is active whilst the mind is receptive. That is awareness.

Awareness is not the same as consciousness. Consciousness is usually associated with the mind and with our thoughts and intellect. Consciousness is a state of wakefulness. When we are asleep we are not conscious, but we are aware of the dreams we may have, even though we may not fully recall them when we wake up. A person having surgery under anaesthetic has been put into a state of unconsciousness in order not to suffer pain, but that patient, as in a dream state, may be aware of activity taking place at another level of awareness. Awareness is independent of mental activity. It is a function of the Spirit which enables us to examine our own thoughts and feelings and become aware of our own sense of 'self' – our own individuality. In your case, you are aware of being you, and in mine I am aware of being me! Spirit has the capacity to absorb and reflect activity that is impressed upon it in any dimension in which it is active, because Spirit has mirror-like qualities – like a crystal ball. It is able to self-reflect – that is, to perceive

its own experiences as another experience. It might be likened to a many-faceted crystal globe that sends out reflections of itself in all directions, or a ball-like lens that is able to perceive in all directions – forwards, backwards, sideways, upwards, downwards – at the same time.

Your Spirit is your 'I' – your sense of identity, your self-awareness – and your awareness is a sense of self-hood in any dimension. Spirit is intangible, but although it cannot be seen, its existence can be discerned when it is active because the Spirit is located where its *attention* is.

Awareness generates a vibration which might be likened to light. It isn't *physical* light, but it has characteristics that are similar. As physical light carries information about what is happening in the physical world around us, and is impacted on the retina of the eyes and then decoded by the brain and translated into visual images which can be interpreted and comprehended by the mind, so this *inner* light carries information about what is being experienced on another level or plane of existence, and from one dimension to another. This inner light is a vibratory state which carries particles – or 'components' – of information. The faster the vibratory state, the more particles there are and the more extended or expanded the awareness becomes. A so-called 'altered state of consciousness' is thus a change in vibratory rate – or frequency – in order that components of information at that level can be conveyed. Indeed, the whole Universe is an information-gathering and information-processing energy-system. And so are you!

In order to carry information from one level or dimension to another, this inner light is channelled through minute vortexes and into thread-like conduits in the 'spatial' substance of multi-dimensional reality. There is no such thing as 'empty' space. What *appears* to be empty is itself a spatial substance. Energy cannot flow through nothing. It must have something to move through in order to be conveyed to perform work. Substance is that through which energy can flow. The substance of the physical Universe is matter. In other realities, as we shall discover, the substance is non-material. As with physical light, this inner light can be distorted so the message being conveyed is unclear and subject to misunderstanding. This inner light can be blocked because the channels themselves are impeded in some way. And it can even be extinguished so no

information of any kind can get through to the consciousness. This is why most people do not remember their dreams on waking. The dream experience has not been conveyed to the consciousness so its message has not got through. This is why most people have no real conception of their Soul – because there is no exchange of information between their Soul, their physical body and their mind. Awareness in each dimension generates a quality that is relevant to that dimension, so there are different states or modes of awareness. Awareness of the physical body, for instance, generates *physical* awareness which is experienced as *sensation*. Awareness on the mental plane generates a quality which allows us to experience *impressions* and to activate thought. Thus it is the awareness – or rather the *quality* of awareness – that undergoes change as movement takes place through the planes or dimensions. Awareness at Soul level generates Soul consciousness, which enables us to have direct access to the source of our creativity and to experience pure *feelings* in our physical body such as joy, elation, ecstasy, fulfilment and, of course, love.

Intellectual speculation about the reality of the Soul is of little avail because there is no direct link between the Soul and the intellect. The intellect deals with separate pieces of information which come from the 'outside' world, and its purpose is to analyse, rationalize, comprehend and explain them. It is the *intuition* – inner-tuition, inner-teaching – that deals with what comes from the *inside* world. So Soul awareness is *intuitive* rather than rational. Only when the Soul and the mind are integrated with the physical body and every aspect of the total being is functioning in harmonic unity is there a channel between the Soul and the mind. In other words, Soul consciousness needs to be conveyed to the physical realm to be decoded and analysed by the mind. Similarly, in order for mental awareness to touch the Soul, it has to go through the physical dimension before it can be conveyed to the Soul. It is the physical body that is the 'transformer' between these dimensions, not the mind. Now do you see the importance and necessity of physical creation? Thinking is not the way to the Soul because the Soul is *beyond* the intellect. It is in a dimension which Tibetan shamans referred to as 'No-Mind' – out of the reach of even the cleverest intellect. The Soul – like the Spirit – can only be *experienced*!

The sense of Self, which I touched upon earlier, is localized within a 'dimension', so only when the awareness is *extended* is there an exchange of information between different 'levels'. Once a human being comes into a recognition of his or her totality as a composite being and multi-dimensional reality, a shift in Life-energy can occur which changes its strength – or 'voltage' if we liken it to electrical energy. This can have the effect of accelerating the perception out of the Space/Time limitations of the physical Universe and into other dimensions. This is how so-called shamanic 'journeys' take place. Shamanic 'journeys' are extensions of awareness into other levels of reality. It is awareness that enables these non-ordinary realities to be perceived, and it is an inner light that conveys information to the consciousness about what is experienced there.

When awareness is shifted shamanically, it is not the Self that moves, for the Self stays at the centre of its own personal reality. A shift in awareness changes the *perception* of reality. So it is not the Self but what the Self *experiences* that changes. This is an important realization. Shifting the awareness is not what some people call Astral Projection. Astral Projection, and similar techniques that seek to project the Self out of the body, can have the effect of leaving the physical body uncentred and unprotected – and therefore vulnerable – and can produce a sensation of disorientation that is uncomfortable and even disturbing. It is not a question of projecting yourself out of your body and into another dimension, because *part* of you – or, rather, an *aspect* of you – is there already and therefore has access to its knowledge. So it is not Astral Projection that I am advocating here, or a psychic skill, but a heightening of the state of awareness. It is improvement in the *quality* of awareness that is true spiritual development and results in an increase in compassion, intuitiveness, creativity and other 'fruits' of the Spirit. This is something very different from the acquisition of methods which serve to expand the Ego and produce vanity and arrogance.

So let us now exercise our awareness in different areas of the physical body, and experience the registering of activity as we do so, as a preliminary to being able to move our awareness to other areas of our composite being.

It is essential that you approach this and future Experiences without worrying about being interrupted. Use a room or

choose a place where you are unlikely to be disturbed for at least half an hour, and ask for telephone calls to be answered for you, or take the receiver off the hook. It may be helpful to record the words of some of the Experiences given in this book. You can then play them back to relieve you of any anxiety about remembering each detail and the correct sequence. For this reason, each action is presented as a single paragraph in the text. Leave a pause of at least 30 seconds between each recorded paragraph to allow yourself time to perform what is described and to monitor its effect. There must be no sense of haste. Everything should be done in a gentle and unhurried manner.

Experience 4: Physical Awareness

Before you begin, loosen your clothing so your body is not constricted in any way, and remove your shoes. It may also be helpful to cover your eyes with a loose blindfold to prevent any visual distractions, but it should be easily removable so that you can make notes. You may undertake this Experience either lying on your back or sitting in a straight-backed chair which will give you support. An advantage of lying down is that the energies are kept well grounded. If you prefer to sit, ensure that the soles of your feet are in firm contact with the floor. Adjust your position until you are comfortable and completely at ease. A relaxed state is an important prerequisite for any shamanic work. Relaxation is not just a release of physical tension, it is also a letting go of the cares and concerns of mundane activity and a release of emotional disturbance and congestion. Relaxation is a state of calm receptivity in which you distance yourself from your ordinary, everyday cares and concerns so that you can be completely at ease within your own energies.

You are now going to move your awareness up through your body and, as you do so, monitor any sensations, impressions, mental images and feelings you may experience as your attention is focused in a particular area of your body. As in Experience 3, no effort is to be exerted at all. There is no force of Will, nor any attempt to analyse or interpret the meaning or relevance of what may be experienced. Just enjoy the experience and make no attempt to 'do' anything with it. Just let it *be*.

Close your eyes and allow your attention to be in your right foot. Wiggle the toes and tighten the muscles as if you are curling your foot around a perch. Then relax those muscles and just be aware of your foot. Write any responses in your notebook.

Let your awareness move to the right kneecap. Tense the muscle there so the kneecap moves slightly upwards, and relax it right away. Check your responses and record them in your notebook.

Your awareness can now be moved to the buttocks. Tense the muscles there so your attention is focused on your buttocks. Relax, and register whatever sensation, mental impressions or feeling you are experiencing. Write these in your book.

Now allow your attention to be on your sexual organs. Tense the muscles in that area and be aware of the presence of your genitals. Relax that tension and monitor whatever response there may be. Make notes of these responses.

Move your attention up the body to your abdomen. Gently pull in your stomach and focus your awareness on the area of your abdomen. Relax, and just be aware of any sensation you are experiencing as your attention rests in your stomach, and of any impressions, shapes or colours you are seeing with your mind's eye. Are you experiencing any feeling as you are aware of your abdomen? Again, write down your experiences.

Now to the area of your chest. Take a gentle, deeper breath as your awareness moves to your chest. Hold it there as you focus your entire attention on your chest. Don't strain in holding that breath for a few seconds. Then, as you exhale, gently monitor any responses. Add this experience to your notes.

Now to the lower arm. Flex the muscles in your lower left arm to help you to focus your attention there; then relax and allow your awareness to be in the lower left arm area. Check for any responses and record them in your book.

To the left hand now. Clench your hand into a fist and bring your awareness into the left hand. Relax, and allow your attention to remain there for a while. Repeat this with your right arm and hand.

Next, the spine. Shift your awareness to the base of the spine. You may tighten the muscles of the anus in order to focus your attention in that area. Then gently move your awareness up your spine. Very slowly allow your awareness to shift from the base of the spine and up the spinal column like an elevator rising gently to the neck and the base of the skull and finally into the base of the brain in the centre of the skull. What are you experiencing as your awareness shifts gently upwards to your head? Again, make a note of responses.

Experience your awareness in the middle of your head. Are there any sensations in any part of your body? A warmth? A coolness? A tingling or pulsating? Have any images, shapes or colours appeared in your mind's eye? Any sudden flashes of inspiration? How are you feeling as your awareness rests in the middle of your head? Is your feeling one of joy, contentment and well-being? Make a note of it all.

Take a few deep breaths. Stretch your arms and legs, and remove the cover from your eyes. Stand up and stretch your arms some more and acclimatize yourself to your surroundings. Then complete the account of your experiences whilst everything is fresh in your mind, otherwise you may forget some of the detail. When you have written your account, go and make yourself a cup of tea or coffee and have a quiet drink before you resume your normal activities.

In this Experience of exercising awareness we have discovered that the focus of our attention can be shifted at will to any area or any part of the body. We have experienced, too, that awareness activates a *response*, sometimes in other parts of the body and sometimes in ways other than the impulses of physical sensation, for awareness may stimulate the mind also and generate a sense of feeling. This shifting of the awareness extends and expands our perception of reality, too. So let us now examine how reality changes in response to where our awareness predominates.

PERCEPTIONS OF REALITY

Reality – according to dictionary definitions – is 'what underlies appearances'. This means that reality is what is *experienced*, rather than what is merely *apparent*. Now that is interesting because in the society in which we live, we have been conditioned into believing that reality is just the physical world around us and what appears to us in it. After all, it is *there*. We can see it, hear it, touch it, smell it, and even taste some of it. The seat you are sitting on as you read this book is solid and supportive. You can feel the firmness of its frame and the suppleness of its seat. If you stand, you will be aware of a solid floor beneath your feet and a hard wall nearby which you can touch and know is there. You can open a door and move into a kitchen and prepare yourself a drink and savour its flavour. Should you then close your eyes and attempt to walk back into the room where you started, the chances are you will bump into a piece of furniture and possibly bruise a shin – proof that it is 'real' enough! However, as the new science of quantum physics is discovering, the physical objects we are aware of all around us are not so solid after all, but consist mostly of space.

Every object in physical reality, including your physical body, is actually composed of whirling bundles of energy – infinitesimal particles that are dancing a pattern of movement that is so fast that they appear to be 'solid'. Indeed, it has been suggested to me that were it possible to remove all the space from the atoms that comprise my physical body, you would need a microscope to examine what was left of me!

Everything we see is just an intricate energy-pattern. What we regard as real and so permanent is only an 'appearance' of what is actually transient. What shamans and mystics of various cultures have been saying throughout the ages is, in fact, more in keeping with what is now emerging from the discoveries of quantum physics than the traditional materialistic concepts with which most of us have been educated.

When I take a short walk to post my mail in the English village where I live, I insert the letters in a red postbox. Now that postbox is real to me and I would swear that its colour is red because that is the colour I see each time. It *is* red, and that is a fact. But that is not the truth. The truth is that my brain does not actually see the colour red at all! The light image reaches my eyes upside down and causes an oscillation of the optic nerve; this is impacted on brain cells which turn the image 'right way up' and translate the oscillation into a colour code. In this particular case the oscillation of light waves contains all the colours except red. So the colour I am seeing is not really there at all. It is the absence of the red end of the light spectrum that makes the postbox appear to be red. So what I think I am seeing is not there at all. What I am seeing is an inner impression of what appears to be real.

A reality is not a finite 'something' outside ourselves, as we have been led to suppose. Reality is an *inner* experience. Although we may separate what appears to be external, what we observe is personal to us because reality – your reality and my reality – is what we each make of appearances. It is what we each perceive to be present within our own circle of awareness. It is what is being *experienced*! So reality is not a static condition. It is constantly moving, continually changing, like everything else, and you are helping to alter your own perception of reality by your thoughts, beliefs and attitudes – creating your own reality. Conditioning what is real to *you*!

Physical reality is only a portion of what it is possible for us

to experience within the *totality* of our being. As reality is what is being experienced and not just what is being observed, it follows that there must be realities other than the one we experience as we go about our ordinary, everyday life. If we regard this everyday reality as 'ordinary' because we are familiar with it, we might call any other reality non-ordinary. Non-ordinary realities differ from ordinary reality, therefore, and are not governed by physical laws that apply in ordinary reality because these other realities are on different levels of existence – in other dimensions – and can only be experienced in different states of awareness.

A dictionary definition of a dimension is 'an extension of measurement in a particular direction'. Ordinary reality is regarded as extending in three directions – with a length, breadth, and height or depth. Our physical senses – especially sight, hearing and touch – enable us to comprehend physical existence as a three-dimensional experience. Actually, physical reality embraces a fourth dimension – Time. Although Time is usually understood to mean *duration*, it can also be regarded as a 'measurement' in which a sequence of events takes place. These other 'dimensions' – other realities, other realms of experience – are not 'way off' but actually close at hand. Indeed, they occupy approximately the same spatial location as our 'ordinary' physical reality. Nor are they *separate* from it. They are merely *out of phase* with it for they exist in different vibrational states – frequency levels – which the physical senses and scientific tools are not able to pick up. These realms of reality – other 'worlds', if you like – actually interpenetrate totally the physical Universe in which we live and move and have our being.

Let us consider an analogy. The many television channels capable of being received on your television screen are all occupying the same air space. In their transmission they are actually passing through the same space that you occupy, even though you are totally unaware of their presence. However, each transmission occupies a particular wavelength frequency band, which needs to be located and 'stepped down' through the electronic transforming devices within your television receiver. The information within those signals is then unscrambled and re-presented in the 'language' of physical reality so that your body and mind can receive the messages and comprehend them.

The different realities can be perceived only by tuning in to their energy-patterns and this can be achieved only by transferring awareness to a more subtle 'vehicle' than the physical body – to a body that functions on those frequencies. This transition results in an altered state of awareness so the 'new' reality can be experienced. An altered state of awareness is a way of 'connecting' the consciousness with another aspect of one's composite being. It is necessary, also, that the knowledge of that experience be retained and brought back into ordinary consciousness in order to be assessed and analysed. Exchanging information between one reality and another is a fundamental skill of the shaman and the shamanist. Indeed, it is this ability to 'travel' into other dimensions and bring back information from that 'journey' that distinguishes the shaman from the medicine man or woman in a tribal group, and from mediums and psychics.

The word 'shaman' is derived from the language of the Tungus people of Siberia and it can be translated as 'Wise One' or 'one who knows', or 'one who knows *ecstasy*'. This refers to a shaman's particular ability to experience realities which co-exist with 'ordinary' physical reality and to bring back knowledge which has relevance to some activity in everyday life – an experience which is frequently ecstatic.

Shamans throughout the ages have acted on an understanding that there are non-ordinary realities which, though distinct in some way, not only overlap physical reality but also affect and influence it. These other realities were regarded by tribal shamans as 'spiritual' because they are non-physical and therefore unseen by normal vision, and they comprehended them as such within an understanding that the physical and the spiritual were complementary polarities.

These other realities can be experienced through a shift of awareness to a 'body' we possess which functions in that particular reality or wavelength. Each body serves as a vehicle in which 'you' – the intelligent Spirit – may function in the appropriate reality. Since, for instance, physical reality is essentially a dense universe of form, a personal vehicle which itself has form and density is required in order that it may be experienced and explored. We call that personal vehicle a physical body. In the reality of the mind there are forms and patterns, too, but these have no density and rapidly change

their shape and appearance as well as their comings and
goings. These are observed mentally through a *mental* body.
There is, too, a reality of the Soul and this is comprehended
through a *Soul* body. Although independent, these different
'bodies' are not separate from us. They are different aspects –
other 'layers' of the one multi-dimensional composite being
that we are.

The total multi-dimensional being, with its different layers
each existing in a different 'dimension' of the multiverse, is the
manifestation of the unmanifest Spirit. Each layer, or body, is
an expression, in its dimension, of the Spirit. Existence thus
encompasses them all – Body, Mind, Soul and Spirit. Each
body or layer is a vessel of the Spirit intelligence that governs
it and is, therefore, just a different aspect or facet of the same
being.

The physical and the spiritual are complementary polarities
of the totality of the All that is, of the All that I am, and the
All that you are. As in a hologram, the All is present in each
facet.

Wholeness is not a quality of the mind but an aspect of the Spirit. That wholeness is a unique presence that is within you – it has only to be rediscovered.

4. The Reality of the Mind

IN ADDITION TO A PHYSICAL body composed of flesh, blood and bones, and an Energic Body of subtle energy, you have a Mental Body which is formed of mental substance. It, too, interpenetrates the physical body and has a similar shape – head, arms, legs, torso, chest, hands and feet. The Mental Body is a vehicle of the personality and is associated with the mind and the process of thinking. It is linked with the Etheric Body and the physical body and brain through the Solar Plexus and Throat chakras.

Personality is defined as the distinctive qualities of a person. Your personality is the sum total of all the characteristics, traits and feelings that belong to you and through which you express your own individuality. From a shamanic understanding, personality may be described as a combination of the energy-patterns you were born with and have developed and through which you express your uniqueness. What you do with those energy-patterns, through the experience of life, 'moulds' your character.

The energy-patterns that contribute to personality are a combination of what you inherited genetically through your parents and what your Soul determined was conducive to the cultivation of your Spirit before you incarnated. The physical environment, especially during childhood, has an effect on fashioning the personality, especially its temperament. The time of year and place of birth are significant because some of these energy-patterns are input from the configuration of Cosmic power in the 'heavens' – the Sun, Moon, stars and planets – and from the influence and movement of natural forces

Earth that are prevalent at the season and time of the year. We shall examine these factors in some detail in Chapter 5.

THE MIND

Before we consider the nature of the Mental Body we need to understand a little about the mind. Educators, scientists, philosophers, medical practitioners and theologians are not entirely in agreement about what the mind is. They know it is not the brain. The brain is a physical 'organ' which the mind uses. Indeed, the brain might be likened to a computer. The bio-computer, which is the brain, can be located and measured because it is physical and an essential piece of the physical body's 'equipment'. The mind, however, cannot be so located and measured because it is non-physical and therefore intangible. So whilst those who have made a study of the mind may not understand fully what it is, they know it exists.

Dictionaries define the mind as 'the seat of consciousness and the emotions'. In other words, the mind is the source of our *thoughts* and emotional feelings. Thought and emotion originate in the mind, but that does not tell us what the mind *is*, only that it is *there* to enable us to experience thoughts and emotions. So although learned people cannot precisely define the mind or locate its whereabouts, and have yet to discover how it *works*, they accept that it is *real*. It exists. But how? And why?

Perhaps part of the difficulty is that we have all been conditioned into regarding the mind as a *thing* – an object which has its own separate existence, like the brain and the body – because science has treated the mind as a complex *machine*. The reality is that the mind is *not* an object. It is not a machine. The mind is a *process*. **The mind is a *processor* of information.**

The processing of information is what the mind is *for*. That is its function and purpose. When we say someone is 'out of their mind' we are recognizing that they have lost the ability to process information – to *think*! When we are asked, 'What's on your mind?', we are being invited to reveal our thoughts. When we are asked to bear certain facts 'in mind' we are being encouraged to think about them, consider them carefully, examine them in detail.

Thoughts are a movement of energy-patterns within the

mental realm, and a *sustained* pattern is that from which the physical is able to take form. So thought provides the mind with the patterns that enable physical reality to be fashioned. When you 'change your mind' you are altering the way you process information and, by so doing, changing the experiences you will have.

When the mind is perceived for what it is – a process, an activity rather than an object – it begins to lose much of its mystery, for we are recognizing its true identity as a process that is intended to serve the Spirit as an *intermediary* between matter and spirit.

In shamanic understanding, the mind functions in a dimension that lies between the vibratory rates of matter and those of the Soul. Your mind was created from a spiral double-helix pattern similar to the DNA structure which contains the master-plan for your entire physical body and is contained in each cell. The DNA structure is a means of materializing patterns that have been inherited from the ancestry of the past and, in resonance with the Soul, enabling potentials to be perpetuated so they can find expression in some way. Your mind came into existence with your physical body in order to process information that would be received by it and through it so you are enabled to manifest your own thought-patterns as a service to your Spirit! Your mind-pattern gathered to itself basic mental substance from the dimension of the mind and built a mental body for you, just as a physical body has been built for you out of physical substance. Your mental body has developed and changed over the years, just as your physical body has changed from infant to child to teenager, and matured into adulthood. Because mental substance is pliable and mouldable, it can be shaped into complex patterns and forms from the information which is conveyed to it by mental consciousness. Mental substance is more changeable than physical substance for it is in a constant state of movement. That is why it is likened to air – or, rather, the *movement* that is *in* air. Substance is generally regarded as something material, but that is not so. In shamanic understanding, substance is that through which energy can flow. Energy cannot flow through nothing for if that were the case it would simply cease to be. The nature of substance differs as we move through the dimensions and relate to the types of energy that flow through it.

Your mental body digests the information that is fed to it as patterns of energy we call thoughts and ideas. These are assimilated into the mental body much as your physical body digests the food that is fed to it for its pleasure, growth, repair and maintenance.

Just as our physical body is sustained by what we eat, so it is with the mind. What is taken into the mind is as much a form of energy as the food we digest in our body. The food that feeds the mind, however, is not physical but *mental* substance – imagery, thoughts, ideas, concepts and beliefs. When those images and ideas are so highly charged that they stimulate the emotions and cause physical sensation, their effect is very powerful. A constant diet of highly-charged imagery that perpetuates cruelty, violence, brutalism, sexual lust and laxity, however innocently packaged as 'entertainment', is as much a health hazard as a diet of junk food, intoxicants and addictives, even though they, too, come attractively presented and wrapped. Although our physical bodies are equipped with natural safety devices to screen out impurities which might have a damaging effect, any overload of toxics will eventually poison the whole system. It is the same with the mind.

Television, with its back-up computer technology, has now become the principal means of information, education, entertainment and escapism, but we need to recognize that it is also a great manipulator. It is so powerful a tool that it can actually change the way we perceive the world! Either we learn to control it, or it will control us.

Parents warn their children not to accept sweets from strangers because they are aware of the danger of child abuse. But how many are as protective by ensuring that their offspring are not seduced by a more subtle purveyor of 'goodies' offered as TV entertainment?

A report in the *British Medical Journal* in February 1994, by consultant child psychiatrist Dr Walter Silveira and child psychiatry registrar Dawn Simmons, indicated that a daily diet of screen violence and sex is wrecking young lives. At Gulson Hospital in Coventry, England, they treated ten-year-olds who were suffering from a condition known as post-traumatic stress disorder after watching a TV drama spoofed up as a documentary about a family in the grip of a malevolent poltergeist. One boy was so scared afterwards that he suffered panic attacks;

when his mother could no longer cope with his distress he was admitted to hospital, where he was treated for eight weeks! Post-traumatic stress disorder is likened to a condition suffered by some people after the trauma of a bad accident or the horror of a war experience. The report followed only weeks after a ten-year-old and an eleven-year-old boy had been found guilty of the gruesome murder of a two-year-old in Merseyside, England, after they had watched a horror video which contained acts of violence similar to those they had carried out on their tiny victim. Despite this and other warnings, cynics maintain that children as well as adults are able to distinguish between real-life and make-believe situations!

As I have indicated, the mind is a process. It is also a *receptacle*. It contains what we ourselves put into it and allow others to put there. Your mind is your mental universe. My mind is my mental universe. We each of us have a mental universe that is all our own because we each have a mind of our *own*. And there is an ecology of the mind just as surely as there is an ecology of the physical world. The word 'ecology' is derived from the Greek word *oikos*, which means 'house'. So the physical ecology is our 'outer' house – the natural world of our physical existence. Our mental ecology is the 'inner' house of our mind and the world of our mental existence. Whilst we would be unwilling to allow garbage to be dumped in our home, are we as reluctant to allow purveyors of mental garbage to tip their rubbish into our minds and our mental universe? After all, we are left with the task of cleaning it up or allowing it to rot there!

The quality of what comes out of our mind is in proportion to the quality of the material that goes into it. As Within, So Without. The world 'out there' is collectively a reflection of the world that is collectively 'in here' – in our *minds*. In a democratic society freedom of expression is a vital principle that is rightly upheld. But freedom of expression can also devolve into freedom to abuse, pervert and influence others for personal gain. So we must never overlook the fact that freedom demands responsibility, in both giving and receiving.

Thoughts and imagery are a movement of energy-patterns within the Mental Realm, and thoughts can take form just as physical matter does. A difference is that the mental substance from which thought-forms are fashioned is far finer and less stable than physical substance. This is why thoughts are quick

to pass into and out of existence. Thought-forms are thought-patterns which are sustainable and therefore more stable and durable. They are fashioned in mental substance by the image – the pattern of energies – created by the activity of thought that has been 'charged' with emotion. Emotion is awareness of movement of energy within the mental body. It is generated in the Mental Realm as the result of an external influence which agitates at mental level. So emotion might be defined as thought with feeling attached, and can be so intense as to be experienced like a physical sensation, resulting in pleasure or pain. Emotion is extremely fluid and unstable. An emotion that persists is what is known as a mood. Thought-forms can be so powerful that when encountered by certain sensitive people they can be mistaken for spirits, because the thought-forms have a human likeness and assume human characteristics. One reason for such encounters is that the dimensions overlap and there is thus a 'veiled' area in which it is possible for people who are sensitive to the finer energies to perceive thought-forms that have become so powerful that they have assumed a 'life' of their own, albeit only temporary.

When, in your imagination, you participate in some kind of activity that seems so real that you experience something of the feelings and sensations you would have if it were physically happening, it is your Mental Body that is involved. Your awareness in your Mental Body is communicating through the consciousness the responses that it is registering.

Your Mental Body is itself a thought-form. It has been given shape and form by the pattern of thoughts and beliefs that you have fed into it, and it has mental self-awareness which is your Ego-self. The Ego-self is who you *think* you are. The Ego-self is *what* you think you are. The Ego-self is what you believe yourself to *be* – and your Mental Body fits that identity. That is why some women who are slim believe they are fat – because their Mental Body is stouter than their physical body. Or a stout man who is overweight may think he is slimmer than he is because he has a slimmer Mental Body. A Mental Body can be more beautiful or less handsome or attractive than the physical body depending upon a person's own concept of his or her appearance. As we get older we find ourselves thinking we are still capable of performing the physical deeds we were able to accomplish with comparative ease when we were

younger, or we find ourselves hesitant about achieving a particular task because the Mental Body has conditioned us not to
attain it.

So let us move on to discover what your own mental self is
like, what kind of qualities it has, and what it looks like. You
need only a notebook and pen for this Experience, which is in
two stages.

Experience 5: Knowing Your Mental Self

For the first stage, write a list of words, each of which describes an
aspect of yourself. These should be single words that describe a
quality, a trait, a recognized strength, an admitted weakness, a talent
– an expression of 'you' as a person. For instance:

Active
Thoughtful
Aggressive
Considerate
Artistic
Impatient
Ambitious
Jealous
Thrifty

There is no limit to the number of words, so take your time over this task
and make the list as complete as possible. It need not be completed
in a single session. The important thing is that it is comprehensive.

When you have completed your list, compose from it a Personal
Profile, using each of the words to describe you in an objective way,
as if you were writing about someone else. What you will then have
is a self-image that is the product of your thoughts and mental
conditioning.

The second stage is to compile a description of how you see yourself physically. Are you tall or short? Stout or slim? What features are
prominent? Are you beautiful, attractive, handsome? Or just plain –
even dowdy? Be honest and objective. This personal description is
for your eyes only, but be as detailed as possible, giving a full description of someone who could be readily recognized from your account.
Look at yourself in a mirror if you need to. Again, don't hurry this
task for it needs to be thorough.

When you have completed this Personal Profile to your satisfaction
you will have a word picture of your Mental Body – the image you
have of yourself in your mind – and of the Ego's awareness of itself.

Let us now experience the existence of our Mental Body by the simple process of shifting awareness into it. This Experience is best undertaken in your usual Quiet Place and when you are unlikely to be disturbed for half an hour or so. All you will need is a covering for your eyes and a notebook and pen handy so you can write an account of your experience immediately afterwards.

Experience 6: Awareness of Your Mental Body

Lie down and cover your eyes to avoid distractions. Make sure your body is comfortable and at ease. Take a few deep breaths, then breathe normally and relax.

Once you are completely at ease, allow your awareness to be in your Mental Body, which occupies the same spatial area as your physical body and interpenetrates it completely. The simple intention of putting your awareness into your Mental Body is quite sufficient. There is no need to visualize or 'do' anything. Remember, intention is what allows activity, and energy follows the intent.

Now, with your physical body remaining perfectly still, move the right arm of your Mental Body and scratch the head of your Mental Body. Was there a sensation in the hand that touched the head? Was the head of your Mental Body aware of being touched?

Again, without moving your physical body in any way, raise the right leg of your Mental Body. Let it down, and then do the same with the left leg of the Mental Body. Then move the Mental Body's right arm upwards, and then the left arm. What did you experience as you moved each limb of your Mental Body?

Next, intend your Mental Body to rise very slowly and hover just a few centimetres or inches above your physical body. Again, just have that intention. There is no need to 'try'. And you are perfectly safe and secure within your own energy-system, so no harm can come to you. Just allow it to happen.

What sensation are you experiencing as your awareness is situated just above your physical body? What mental impressions do you have? What are you seeing in your mind's eye? What does it feel like to be lying on the floor but seemingly hovering a little distance above its surface?

Allow your Mental Body to rise just a little higher and turn the head of your Mental Body to look down on your physical body. What are you experiencing as your awareness is outside your physical body? Do you have any sensations or feelings? What does your physical body look like as it is lying there? Is there anything especially noticeable about your physical body?

Now allow your Mental Body to gently lower itself into your physical body, and experience your awareness being in both your Mental Body and your physical body.

Take a few deep breaths and stretch your arms and legs. Remove the covering from your eyes and look around to familiarize yourself again with the room and the furnishings. Sit up slowly and take a few more deep breaths before you get up from the floor and write an account of your experiences.

THE EGO

The Ego is a mental self-image – a concept of self that exists in the mind. It is a false concept because the self – the True Self – exists not in the mind but in the Spirit, as we shall later discover. The Ego itself is quite complex. It has three aspects which we might consider as 'layers'. The outer or 'surface' layer is concerned with serving the needs of the physical body and gratifying the senses, although the Ego itself is never satisfied for it desires more and more of what it wants and less and less of what it needs. The second layer is more concerned with mental appetite and feeding its sense of self-importance and separation. It makes judgements and comparisons that produce vanity. The third aspect is concerned with its sense of self-justification. So powerful is the Ego that it leads us into believing that it is all we are – that it is the True Self, rather than the illusory, temporary and limited 'self' that it really is.

The Ego concerns itself primarily with attachment to the things that it believes will bring pleasure, and the avoidance of pain; and our physical body in some way identifies itself with what has originated from this mental process. So it is that we act as if we are our thoughts, as if material things around us – even some human beings – actually belong to us: *my* house, *my* car, *my* wife, *my* partner, *my* child, and so on. All are *attachments*. They are attached to our Ego. They belong to our Ego because they belong to our thoughts! The Ego wants to hold on to what it is attached to and has created for itself. It causes us to make comparisons with others, and judgements about other people because of the way their actions and opinions affect our own. We behave in accordance with the expectations that are foisted on us and this puts further pressure on us and

causes us stress by our endeavours to keep up. So it is that we become trapped in a constant round of unsatisfied desires, locked into behaviour patterns from which there appears to be no escape, imprisoned by a conditioning that has been brought about by our own thoughts and beliefs. There is a way of escape, but it can come about only by breaking the pattern of that conditioning and bringing the mind more in harmony with the Spirit and in resonance with the Soul. 'Conditioning' is fundamentally a form of energy that affects the way we perceive reality. It is composed of energies that are limiting and restrictive because they confine us to a single plane of existence and prevent us from experiencing our greater reality. All conditioning is generated by limiting beliefs that are activated by fear. Not the real fear of physical survival but imaginary fear which is 'real' enough to the mind and the Ego and has a debilitating effect on our vitality and health. Such fear is identified by 'What will happen if . . .?' questions and 'What will so-and-so think of me if I do such-and-such?' concerns. Conditioning is so real that it accumulates in the physical body to impose further limitations on us. Many physical ailments and impediments are conditions brought about by our mental conditioning. Remove the conditioning and the condition it has brought about will be removed also. More of this later.

Shamans of different cultures and over many centuries have regarded the mind not as a *controller* but as a *servant* – there to help and to serve, but not to take control of our lives or be *venerated* by us. When reality is experienced through mind alone, we perceive the separateness of things. We define and categorize what is observed. We analyse, make comparisons and draw conclusions. When reality is experienced through the Spirit – with the 'Heart' – we perceive the holistic nature of things and the relationship and interdependence that exist at all levels. Only when we come to a realization from within that the mind is but an 'extension' of the Spirit into the Mental Realm can we understand that it is only our beliefs that have separated and isolated them, and in this way we have created an Adversary to our own Spirit!

An ultimate purpose for mankind is that the mind and Spirit come together in perfect harmony so their 'sound' is one – a total unity. The marriage and union of man and woman was intended to be an example of this and a teaching of great

intimacy. Isolation of the Spirit from the mind has caused this union to be regarded primarily as a sexual relationship.

Your mind belongs to 'You' – the real You who is a Spirit. Your mind is yours to use, but you must control it for it is so powerful that otherwise it will control You and lead you into believing that your Ego-self is the only 'you' and will continue to fashion your life accordingly.

THE SHAMAN'S COSMOS

Since prehistory, shamans have perceived the mind as functioning on three, or possibly four, levels. A tree was often used as a symbolic aid to an understanding of different states of mind and other dimensions of existence. Materialistic science accepts that trees serve as protectors of the environment and that without them the atmosphere would be contaminated with an excess of carbon dioxide. In ancient times, trees were regarded also as symbolic 'guardians' of levels of the mind. This

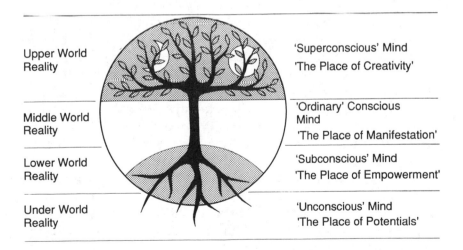

Figure 8. The Cosmos of the shaman, represented by a 'cosmic' tree which indicates its multi-dimensional nature

was because, in the transition from ordinary to non-ordinary reality, the patterns of protective forces between the dimensions were frequently imaged in the mind as trees. Trees have long been a symbol of the reality of multi-dimensional existence. The trunk of a tree represents the individual in relation to physical existence, grounded to the Earth and with access to the deepest levels of the Unconscious, where potentials lie hidden beneath the surface. The noblest aspects, represented by the topmost branches, reach upwards to touch the sky and Cosmic consciousness and 'the Place of Creativity'. The trunk was often referred to as the 'Middle World' – 'the Place of Manifestation' – between Heaven and Earth. The surface of the ground where trunk meets roots, indicates a need to be grounded so that personal development and the cultivation of the Spirit can take place in an organic or natural way. This is the realm of subconscious activity and it was often referred to as the 'Lower World' and 'the Place of Empowerment'. The deeper roots, reaching down into subterranean levels, indicate contact with the depths of the Unconscious where our potentials lie hidden. This 'Place of Potentials' was also called the 'Under-world'. The branches of the tree indicate spiritual aspirations reaching up to the Heavens, with the leaves quivering in expectancy of the Divine touch. This is the Realm of the Soul and was often referred to as the 'Upper World'. Indigenous peoples thus had high regard for trees. Native Americans called them 'the Standing People', because they stayed where their roots were and could impart great wisdom to humans whose hearts and minds were open enough to receive their message. They treated trees with respect and were not only attuned to them but could actually *communicate* with them! Cynics may scoff at the idea that communication is possible between trees and humans, but that cynicism is born of an ignorance of the spiritual ecology and they are thus cut off from any knowledge of such realities. Of course, communication is not possible *physically*, because trees have no mouth or larynx; nor is it possible on a *mental* level, except in a fantasy of the imagination. But it is possible for the *Spirit* of a human being to communicate directly with the Spirit of a tree!

Trees draw their sustenance from the Sun and from the Earth and the atmosphere that surrounds them, and they vibrate in harmony with the life-pulse of the Earth itself. Indeed, what

the Earth experiences in her nurturing of trees is similar to the feelings a human mother has whilst breast-feeding her baby. It is appropriate, therefore, that our early work with Shamanics should include experience of being still. We need to learn not only how to be physically still, like a tree, yet fully alert, but also how to still our thoughts so our awareness can be focused on inner growth and inner development, as a tree's is. We need to be able to stem the constant flow of thoughts that rush through the mind and intrude on our awareness, and to be able gently to push aside the Ego so that it is no longer 'in control'. We can then become 'connected' with our own Spirit just by allowing ourselves to 'be'. Here, then, is a learning experience that has been gathered personally from a tree. It is what a tree taught me about how to be 'actively' still.

Experience 7: 'Active' Stillness

Standing without moving is not doing nothing. It is a powerful energy generator which can have a profound empowering effect. It can increase vitality, rejuvenate the physical body and stimulate the mind. It can improve the body's natural immunity and help to regenerate the nervous system. And for older people it can even slow the ageing process.

Standing in the midst of the elements, a tree draws its strength from the Earth and from a field of energy around it. You can do likewise. The ideal place to undergo this standing Experience is out of doors in the presence of a tree or trees.

Stand with your feet shoulder-width apart and your toes pointing forward or just slightly outward. Bend your knees slightly but keep your back straight, assuming a stance like riding a horse. Your body weight should be evenly distributed and balanced on the soles of your feet. Keep your head erect. Your arms should hang loosely, with the palms of your hands upturned to form a bowl and the middle fingers just touching in an area slightly below the navel (see Fig. 9).

Breathe normally. Don't tense yourself in any way. Breathe in through the nose and out through the mouth.

Close your eyes and focus your attention on the top of your head. Just allow your awareness to be on top of your head. Don't exercise any particular thought about it, but do take notice of any sensations you may experience as you do so, or any impressions or images that spring into the mind, or any 'gut' feelings you may have.

Next, move your awareness to your eyes. Open your eyes and look forward and slightly downward, but don't focus on any particular

Figure 9. Practising 'Active' Stillness. Stand in the horse-riding stance with the feet shoulder-width apart and knees slightly bent. The palms should be cupped upwards just below the navel.

spot. Just allow your eyes to relax. What are you experiencing with your eyes? Not what are your eyes seeing, but what are your eyes experiencing?

Next, pay attention to your throat and release any tensions in your neck. Experience the freedom in your throat and neck.

Now to the shoulders. Relax the shoulders and back muscles and allow your chest to drop slightly. Experience the comfort in your chest, back and shoulders.

Shift your awareness to the belly and release any tension there. Then to the buttocks and the base of the spine. Move your attention to your thighs and then your knees. Bend your knees slightly to check that they are not locked or stiff but springy.

Put your awareness into your feet and their connection with the Earth, as if the soles of your feet are sending down roots into the ground. Sense those roots going down. Notice any sensations, visual images in the mind, or feelings you may have as your attention is focused in your feet.

Now, with each in-breath you are going to bring your awareness

slowly and gently up from your feet and through your body to the top of your head. Experience the flush of energy as it rises, bringing a warm glow to your abdomen and chest, up into your neck and head, and finally jetting out through the top of your skull like a water fountain.

As you breathe out, allow your attention to return slowly to your feet, and repeat the cycle as you breathe in again. Continue this for a couple of minutes or so until you feel thoroughly invigorated.

Then take a few deep breaths, stretch your arms and move your legs, and breathe normally.

This entire Experience should take only ten or fifteen minutes and, quite apart from invigorating your body, it will transform your whole day in many ways. Although very simple, it is very effective, and is another example of a shamanic principle in operation: 'maximum efficiency with minimum effort'. The 'effort' required is that of 'not trying'. As with much shamanic work, you don't 'try', just 'do'. Knowledge – or, rather, know-ingness – comes from the experience of doing.

PORTALS

The mental body is connected to the brain and attached to the physical body by channels like very fine umbilical cords. The openings to these thread-like conduits were referred to in some mystical traditions as 'portals', or symbolized as 'gateways', because they were regarded as entrances not only to levels of the mind other than ordinary conscious awareness of the external physical world, but to other states of being-ness and 'inner' realities. These portals or gateways may be perceived also as transition chambers or switch-over points, where changes are made from one level to another.

These switch-over points are where seven of the chakras are located – from Brow to Base-of-the-Spine. Each is an opening to a different quality of awareness and acts as a filter to allow the attributes of that particular quality to pass through. Their functioning might be likened to that of a colour filter that screens out light other than that particular ray. Through ignorance, neglect or abuse, these filtering channels become blocked or congested so that information between levels cannot be exchanged with clarity, and that which does get through may be distorted, diluted or diffused. The channels malfunction

when they come out of attunement with themselves and with one another.

The portals, their location in relation to the chakras, and their qualities and colours are as follows:

Base-of-the-Spine	Self-preservation Determination to survive	Red
Sacral	Human relationships Sexuality Sensuality	Orange
Solar Plexus	Self-identity 'Lower' emotions Desire Absorption	Yellow
Heart	Affections Love and compassion 'Higher' emotions Balance	Green
Throat	Communication and expression	Light Blue
Base-of-the-Brain	Aspirations Inspiration	Dark Blue
Brow	Imagination Intuitiveness Mental dexterity	Indigo

The portals are spiralling, free-flowing vortexes whose basic movement might be likened to a figure of eight. Indeed, the ancient symbol of a sideways figure 8 – a line without beginning or end – indicates movement whose source is at its own centre. The centre itself is a point of transition where the direction of flow is reversed and is thus a switch-over point.

The figure of eight also symbolizes the closeness of the relationship between the 'spheres' or 'worlds' – between the seen and the unseen, the tangible and the intangible, the physical and the non-physical. But it is more than a symbolic 'switch'. It is a means of establishing direct personal communication with other levels of existence. The swirling current of the figure of eight movement runs in both clockwise and anti-clockwise directions which intersect at the point of balance, and it is there that a change of direction occurs. This intersection and point

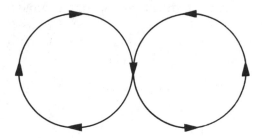

*Figure 10. The Figure of Eight free-flowing energy-system, with its 'source'
and switch-over point at its own centre*

of balance and change is equivalent to the eye of the labyrinth – another ancient symbol – which is the place of transition. The eye of the labyrinth – the switch-over point – is where energy is transformed and where the physical aspects of one's being connect with the non-physical and make it possible for the awareness to make a transition from one dimension into another.

In Taoist understanding, the figure of eight indicates the energy-movements of the Yin and Yang – the two complement-ary polarities – coming together in a balanced unity of giving and receiving for the purpose of creating beauty and harmony. By simulating the figure of eight movement with our physical body, coupled with our intention, we make contact with the non-physical aspects of our being – both the mental and the spiritual – and by so doing help to harmonize our entire energy-system. By exercising our physical body in figure of eight movements we acknowledge the DNA double-helix wave pattern that is contained in every cell, and we actually 'tell' it, through the impulses of those movements, that we not only recognize and respect it but have a loving regard for it!

The Figure of Eight Movement can be performed almost anywhere, indoors or out, at any time, and need take only a few minutes.

Experience 8: The Figure of Eight Movement

Stand erect, feet shoulder-width apart, arms hanging loosely at your sides, and be perfectly relaxed. Without moving your feet, rock your pelvis forward, backward and sideways in a figure of eight move-

ment. It may help to imagine that you are tracing a figure 8 on the floor or ground with an invisible crayon reaching down between your legs.

Put your full attention into your pelvic region so your awareness is in the continuous flow of the movement itself, and enjoy the sensation of it! Dance the hula-hula!

Without moving your feet, but still rotating the pelvis, trace a figure of eight pattern with your left hand by rotating the wrist. Switch your awareness of the figure of eight movement to your left hand and wrist. When your left hand and wrist are moving fluidly as well as your pelvis, start moving your right hand and wrist in figure of eight movements also, and focus awareness there.

Now focus your attention on your shoulders and move them in a figure of eight pattern, and then your head.

Finally, still staying where you are, just allow your whole body to 'dance' the Figure of Eight Movement. Be aware of your entire body as it becomes absorbed in the sheer delight of uninhibited movement, as if becoming the very figure of eight pattern itself! Enjoy this experience for a few minutes until you feel invigorated and energized.

Shifting your awareness to different locations in the body helps you to develop a vital shamanic technique. The exercise climaxes as you extend the figure of eight movement to your entire body to the point where you experience the movement itself.

This entire Experience should be performed regularly every day. Its enjoyment can be enhanced by performing it to a piece of melodic, easy-listening music.

The figure of eight pattern is symbolic of a primary Power of the Universe and the DNA wave pattern, which contains within it coded instructions not only of how you look – your physical appearance – but also the basis of your mentality and what you are like as a person. So let us now examine personality.

Where does the acorn obtain its power to become a mighty oak? Or the bud of a rose its ability to blossom into so magnificent a flower? From a Source that is within itself. So it is with you. Are you of any less value than a tree or a flower that contributes its strength and glory to the beauty of the Whole? Accept yourself for what you are, for only then can the potential that is inherent within you come forth to add its unique quality to the All.

5. Your Earth Personality

MODERN GENETIC SCIENCE IS COMING to conclusions that have been shamanic understanding for centuries – that not only our basic physical and mental characteristics are pre-determined before our birth, but also the way we are as individuals. To genetic scientists it is the genes – the DNA code that is inherited through our parents – which determine our basic physical features, our mental attributes and dexterity, and also our personality traits. Indeed, genetic scientists are now advancing the view that it is our genes, not social and environmental factors or personal circumstances, that largely determine how we are as individuals. And genetic research over recent years has indicated that the brain is 'wired' by the genetic program within us to respond to certain energy-patterns received from the surrounding environment. Psychologists call these responses 'behaviour traits'. We are affected, of course, by social and economic factors, and by racial and cultural influences and other circumstances; consequently we do not always respond to situations in quite the same way.

However, none of this implies that we are little more than bio-robots who function in accordance with a predestined plan, because we each have a quality which no other life form on Earth possesses – free will. Will is the power to *effect* a cause. In other words, the Will is what determines a *cause*. So free will is the freedom to **cause** things to *happen* – to cause something to *be*. It is an ability to make choices unconditionally and so be responsible for our own life and in control of our own personal destiny. Our destiny is not what is *fated* to happen,

but the outcome of the choices we make and of our reactions to the choices of others that in some way affect us also.

The genes contain the inherited traits and the blueprint of the basic personality structure through which we are each enabled to present ourselves to the world. How we develop those traits and that personality as a result of our upbringing and our life experiences and develop character is a matter of free will.

Personality might be defined as the total pattern of qualities that determine behaviour. Character is what adds ethical and moral values. So your personality is not 'You' but a way you are enabled to project yourself to others as an individual and the way you respond to others and to yourself! Personality is thus linked with the way behaviour-patterns are structured. Psychology is a comparatively new science which explores behaviour-patterns and the way we relate to other people, and has in many ways assumed the role which was regarded by some people in past times to be the province of astrology.

In all cultures there has been an underlying belief that the time and place of birth has some significance in the way we experience life. Astrology is a very ancient method of discerning celestial energy-patterns and how they relate to us on Earth. It indicates that we contain within us an imprint of the stars from which we originate. It is based on the principle, 'As Above, So Below' – that movement of energies in the Universe 'up There' is indicative of the formation of corresponding forces 'down Here' – and has application both generally and individually. Astrology, which has been trivialized through media emphasis on foretelling the future as 'entertainment', is incomplete for it is Sun-oriented and outward-looking. There is, however, another aspect – an intuitive 'inner' influence created by the pattern of Earth forces prevalent at the time of birth through changes in the turning of the 'Wheel of the Year'. This complementary system formed part of an ancient wisdom that was 'lost' in antiquity but is now being reclaimed. It looks within for explanations of what is happening 'outside' ourselves and is based upon the principle, 'As Within, So Without'. It helps us to comprehend the Earth nature we have been given for the education of the Spirit for this lifetime. I have called this system 'Earth Medicine' because it is concerned with down-to-earth practicalities and

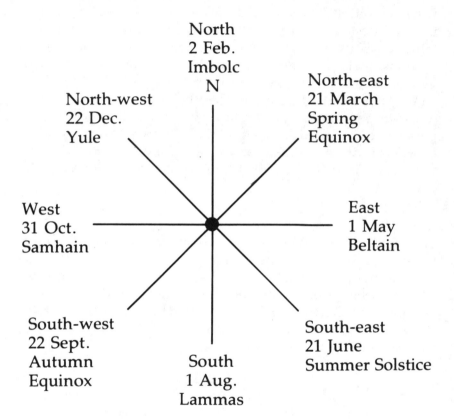

Figure 11. The Wheel of the Year

emphasizes personal empowerment – what Native Americans call 'Medicine'.

Your power is your 'medicine', for among Native Americans the words are synonymous. Earth Medicine means Earth *Power* – the power of the *natural* forces on, in and around the Earth

– that influence and affect the way we are. It is a power that merges at the time of birth with those attributes we have inherent within ourselves, to influence broadly the way we are to perceive and respond to physical reality. Earth Medicine is based upon the Wheel of the Year – the natural cycle of the Earth's orbit of the Sun – and on the Medicine Wheel, which itself is a *catalyst* of ancient wisdom and also a 'map of the mind' enabling us to come into an understanding of ourselves as individuals and our relationship with Nature and other living beings. Earth Medicine might also be called *Nature's* Horoscope because it is a means of helping us to understand our own personality and arriving at an indication of the purpose for our incarnating at this time. Your personality is an expression of who and what you are *inside*. It is not the *real* *'You'* but it is a 'face' the Real You presents to the world.

THE MEDICINE WHEEL

The Medicine Wheel is a hoop or circle that puts a limit on the limitless. It symbolizes the container of all that *is*. Within the circle is an equal-armed cross – a symbol of balance, and the blending of opposite potentials represented by the vertical and horizontal lines and their polarities. It is the Taoist 'masculine' Yang and 'feminine' Yin locked together, absorbing and distributing energy in perfect harmony.

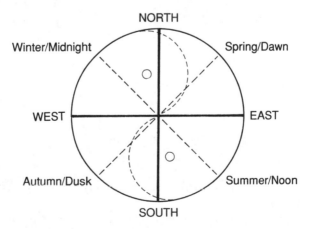

Figure 12. The encircled cross and basis of the Medicine Wheel mandala also encompasses the Taoist Tai Chi symbol of the Yin and Yang polarities.

This two-dimensional symbol of the encircled cross actually incorporates three interlocking circles, so it represents the length, breadth and height of physical manifestation, conditioned by a fourth dimension – the duration of movement and change – Time.

It establishes direction – North, South, East, West, Above and Beneath; or in front, behind, left, right, Sky and Earth. By establishing the non-cardinal directions of North-east, South-east, South-west and North-west, a further four 'spokes' are added, resulting in an eight-spoked wheel which is indicative of four primary creative principles in their dual nature and contained in perfect balance and harmony within the whole. It establishes four seasonal quarters and four transition points in between which trigger significant changes in the turning of the Wheel of the Year – the Spring and Autumn equinoxes when day and night are of equal length, and the Summer and Winter solstices which mark the longest day and longest night.

When each seasonal quarter is divided into three, twelve segments of Time are established. In ancient numerology twelve was the number of organizational structure or arrangement – categorical measurement. So it establishes twelve Time segments in a solar year, which is the Earth's complete orbit of the Sun – each of approximately equal duration, and each affected by lunar influence resulting from the Moon's orbit of the Earth.

The twelve segments provide not only twelve Time periods of change within the natural cycle, through which physical reality may be experienced, but twelve different 'locations'

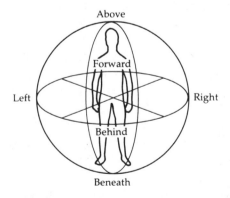

Figure 13. The three interlocking circles establish directions.

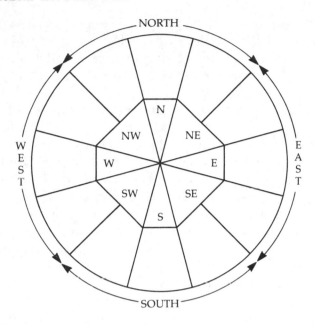

Figure 14. The eight directions and the twelve divisions

from which it may be perceived – twelve broad categories through which it can be *faced*. The Medicine Wheel thus provides a very valuable device for self-knowledge. It enabled Native Americans to identify with the characteristics of the season in which they were born, with the qualities of the Moon or month (Moon-th) of their birth, and with other aspects of the changes taking place in the natural environment. These provided clues to the individual's own essential nature: likely strengths and weaknesses, and possible assets and disadvantages inherent in that 'portion' of Time. Weaknesses were not perceived as liabilities, but rather as *opportunities* for acquiring new strengths, as *challenges* for the fashioning of character, and a further means for the development of personal empowerment.

EARTH MEDICINE

Nature's 'Horoscope' is thus not about what may be fated to happen in spite of ourselves, but the opportunities that are

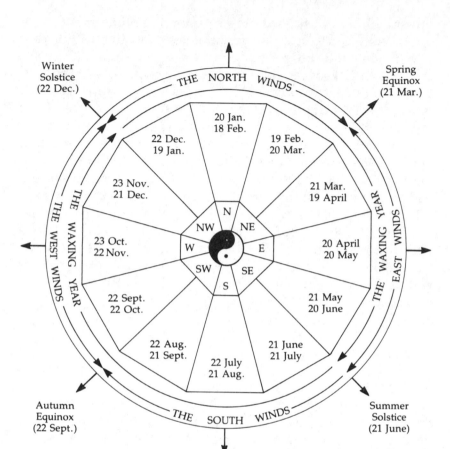

Figure 15. The twelve time segments on the Wheel of the Year

with us in the present and with which we fashion our own future as a result of our responses to those experiences.

Earth Medicine* indicates how before birth the Soul equips the vehicle of the physical body with the qualities and potentials that are needed by the individual to face the situations and circumstances of life on Earth that will enable development to take place in a *natural* evolutionary process.

The Moon plays a significant part in all this. It regulates the cycle of menstruation. It governs the gestation period for a

---

* *Earth Medicine* (Element Books, 1989) is a comprehensive guide to the system and contains detailed profiles of each birth 'totem'.

human embryo in the womb: nine months – nine moons – or forty weeks from conception. It influences not only the tides but also the ebb and flow of emotional forces within us. It reflects the light and life of the solar source at the centre of our physical Universe and also indicates the forces within ourselves that reflect the light of our own spiritual 'Sun' at the source of our own being. In other words, the Moon mirrors what your Spirit expression is – the essence of what you *are*. So it is a reflection of your *authentic* Self. No wonder shamans had an understanding that the characteristics of the Moon – the month of birth – had an influence on the sort of personality one was to become.

Your Earth life is thus experienced through a perception 'window' to the world, which is 'positioned' in accordance with the place on the Wheel of the Year at which you were born. Your Earth life is not only an experience of the Spirit within 'looking out', but also a means by which it may find expression in a particular way.

Totems

Earth Medicine is derived from an understanding that energy-patterns within the genes formulate our personality traits and the potentials we have, and culminate at birth to merge with the natural forces influential at that period of the Earth's seasonal cycle. These qualities are represented as *totems* rather than as glyphs or symbols. A totem is a symbolic 'sensor' that helps in the discernment of the interplay of non-physical forces. As a totem expresses the characteristics of a living being, it is a more effective aid than a glyph or geometric symbol. Whereas in astrology birth is associated with a constellation of stars – Aries, Gemini or Scorpio, for instance – in Earth Medicine it is related to an animal totem on the Medicine Wheel, such as Wolf, Beaver, Hawk, Owl or Salmon, which is more readily communicative than a cluster of stars. Earth Medicine recognizes the influence these energies have on the 'inner' pattern from which our individual physical life is moulded. It also indicates the connectedness with Nature and animal forms, that teach, help and support us on our Earth 'Walk' and enable us to thrive and develop in all aspects of our total being.

Earth Medicine provides us with clues about how we were

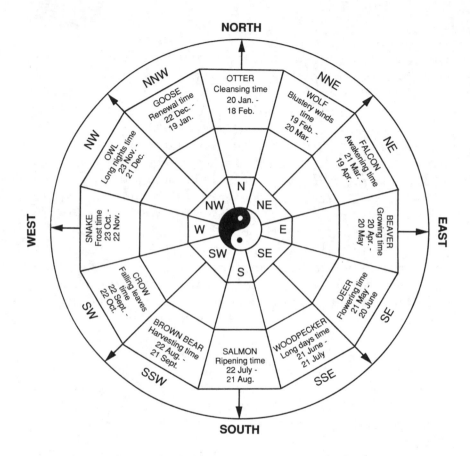

Figure 16. The Earth Medicine Wheel with the totem animals associated with the twelve time periods – the influencing 'moons' or months (moon-ths) of the year.

put together as personalities and the kind of challenges and life lessons that are likely to arise in order to cultivate our innermost Self and thus further our evolutionary progress.

So Earth Medicine can help you to get to know yourself more fully, and through that understanding to get from where you are to where you want to be.

Here is just a brief summary of the characteristics associated with each of the twelve time periods and their respective totem animals.

21 March–19 April   *Falcon*
The Awakening Time

You were born at a time in the yearly cycle when Nature's dormant forces are bursting into newness of life. You, too, are enthused with exuberance, revelling in what the moment holds, oblivious of the past and little concerned about the future. Your joy is in what is happening *now*!

Like your totem animal, you like to explore new places, new experiences, new ideas. And as a falcon flies to great heights, you, too, enjoy having your 'head in the clouds' of lofty aspirations. You enter each new challenge with enthusiasm, taking off with ease, but lacking staying power if what you are looking for eludes you or cannot be obtained quickly.

Part of your Life Purpose is to learn persistence and to stay long enough with a situation to nurture it into fruition. Your need is to study Nature and learn from her: first the seed, then the shoot, stem, branch, bud, flower, fruit, and back to seed again – all in its rightful sequence and in its own good time.

Falcons are enthusiasts – quick to goad others into action in support of their latest project, but just as quick to lose interest when something new catches their eye. A lively imagination coupled with infectious enthusiasm produces a tendency to fantasize, and that can lead to making judgements that may be regretted later.

Your essential nature is that of a 'high-flyer' – energetic and enthusiastic, but with an impulsiveness that can tempt you into making hasty judgements and unwise decisions. The underlying challenge in your life is to bring your aspirations down to earth, and this requires the attribute of persistence. Situations are thus likely to recur to provide opportunities for you to curb your impulsiveness and develop both patience and humility.

Principal lessons: Discovering that happiness comes through sharing, and that individuality need not be selfish but can be expressed more fully when it is in harmony with others.

20 April–20 May
The Growing Time

Beaver

Your birthday comes during the period of dramatic change in the yearly cycle when new life puts down roots to secure stability. You seek solid progress – the sort that provides a firm foundation on which to build – and a sense of permanence. Your energy-expression is constructive, and with it you display organizational skill, even to the point of 'engineering' the lives of others.

Like Beaver, your totem animal, you have a capacity for hard work and persistent endeavour, busying yourself with making alterations and improvements to your surroundings and working conditions. You are quick to learn, but slow to make up your mind; creative, but inclined to be concerned more with material prosperity than with idealistic principles. Although warm and affectionate by nature, you can be inclined to be austere and vengeful towards those who cross you in any way.

Beavers find satisfaction in having possessions that bring comfort and pleasure, but need to guard against the excesses of self-indulgence and possessiveness.

Your essential nature is one of industriousness, with a capacity to manage things even within strict limitations, and a determination to consolidate and make secure.

Part of your Life Purpose is a recognition of the difference between what is temporal and what is lasting.

Principal lessons: Your worst emotional traumas are likely to be in those areas of your life in which the tendency to form attachments extends into close personal relationships and becomes possessive. Through the grist of experience you are cultivating flexibility, adaptability and compassion. You need to give others the 'space' to be themselves, just as you demand the space to be 'you'.

21 May–20 June
The Flowering Time

Deer

You were born during the last cycle of Spring, when trees are in full leaf and flowers are blooming – a time of expansion in

Nature – and your nature is one that seeks stimulation and variety. Your energy-expression is one of sudden change – blowing hot and cold over some issues, showing abundant vitality over what is immediately appealing and lethargy in other matters.

Like your totem animal, you are sensitive – quicker to recognize the needs and feelings of others than you are to understand your own – and prone to moodiness. You are resourceful, able to make the best of even the most basic materials. Like deer, you have boundless enthusiasm for the things that catch your attention, but are easily distracted and all too ready to leap from one attraction to another.

Restlessness and lack of concentration often distract you from accomplishing what you are capable of. You have a warm temperament and an affectionate nature, but your moods can undermine even your closest relationships unless you learn to cope with them. You have a strong sense of curiosity and a love of variety which draws you towards new experiences. Although you thrive on versatility, a warm and cheerful atmosphere and companionship with a positive attitude bring out the best in you.

A principal Life Purpose is learning the value of self-discipline and consistency. Many of your traumas are indications that you have not persisted long enough to gather fruits from your endeavours or learnt that lasting success comes from endurance.

Principal lessons: The rifts you have with others indicate divisions within yourself. You are learning how to co-ordinate that which appears to be contrary but which truly is complementary.

21 June–21 July　　　　　　　　*Woodpecker*
The Long Days Time

The month of your birth marks the beginning of the Summer season when the promises of Spring are coming to fruition. A person born at this time expresses the qualities of nurturing and protecting which are evident in Nature at this period of the Summer Solstice and the year's longest days. Your energy-

expression is concerned with the channelling of devotion. It is shown in your willingness to make sacrifices for the benefit of others close to you, which might, however, be converted into self-inflicted martyrdom.

Like their animal totem, Woodpeckers are clinging – reluctant to let go of what they consider is rightfully 'theirs', and this tendency applies even to personal relationships. Emotional and sensitive, yet possessive and vulnerable, Woodpeckers are warm and responsive to those closest to them, but often cool and aloof to strangers. They are easily hurt, and any disappointment or setback can trigger an attitude of self-pity, and even recrimination and bitterness.

Although affectionate by nature, you are likely to be unforgiving to anyone who brings an inadequacy of yours into the open, or poses any kind of threat to your security. Your fertile imagination may cause you to exaggerate and 'make mountains out of molehills', or to worry over issues that have no reality other than what is in your own mind.

Principal lessons: To learn to treasure the moment. Not to dwell on regrets of the past or on expectations of what may be in the future, but to recognize that the power to make changes is always in the Now!

The challenges facing you on your Earth 'Walk' are to enable you to mature through the experience of closeness. Much stress and anxiety may be caused through tenaciously holding on to what has served its purpose, and through mistaking attachment for love. The ability to let go is often a test of true love.

22 July–21 August　　　　　　　　　　*Salmon*
The Ripening Time

Your birthday falls at a time in the Northern hemisphere when the Sun is at the peak of its power and the whole of Nature is bringing forth its fruit in abundance. So this is a time of openness and bountiful activity. Your energy-expression is thus one of caring concern and zestful activity that thrives on close relationships and a strong sense of being wanted.

Your energy, enthusiasm and warm-heartedness are great assets, but there is a need to ensure that self-confidence does not develop into self-importance through arrogance and an uncompromising attitude. You may be well equipped to take charge and to run things – and that is fine – but difficulties can arise if you try to live other people's lives for them. You need to emulate your totem animal by not causing waves of disturbance and undue friction as you move through the waters of life.

Disappointment of any kind, or adversity, can quickly cause your usual optimism to crumble into gloom. Love and affection are essential ingredients for your well-being, and you feel things so intensely that you are more vulnerable to emotional upsets than most people. You are having to learn, in this lifetime, the necessity of attaining mastery of the emotions.

Principal lessons: You are frequently faced with situations which challenge your stubborn resistance to change, and with the need to become more flexible and adaptable through developing a regard for the emotional needs of others. You are learning to recognize that fulfilment comes not so much through the forcefulness of making things happen, but through allowing things to be.

22 August–21 September　　　　*Brown Bear*　
The Harvesting Time

You were born at the time in the yearly cycle when what has been sown is ready to be harvested. Your energy-expression is thus one of practical endeavour in order to harvest in full the potentials that lie within you.

Like their totem animal, Brown Bear people can stand on their own two feet in preference to reliance on others. Slow to make changes, they prefer the familiar to that which is new and unknown.

You are good at fixing things, whether they are objects requiring repair or situations which are causing a malfunctioning in the lives of others with whom you have an affinity. With a good eye for detail, you enjoy taking things apart and putting

them together again and seeing an improvement in the way they function. Although essentially a practical person, you have a vivid imagination and your fantasizing can lead you into assuming that things are different from what they are. Let your ideas and aspirations be incentives to practical achievement by keeping your feet firmly on the ground. Dreams become physical realities only when they are grounded.

Principal lessons: Whatever you are searching for is to be found where you are. You are learning to know when to exert energy to effect a change, and when to accept circumstances that cannot be changed.

22 September–22 October   *Crow*
The Falling Leaves Time

This is the period when the Autumn Equinox signals a slowing down of Nature in preparation for the Winter period of renewal that lies ahead. So the essential energy-expression of people born at this time is one of consolidation and the development of inner resources to deal with outer challenges.

Like their totem animal, Crow people require the company of others to provide them with a sense of security, and work best in partnerships or groups. This tendency provides them with an empathy for others and consideration of points of view other than their own.

You have an easy-going nature, disliking contention, muddle, confusion and emotional upsets, preferring to keep the peace at almost any price. You are a good organizer and an enthusiastic communicator, but reluctant to be hurried into making decisions you may later regret.

Challenges will arise in your life to test your capacity to share and co-operate with others whilst still retaining your individuality and independence.

Principal lessons: To gain the inner strength that comes from acting firmly on your convictions, and acquiring the wisdom that results from making sound judgements.

23 October–22 November   *Snake*
The Frost Time

This is a twilight period in the yearly cycle, just before Winter, and compares with sunset in the daily cycle. People born at this time have an affinity with both the visible and the invisible aspects of life. They have a probing curiosity to uncover what is not always apparent.

Like Snake, your totem animal, which is able to shed its skin and renew itself, you have a capacity to free yourself from former attachments and to leave the past behind and make dramatic changes to your life much more readily than most people. You abound with ideas, though they can cause you frustration if the changes you want cannot be made immediately or the time is inappropriate. You are adaptable to new situations and have the strength and endurance that enables you to make the best of even adverse situations and circumstances. Like Snake, you can climb to heights of elation or plummet to the depths of despondency.

Principal lessons: Your impatience causes you pain and discomfort, but such traumas are teaching you the need for proper timing. Being confronted with seemingly formidable tasks and difficult tests is part of the regenerative process inherent in your nature, which can enable you to transform what was into that which may now be. Such challenges push you beyond your own self-limitations.

23 November–21 December   *Owl*
The Long Nights Time

This is the period in the yearly cycle in the Northern hemisphere when the air is crisp and clear, and people born at this time have a clear sight of what they need and where they want to go.

Like Owl, your totem animal, you have a keen eye for detail and an inquisitive nature; you will break away from tiresome situations in which you are sometimes involved, preferring

your own company in which to reflect and consider. You are resourceful, self-reliant, and with an ability to adapt to a new environment or a changed situation without too much difficulty. Urged on by an inner drive, you are motivated to grasp fresh opportunities and accept new challenges. You require the warmth of close relationships and tend to cling to those who are responsive or supportive. Disliking confinement of any kind, you thrive best when allowed the freedom to express yourself.

Principal lessons: Learning to manage your potentials by not dissipating your energies in too many directions at once. Attainment of inner sight so you can perceive beyond the obvious, and a warm heart so you can be compassionate towards those who stumble around in the dark.

22 December–19 January   *Goose*
The Renewal Time

Your birthday comes at the most barren time of the year, and also at the beginning of a new pattern which, though dormant, is about to be quickened.

Like Goose, your totem animal, you are far-sighted with a willingness to explore unfamiliar territory. When that is coupled with purity of intent, the seemingly impossible becomes attainable, provided you never lose sight of your objective. You prefer to keep on the move and to accomplish, so you tackle tasks with enthusiasm. Your innate drive to be a perfectionist enables you to perform even quite ordinary jobs extraordinarily well. If you are in the company of others whose standards are lower than your own, or comparatively minor issues are dominant, you are easily provoked. Prudent by nature, you have a shrewd sense of values, but your idealism may cause you to be misunderstood.

Your challenge in life is to learn how to bring things to completion and thus gain the understanding that can come only through attainment.

Principal lessons: These are derived from your efforts to arrange

and conserve, for their purpose is to teach you self-reliance and self-sufficiency in order to establish your own identity.

20 January–18 February   *Otter*
The Cleansing Time

This middle period in the Winter season is a time when the Earth is being cleansed in preparation for new life. People born in this month are conservationists and visionaries.

Like Otter, your totem animal, you excel in orderliness, and require cleanliness both at home and in a work environment. You have a busy mind and enjoy getting involved with people, though you are prone to take on too many commitments. You are reforming in a constructive way, but shy away from too many rules and regulations which are inhibitive. You have a flair for originality and can be quite inventive, although your ideas are sometimes impractical.

Principal lessons: To help you to find the courage to act more on an inner 'knowing' than on other people's expectancies. You are learning to turn visions into practical realities through struggle and even adversity.

19 February–20 March   *Wolf*
The Blustery Winds Time

You were born at an 'in between' period in the yearly cycle and at a time of rapid change in anticipation of the vigour of new life which is about to come forth in Nature.

Like Wolf, your totem animal, you are highly sensitive and intuitive, able to discern the attitudes and intentions of others, however well hidden. Your sensitivity and compassion can cause you to be gullible and vulnerable to suffering emotional turmoil, if you allow sentiment to influence you. You have a love of what is pleasing to the eye and to the ear, and enjoy creative endeavours. Spend time on ways of self-expression that can provide you with the means of recuperating from the

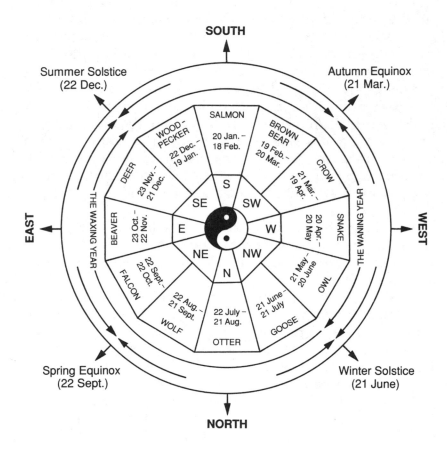

Figure 17. The Earth Medicine Wheel for the Southern hemisphere

demands that are often placed upon you – for refreshment and renewal come from within.

Principal lessons: To learn to become more discriminating in facing the demands that are constantly made upon you. The

challenges of your life are for the purpose of enabling you to break free from entanglements that are limiting and restrictive, so your horizons can be extended.

As the time segments in Earth Medicine are related to the seasons and the natural cycle of the year, the orientations in the Southern hemisphere are different, and so are the totem animals associated with the dates. For instance, in the Northern hemisphere Spring begins at the Spring Equinox around 21 March, and Falcon is the totem animal affecting the period 21 March–19 April. However, in the Southern hemisphere the Spring Equinox is around 22 September, so the period 22 September–22 October is the first portion of the Spring season and is the one associated with the Falcon. On the Earth Medicine chart, North and South exchange positions and so do East and West (see Fig. 17).

In astrology the Sun signs are the same in both hemispheres since they are determined by the Zodiac, a fixed imaginary belt encircling the entire Earth on which the constellations of stars are represented.

Astrology was originally a study of the energy-patterns of the Universe and how they affect and influence human development because they are imprinted within each individual. Earth Medicine is an awareness of the energy-patterns in the Earth's environment which are absorbed within us and help to fashion human personality and behaviour.

Although people born in the same month, or on the same day, share similar basic qualities it must be stressed that each individual is unique. Earth Medicine provides only indications that will help us to understand the nature of our own energy-patterns and potentials. But more importantly, it indicates the need for each of us to look inside rather than outside for explanations of why we are as we are.

Only by living in the Present can we experience the Living Presence that is not outside us and beyond reach, but within us every moment of an ever-present Now.

6. Cosmic Influences

YOU ARE A UNIVERSE. The universe that is 'You' is a miniaturization of the greater Universe and functions in accordance with similar laws. Understand yourself and you understand the way the Universe 'works', and vice versa, because you are it and it functions in you, too. You absorb subtle energies from the stars, planets, constellations and other cosmic influences, and these affect, to an extent, the way you are and the effect you have on others. Among the powers of the Universe are Cosmic influences which are charted on the Medicine Wheel as spokes. These are indicated as cardinal and non-cardinal 'directions', but they are not geographical orientations, as some have assumed, but ways in which powerful forces that influence energy-flow may be *approached*.

These powers are not limited to a specific direction or confined within a compartmentalized segment of a symbolic Circle of Awareness. They exist all around us, above and below us, outside and inside us. They impregnate and saturate all levels of our being – physical, mental, emotional and spiritual. So a 'direction' on the Medicine Wheel is not about where certain powers may be *located*, but how they may be *approached*, for the direction from which they are approached influences and affects the way they *respond*.

SELF-KNOWLEDGE THROUGH THE MEDICINE WHEEL

Before we examine the nature of these Cosmic powers, let us first understand a little about the Medicine Wheel itself. Its

86

basic purpose is to serve as a symbolic multi-dimensional device that enables connections to be made with Cosmic forces and natural energies, and balance to be attained with Nature and oneself. It functions at all levels – physical, mental and spiritual – and can be employed for many specific purposes. Here, we will confine our examination to its primary purpose as a means of obtaining self-knowledge through attunement with the natural energies that affect and influence our lives and the environment all around us.

The Wheel itself is an encircled cross. The circle represents the totality of space in the entire Universe. It is also our own personal space and everything that is within and around us as individuals.

The Medicine Wheel is a universal mandala that is beneficial to all human kind and not just to the Native Americans who have preserved and honoured it, because it is a catalyst of all other systems. A catalyst is something which brings about change without itself undergoing change but the Medicine Wheel is something more. It functions also as a process of *integration*. Integration is a bringing together of segmented portions into a unified and co-ordinated whole. So the Medicine Wheel is not only a means of bringing together those aspects of ourselves that we have been conditioned to assume are 'separate' – body, mind, soul and spirit – so that they might function together in unison, but also a means of bringing us into harmonious relationship with other beings and with the very powers of the Universe! Like a catalytic converter on a car that converts polluting gases into ecologically-friendly ones, the Medicine Wheel is a means of converting our polluting self into a self that is in harmony with the Universe. A pollutant contaminates, defiles, corrupts and violates the natural environment, which is precisely what we humans are doing to the Earth and to the Cosmic forces of the Universe through mis-use of the mind and in choosing to serve and satisfy the Ego-self.

In some mystical traditions relationships between different beings, bodies, objects and things that share a similar quality or qualities were called 'correspondences'. The word 'correspondence' is derived from the Latin *cum respondere* which means 'to promise or pledge with'. It is concerned with responsibility – the ability to respond and relate to. So 'correspondences' in

shamanic understanding denote a relationship between different beings, powers, substances and energies that triggers a response. Our response-ibility as human beings is to recognize that life is the same outside as it is inside. To change the outside we must first make changes to the inside. That is what the Medicine Wheel is truly about. Making changes to ourselves on the *inside* so that we may ultimately bring harmonious changes to the world 'outside', for our first responsibility is to ourselves as individuals.

When set up outdoors, the Medicine Wheel's centre is marked by eight stones to represent not only the hub around which everything revolves – individual awareness – but also the Source of Life and Light, Love and Law, that comes from within. They indicate the twin aspects of the use of energy – Giving and Receiving, and Holding and Determining (or Choosing). Another eight stones mark the perimeter of the circle and are placed at the cardinal and non-cardinal directions. These stones represent powers within the Universe and the individual, arranged in balance as a reminder of the Cosmic Law of Harmonics or Octaves. Eight further stones are used to form the arms of a cross and indicate paths to inner empowerment and self-cultivation. The Medicine Wheel can also be represented on a working surface as an encircled cross – a Circle of Awareness that serves as a reflective mirror to reveal how one's own life is being energized and shaped and how all things are related in some way to everything else. My book *The Medicine Way* is a practical guide to the Medicine Wheel as a personal development system.

The Medicine Wheel of the North American Indians and the Mystic Circle of Western traditions are identical symbols, but as they are aligned differently the effect and outcome is not the same. The Mystic Circle puts the emphasis on determining with the mind – that is, making choices and decisions through exercising the intellect and by what appears to be desirable, appropriate and beneficial to the Ego-self.

The circle is aligned in order to shape and mould in accordance with the Will. It is a way of obtaining the power to get what you want. It is the setting of the manipulator in order to exert control. It emphasizes the way of self-interest.

Dictionaries define the Will as the ability to effect a *cause*. Not to cause an effect, but to actually cause something to be. So

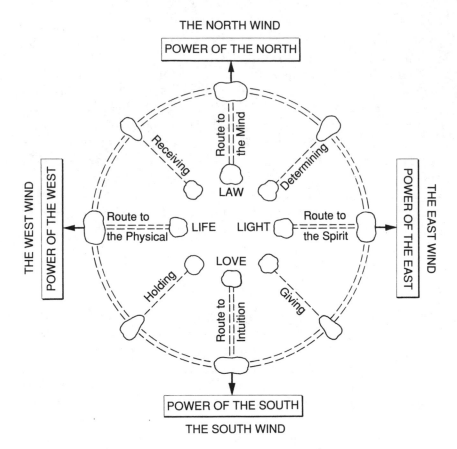

Figure 18. A Medicine Wheel representation indicating at its centre the source of powers that lie within, the twin powers of the use of energy which affect personal empowerment, and the routes or approaches to the Cosmic powers of the Universe

Will is what creates a happening. Free Will, then, is the freedom to cause something that is desired to come into being. It is the ability of a creator of both objects and situations. **It is a creative power of the Universe**! And we each have it and use it either to serve self-interest, which takes from others and other life forms in order to satisfy the desires of the Self, or as an exchange of energy that produces harmony because it is *shared* with others. The Will is what directs the creative powers we possess, and can be controlled by the Ego or the Spirit.

Medicine Wheel alignments show the approach of determining with the *Spirit*. This approach implies willing participation and co-operation at all levels of being and with all realms of existence. It is the way of establishing balance, harmony and beauty within the environment you are in. It is using energy to express what *you are*. It is 'the power to give what *you are*' rather than 'the power to get what *you want*' and, thereby, to express your essential energy in harmony. Harmony is a power that balances the development of the individual with that of the Whole, and functions at multi-dimensional levels of the Universe.

THE FOUR DIRECTIONS

The so-called Four 'Directions' are actually four mighty *Powers* – Cosmic Intelligences whose presence affects all living things as well as the Earth's environment and the atmosphere around the Earth. These Intelligences belong to a dimension which transcends physical and mental reality, and in generating *movement* they affect the nature of what is coming into manifestation. They are, therefore, far more than philosophical concepts, metaphysical principles or religious beliefs. They are spiritual *realities* that actually regulate Nature and the Universe! In some cultures they were known as the Four *Winds* because, as Spirits, they could not be seen, but like winds their presence could be experienced through the effect they had on their surroundings. Some worshipped them as 'gods' or venerated them as archangels – the highest-ranking celestial beings – because they control and manage the life-support systems of the Universe. Some Native American tribes referred to them as 'Spirit *Keepers*' because they are the guardians and caretakers of the Universe. Although possessing such awesome powers, they were not

regarded as fearsome, but approachable and benevolent. These Cosmic Intelligences, concerned with upholding the nature and structure of things coming into manifestation rather than the forms themselves, were understood to be enabled to express themselves without the vehicle of a body.

Totems were used to represent these 'Spirit Keepers' and to serve as symbolic 'connectors'. The totem of the **North** is Buffalo, an animal which provided native peoples with everything necessary for survival, so it indicates orderly *compacted power*. The totem of the **West** is Grizzly Bear, which is characteristic of *inner strength* and introspection. The totem of the **East** is Eagle, a bird that reputedly flies closest to the Sun – the source of light and *radiance*. The totem of the **South** is Mouse, a tiny animal associated with *rapid growth*, and which stresses the importance of not confusing power with size. Its whiskers indicate the importance of 'closeness' to things and the power of emotion.

Whatever is associated with a Directional Power through a spiritual, mystical, magical or metaphysical system, actually aligns it with an energy-expression and affects its mode of activity. In other words, the individual sooner or later experiences the consequences of the approach. Direction is thus of prime importance. So is motive and intention.

Motive is what initiates movement and causes action in a particular way. It is a generating force that actually *drives* an activity. Intent has to do with *aim*. In Shamanics the motive is always that of Love and Harmony, so that what is attained is always for the ultimate benefit of the person, persons, or beings involved in order to restore or maintain harmony and balance. The intention, however, is always focused on a specific purpose.

Feng Shui

Coming into harmony with the Cosmic forces that uphold the environment was called in ancient China, *Feng Shui*. Feng Shui means 'Wind and Water', indicating that these hidden forces act like air and water in the way the environment all around us is maintained. Indeed, the advice of Feng Shui Masters was sought regarding where best to build a house and place its doors and windows so that every aspect of the building could

be aligned harmoniously with the Directional Powers. Even today there are Feng Shui consultants working among Chinese communities in some of the world's major cities and practising this ancient tradition which is said to be at least three thousand years old. Its origins, however, go back much further for they are derived from the shamanism of much earlier times.

Wind and Water are terms that describe not only the powers that fashion our natural surroundings, but also the very *aliveness* that enables them to continue to influence the environment. Feng Shui, however, was not a means of controlling the environment and bringing it under subjection, but rather of living respectfully and harmoniously within it by aligning with its positive effects and being aware of any negative influences. In other words, like Shamanics and the spirit of shamanism from which it originated, Feng Shui was a practical way of dealing with reality – with the way the Universe is.

CONNECTING WITH THE CARDINAL DIRECTIONS

If we harmonize and co-operate with the forces of Nature, the environment will support and uphold us. If we tamper with Nature, or are motivated in our approach by a selfishness that generates disharmony and chaos, its equilibrium will be disrupted, with threatening and sometimes disastrous consequences. So how are we to establish the directions and recognize the powers that are inherent in each one?

In the Northern hemisphere the pivot around which the stars appear to revolve is Polaris – the North Star. On a clear night, Polaris is easily located for it is positioned in a direct line above the 'container' of the Plough – a group of distinctly-shaped stars in the constellation of Ursa Major – which is also known as the Big Dipper. The polar star shines quite brightly. On the Medicine Wheel, North is positioned at the top of the circle because the perspective is grounded to the Earth as if one is looking towards the North Star. In astrology and in Taoist chartings, South is at the top because the perspective is a 'heavenly' or Cosmic one, as if one is looking from the direction of the North Star. Either way, a position is being established in Time and Space in relation to a 'fixed' and immoveable point – in this case the polar star.

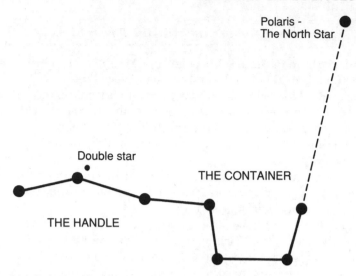

Figure 19. *Polaris, the North Star, is in a direct line from the first star of the 'container' of the Plough, or Big Dipper, a group of seven stars which turn around the seemingly 'fixed' position of Polaris in the northern hemisphere. The sixth star in the group is a 'double' star.*

On the Medicine Wheel, East is on the right, West is on the left, and South is at the bottom of the circle.

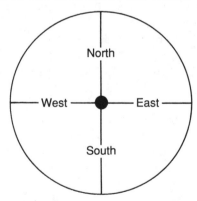

Figure 20. *The cardinal directions on the Medicine Wheel*

You can actually obtain a 'feel' for each of these cardinal directions and receive a personal teaching from connecting with them by undertaking the following Experiences.

Experience 9: Connecting with the Power of the North

Wait for a time in the month when the Moon is waxing to Full and you can go outside at night and see its silvery light.

Locate the North Star and align yourself with that direction so that you are facing due **North**. Now focus your attention on the North Star and become aware of the perfection of the almost imperceptible movement as the whole galaxy moves around that seeming pin-prick of a pivotal point.

Now 'connect' with the Power of the North. You can do this simply by making a clear intention to do so in an attitude of positive expectancy that entertains no doubt.

A quality of the Power of the North is *renewal*. So by connecting with the Power of the North you can receive from it energy from that quality and absorb it into yourself – an ability to renew *yourself*: make a fresh start and put the past with all its 'mistakes', pains, sorrows and disappointments behind you. **To be made 'new'**!

There is nothing you have to 'do' except to be receptive so your mind may be open to receive information, and relaxed so your body is ready to experience any sensation. Just allow the Power of the North to energize you. *Clarity* is among its many other attributes, so let the Power of the North remove the conditioning that in the past has prevented you from seeing things as they truly are and not as others have led you to believe them to be, and ask the Power of the North to give you a personal teaching about clarity.

Afterwards go back indoors and make notes of what you have experienced and the personal teaching you have received.

Experience 10: Connecting with the Power of the West

For this Experience it is best to choose a time when you can go outdoors and watch the Sun set.

As you face **West** and watch the Sun sink slowly down onto the horizon, simply relax and allow yourself to be absorbed in the soft blanket of golden colours and 'connect' with the bounteousness of the Power of the West.

A quality of the West is *transformation*, which you are now experiencing physically, so just allow yourself to be touched by the power that brings *change* – the power that can enable you to be transformed from what you have been, and from the limitations and constraints that have gripped and confined you, into what you are capable of becoming: a greater, more *complete* you.

Experience that change actually taking place within you now. Don't just *think* about it mentally, *feel* it physically.

Then ask the Power of the West to give you a personal teaching about change, transition and transformation, and wait for a response.

By the time all this has happened, the Sun will have dipped below the horizon and day will have become night, and that very act of Nature will help you to understand the need to ground your visions and bring your own spirituality down to Earth into physical reality.

Go back indoors and write up your experiences and the messages you have been given.

Experience 11: Connecting with the Power of the East

Get up before dawn and go to an outdoor location which is natural and undisturbed by obtrusive traffic noise. If it is your own garden, fine. But if you live in a large town or big city, it may be necessary to arrange a day or two in a country area where it will be more convenient for you to experience a dawn.

Stand facing **East**, where the dawn will break, and listen to the stillness of the night. Be warmed by its blanket of silence and recognize that in the silence there are sounds. Then, just before sunrise, those silent sounds will expand into the beginnings of the dawn chorus as birds awaken from their slumber and are touched by the gentle movement that heralds a new day.

As the distant horizon begins to lighten, connect with the Power of the East and experience the power and vitality that generates the dawning of a new day. Feel a power within you 'awakening' and bringing light into those areas of your life which you have not understood.

A quality of the Power of the East is *enlightenment*, so ask the Power of the East to enlighten you with a teaching *now*.

Afterwards, write an account of your experiences and the teaching you have received.

Experience 12: Connecting with the Power of the South

Plan to be in an outdoor location at around noon. A garden will do, or a quiet place where you can be surrounded by natural things. Face **South**, which is the direction the Sun is in at midday.

Stand relaxed but alert, and lift your left arm as if you are reaching out to touch the Sun with your hand. Do not stretch or strain in any way – just a gentle, easy movement as you connect with the Power of the South to experience the *closeness* of its radiance. As you breathe in, become aware of an inner glow as you receive its *strength* into yourself. Continue this for a while, then let your arm relax to your side.

Adaptability is a quality of the South, so you can ask the Power of the South to help you to move more easily with the flow of life and *adapt* yourself to its changing circumstances. Ask the Power of the South to empower you with the flexibility to *adapt* to change, and to give you a personal teaching that will help you to become more *intuitive*.

Immediately afterwards make notes of what you have experienced and the teaching you have received.

So the powers inherent in these Spirit 'Keepers' respond in accordance with the direction in which they are approached and the motive and intention which colours that mode of activity; and although they transcend the Dimensions, they generate movement within them all. Each also has an influence on the development of our total being. For instance:

The *Power of the West* activates the intelligence of the physical body and enables it to work with the material substances that constitute our flesh, blood and bones.

The *Power of the North* clarifies the mind and purifies our mental being.

The *Power of the South* empowers and strengthens the intuitive 'self'.

The *Power of the East* enables us to be enlightened with sudden flashes of inspiration and understanding through our innermost 'self', which is the noblest aspect of our total being.

Colour and the Four Powers

Each of the Four Powers is associated with a colour on the Medicine Wheel – white in the North, black in the West, yellow in the East, and red in the South – because the colour is a vibratory expression of its inherent qualities and it, too, has an impact on the human energy-system. It is not without significance that white, black, yellow and red (brown) are the colours also of the four primary races of mankind.

The Spirit 'Keepers' are intangible creative powers that might be beyond the range of human comprehension but are contactable shamanically. Here are some of their essential qualities,

their principal areas of influence on the human condition, and their totems.

Power of the North
The power of renewal
The power of quickening
The power of purity
The power of clarity
Principal human aspect: The mind
Chief characteristic: Intelligence
Emphasis: Purity and intensity
Totem: Buffalo

Colour: White

Power of the West
The power of transformation
The power of introspection
The power of consolidation
The power of grounding
Principal human aspect: The physical body
Chief characteristic: Endurance
Emphasis: Stability
Totem: Grizzly Bear

Colour: Black

Power of the East
The power that enables Light to be
The power to disperse darkness and ignorance
The power to illuminate and make known
The power of awakening
The power of newness of life
Principal human aspect: The Spirit
Chief characteristic: Far-sightedness
Emphasis: Spirituality
Totem: Eagle

Colour: Yellow

Power of the South
The power of organic growth
The power of discovery
The power of teachability
The power of unfolding
The power of inner sensing – intuitive knowing

Principal human aspect: Emotions
Chief characteristic: Closeness
Emphasis: Vitality
Totem: Mouse   *Colour*: Red

WAKAN-TANKA

Figure 21. The Wakan-Tanka symbol of energy spiralling into manifestation and of form reverting to energy within the Circle of Creation

The movement I have indicated on the Medicine Wheel, by starting at the North, moving counter-clockwise to the West, across to the East and clockwise to the South, is a spiralling one. If traced on a two-dimensional circle it produces an S-shape which, among the Plains Indians of North America, was a symbol for Wakan-Tanka – the Great Spirit in manifestation. This is represented here as arising out of the Mind of the Great Spirit in the North, moving West to manifest in physical form, then to the East to be activated by Spirit, and then to the South to live as a Child of Nature in order to enable Spirit to experience involvement with matter. The symbol also indicates movement of energy into form and form into energy. By joining together the polarities of North and South, the S-shape is converted into another symbol, a figure 8, which is the twin circle of motion between two polarities – the visible and invisible, physical and spiritual, mind and matter, Yin and Yang – in a never-ending continuity of existence.

YANG AND YIN

The origin of all movement and, indeed of Life itself, is expressed in the ancient Chinese symbol of the Tai Chi – the Supreme

Figure 22. The Taoist Tai Chi mandala is symbolic of the active and receptive, masculine and feminine, aspects of the Original Source, held in perfect and dynamic balance to emphasize the relationship of the forces of complementary opposites inherent in everything in manifestation.

Ultimate – which combines within it the essences of Heaven and Earth, spiritual and physical. It embraces a similar meaning to the Wakan-Tanka symbol. This singular Original Source polarized the energy within Itself into two – Yang and Yin – each delicately balanced in harmony with the other and comprising a dynamic cyclic power of movement and rest which enables force to become form.

Yang and Yin are not static states of different energies, but *relative values* – interchangeable phases of the same basic energy. Active and passive, positive and negative, hot and cold, masculine and feminine. Expansive and contractive aspects of the same thing and derived from the same Source. Yang transforms and transports. Yin assimilates and stores.

The Chinese ideogram for Yang means the sunny side of the hill. For Yin, it is the shadowy side of the hill. These images express how, through natural movement such as the orbit of the Earth around the Sun, each is transformed through the other, just as the sunshine side of a hill becomes the sunset side in the great creative process of change.

Yang and Yin are thus two Original Forces that govern the Universe and themselves symbolize Harmony. All things contain a varying degree of Yang and Yin which are in a constant state of movement and change. Hence, nothing forever remains the same. Everything, however static or solid or apparently immobile and permanent, vibrates and pulsates. Everything is

energy coming into form, remaining as form for a duration, and then reverting to energy in a magnificent circular, cyclical and spiralling Dance of Life.

THE DYNAMICS OF LIFE

Understanding the reality of Yang and Yin is important for it helps us to comprehend the *dynamics* of Life – the way natural energies flow and change. The whole Universe is in a state of constant change because of the creative interaction of Yang and Yin, and so are humans because we are ourselves mini-universes. The changing pattern of the seasons in the cycle of the year is not haphazard but of the very nature of Reality, and this has its effect on everything else that is coming into manifestation, including us, and we are partly fashioned by it. The garment of flesh that clothes the human Spirit contains an expression of the changing nature of the Earth itself at the time and place of our birth, as well as an imprint of the Universe (as discussed in the previous chapter), for the Cosmic Laws that govern the Universe function also within us, and the same Powers, conditions and processes that comprise the Universe comprise us too.

What has been called 'Creation' is thus in Reality a *transformational process* – from that which is invisible to that which is visible: the intangible becoming tangible, and energy being transformed into matter and matter being transmuted back to energy.

According to ancient wisdom, Creation was dependant on Four Principles: the active and initiating being attracted to the passive and receptive and forming a *Unity* in equilibrium and harmony to produce a new creation through its inherent power of Love. So the Two produced a Third as a result of the bonding power of Love that united them and *is* them. And the Third brought into being the Fourth, which is the multitude of all that manifests.

Taoist shamans referred to this Source as a spiritual 'Sun' that emerged from a Great Emptiness they called *Wu Chi*. Native Americans called this Void 'Great Mystery', out of which Great Spirit emerged. Among ancient Hebrews the word YHVH was understood as 'the One that cannot be Named' and

translated also as 'I Am That I Am'. Yahweh, or Yeywah (vowels are not contained in the Hebrew alphabet of twenty-two characters) can mean also 'I Am Absolute Love and Absolute Love is What I Am'. The spiritual 'Sun' – or Great Star – according to this ancient shamanic understanding, contained within its One-ness a trinity of Original Beings who brought the Universe and all that is contained within it into existence as it became self-aware and extended itself. As the expansive power of this Great Star expanded outwards in a great spiralling movement – blending, dispersing and absorbing pure energy as It extended Itself *from the inside out* – particles of It flowed throughout Space as Cosmic dust. This subsequently became the soil of the Earth and also the substance from which human flesh was formed. That is what is truly meant in the sacred writings of Judaism and Christianity in referring to the human being: 'Dust thou art, and unto dust thou shalt return', (Genesis 3:19). **We are each a self-aware particle of Light from a Great Star. Star Dust!** An individuated spark from a Solar Being. A Spirit expression of a Greater Spirit. Thus the Nameless One is able to experience Itself in an infinite number of ways through reproducing Itself in an infinite number of ways. So it is that we live in a holographic Universe and we ourselves are a holographic system. (A hologram is a three-dimensional image in which every part of the picture contains an image of the whole, and information about the whole picture is contained in every individual part.) This was the knowledge of the 'Wise Ones' which has been 'hidden', obscured or suppressed.

The first Original Being of the Triple Unity, according to this understanding, is a Cosmic Intelligence that forms *particles*.

The second Original Being of the Triple Unity forms *wave patterns* by which It is able to pervade everything and through which everything is enabled to be supplied with energy.

Through the bonding power of Love – of the Yang and the Yin positively and negatively 'charged' – these Two produced a Third, co-equal with them, in order that *manifestation* could take place.

In Native American understanding, Great Spirit and Great Mystery are not identical, but individually complete. European settlers and their missionaries, with a concept of a God with human-like attributes but supernatural powers who could express great love and compassion on the one hand and violent

jealousy and condemnation on the other, could not comprehend such an understanding. Great Spirit came out of the Void
– which is the Great Mystery – to direct the creation of all life
forms and to perform it in love, beauty and harmony. In the
East, Taoist shamans shared a similar understanding, though
expressed in a different way. Lao Tzu, the Chinese sage, described the Void as 'the Nothingness out of which everything
came'. The Three Great Beings contained within the Nameless
One became represented in Taoist mythology as three 'Emperors'. These Three were perceived as controlling the three principal bodies of a human being – the physical (which includes
the Energic and the Mental), the Soul and its body of Light,
and the Spirit which is the essential being. The Three Emperors
were said to reside in three 'palaces' – *tan-tiens* or 'heavenly
places' – the 'three treasures' of a human being. A Lower tan-
tien is positioned in the Energic Body and located just below
the belly button and about 5 centimetres (a couple of inches)
beneath the surface. It is a storage place for a vital essence (see
Chapter 7). From its 'reservoir' it distributes this life-sustaining
essence through electro-magnetic and biochemical substances
and body fluids. The Middle tan-tien is in the area of the chest.
As a person experiences an expansion of consciousness and becomes more spiritually 'aware', this tan-tien moves towards the
central chakra column. The Upper tan-tien is located in the
head and is concerned with the perception of non-physical
things. All three develop naturally in accordance with a way
that is best suited to the individual.

THE FOUR ELEMENTS

Within this understanding the Third Original Being was perceived as having brought into being what became known as
Elements – Energy Beings responsible for the structure and
substance of matter. Through them energies are enabled to
take form in physical manifestation. The Elements are transformational processes that not only *possess* specific qualities but
have *intelligence*, because Spirit directs their movement. Each
Element has a direct influence on the physical, mental and
spiritual processes of human beings, so understanding something of their nature can help us to come into harmony with

them. There should be no attempt to manipulate and control them for that way brings about adverse consequences.

According to Western mystical traditions there are four Elements: Air, Fire, Water and Earth. These four were regarded as basic 'components' of whatever exists in physical reality although they were not understood to be *physical* substances, but metaphysical *principles* which governed the way matter appeared. However, the Elements can best be understood as energy *movements*. They indicate the way energy *moves* and is *transformed* or *transmuted* in a *natural* process. The Four Elements were sometimes symbolized as an equal-armed cross contained within a circle to represent them in a state of equilibrium and balance. Each associated with a Direction, but this indicated a *mode of activity* in relationship with a Directional Power or 'Spirit Keeper', rather than a location. For instance, an approach which places Earth in the North, Air in the East, Fire in the South, and Water in the West, is one in which the emphasis is on control and manipulation; whereas when Air is approached in the North, Fire in the East, Water in the South, and Earth in the West, the mode is that of harmony and balance.

Each Element is Spirit, but it is not individuated like 'human' Spirit, nor is it a 'group' Spirit, as with animals and trees. Rather, it is a *class* of Spirit. This is why Native Americans referred to the Elements as Spirit *clans*.

All the Elements were responsible for moulding the very substance and structure of the planet Earth when it came into manifestation, and they are still actively involved in this process and in the organization and arrangement of what is coming into form. Each Element has identifiable qualities and characteristics:

Fire is creative, expansive, vigorous, explosive, consuming.
Water is fluid, adaptable, absorbing, contractive, dispersing.
Air is boundless, quick, impatient, unpredictable.
Earth is stable, patient, nurturing, stubborn.

Each Element predominates in one of the four principal bodies of a human being:

Element of **Earth** predominates in the *physical* body.
Element of **Water** predominates in the *energic* body.
Element of **Air** predominates in the *mental* body.
Element of **Fire** predominates in the *Soul* body.

Each element governs an aspect of Life itself:

Fire – the *spark* of Life.
Air – the *breath* of Life.
Water – the *flow* or *river* of Life.
Earth – the *substance* of Life.

The Spirits of the Elements, though classes rather than groups – in some sacred writings they are referred to as *Choirs* – have no gender, but they do have individuated *expressions* of themselves and these are what are sometimes called Elementals. Elementals may be regarded as the *builders* of Nature and work at an unconscious level, whereas Elements are the *designers* and function at a superconscious level. Elementals do not have bodies, but they can appear to humans in the form of images which indicate their elemental nature: *Air* spirits as fairies with wings, for instance; *Fire* spirits as salamanders; *Water* spirits as nymphs; and *Earth* spirits as gnomes. Nor should they be confused with Devas, as they often are. The word 'deva' is derived from a Sanskrit word which is interpreted as 'shining one' – meaning a Celestial Being or archangel. Devas are Spirits that are concerned with the guidance of an entire planet and the life forms a Planetary Being sustains. The Elements, when perceived as *living* Realities rather than as principles or concepts, are identified as creative and formative Intelligences that emanate from the Great Spirit and function in dynamic relationship *within* Nature, each expressing a quality of movement through their presence.

Animal Totems

In American Indian traditions, each Element was associated with an animal totem which provided further understanding of its essential qualities as well as serving as a 'connector'. For instance:

Fire with Hawk

Water with Frog

Earth with Turtle

Air with Butterfly

To American Indians, **Hawk** is a 'Fire-bird', not only because, like Eagle, it flies nearer the Sun, but because in their mythology it was associated with thunder and lightning. So Hawk characterizes the instantaneousness of understanding, like a sudden flash of lightning, and the power of transmutation, like thunder that heralds weather changes. So Hawk – the Element of **Fire** – brings inspiration, generates enthusiasm, and invigorates and purifies.

Frog characterizes the Element of **Water** because of its adaptability – from tadpole to four-legged creature – and its flexibility in being able to adjust to changes of environment – from water to land. So the Element of Water is a Spirit of adaptability, sensitivity, and adjustment to changing circumstances.

Turtle is characteristic of the Element of **Earth** because of its solidity and inertia. The Element of Earth, like its totem, brings with it qualities of persistence and tenacity.

Butterfly is the totem for Air, primarily because of its constant changes of movement and its ability to transform itself from grub to chrysalis to winged creature. The Element of **Air** has the capacity to make constant changes of movement and to transform the environment through its power of movement in its presence.

Totems are thus a tangible means of making connections with intangible powers and can be highly effective in giving instant access to the qualities inherent in the power-source which they represent. By associating a totem with an Element we are thus enabled to relate to it more easily and share in its essential qualities.

THE FIVE ELEMENTS

In the so-called Eastern tradition, there are *five* Elements – Wood, Fire, Earth, Metal and Water. These are often symbolized

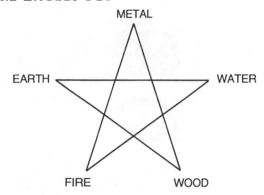

Figure 23. The pentagram is a symbol of the Elements in their functional relationship.

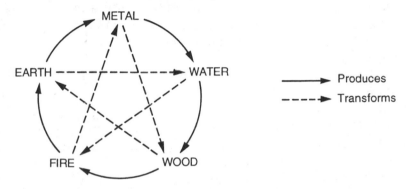

Figure 24. The Five Elements in their productive and transformational modes

in the form of a pentagram – a five-pointed star – which serves to indicate their functional and transformational relationships. The two broad traditions – East and West – are not, as it might appear, contrary or even *different* understandings. They are *complementary* **polarities** of a totality and indicate what are essentially *different modes of activity*. In Chinese, the names of the Five Elements are the names also of the five major planets. Wood is Jupiter, Fire is Mars, Earth is Saturn, Metal is Venus, and Water is Mercury. The significance of this is that the planets are not perceived solely as objects that are way off in the Universe, great distances away from where we are on Earth. They share a relationship in the energy-system of the Universe which is identical to the way certain forces function within the energy-system of the miniature universe that comprises our own total being. As the planets can be viewed as

properties of the Universe with a relationship with the Earth, so the planets can be viewed as properties of the Soul with a relationship with the physical body. This is why in ancient astrology, planets were assigned to different organs of the body and were considered as relating to and influencing them in some way: Mars (*Fire*) to the heart, Venus (*Metal*) to the lungs, Mercury (*Water*) to the kidneys, Saturn (*Earth*) to the spleen, and Jupiter (*Wood*) to the liver.

This very ancient understanding, in which Earth is linked so closely with Saturn, is made more intriguing by the news that a space mission is to be launched from Cape Canaveral, Florida, in October 1997. It will take seven years for the space vehicle to get close enough to Saturn to launch a mini flying saucer to explore Titan, one of Saturn's eighteen moons, which researchers believe may resemble what Earth itself was like some 4.5 million years ago before life on the planet began.

In this understanding, the heart (*Mars/Fire*) is seen to support the spleen (*Saturn/Earth*), the spleen supports the lungs (*Venus/Metal*), the lungs support the kidneys (*Mercury/Water*), the kidneys support the liver (*Jupiter/Wood*), and the liver supports the heart. A similar cycle applies to other organs – the small intestine (*Mars/Fire*) supports the stomach (*Saturn/Earth*), the stomach supports the large intestine (*Venus/Metal*), the large intestine supports the bladder (*Mercury/Water*), and the bladder supports the gallbladder (*Jupiter/Wood*). If there is an energy imbalance within a organ it will not support the

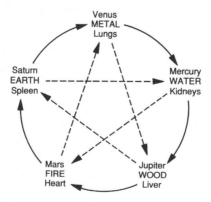

Figure 25. The Five Elements and their relationship with the five major planets and the five principal organs of the physical body

succeeding organ in the cycle, so that will be adversely affected also. In this mode of motion and flux, each property generates or breaks down another. Chinese medicine is founded on these fundamental principles.

Elements are thus not themselves energies but energy **movements**. They indicate the way energy *moves* and *transforms* itself in a natural and cyclical process. For instance:

Wood **burns** and *produces* Fire.
Fire **leaves** ash, which is Earth.
Earth **contains** ore, which *produces* Metal.
Metal **melts** and *produces* Water.
Water **nourishes** plant life and *produces* Wood.

And thus the cycle is completed. However, in a dispersement cycle:

Wood **destroys** Earth by drawing on its strength.
Fire **melts** Metal.
Earth **pollutes** Water.
Metal **chops down** Wood.
Water **extinguishes** Fire.

When the Five Elements of the Chinese system are positioned on the Medicine Wheel:

Wood – as the **generating** force – is in the East.
Fire – as the **expanding** force – is in the South.
Earth – as the **harmonizing** force – is in the Centre.
Metal – as the **introverting** force – is in the West.
Water – as the **reverting** force – is in the North.

Although the Five Elements of Chinese understanding are the movements of energies in a process of *transformation* and *evolution* or *devolution*, rather than a mode of *equilibrium* as with Western traditions, when positioned on the Medicine Wheel the two understandings are seen to harmonize. With the Five Elements of the Chinese approach, Earth at the Centre is seen as a great balancing and uniting force. With the Four Elements of Western traditions, there is a 'hidden' Element at the Centre. Theosophists called this fifth 'Element' *Aether* or *Ether* – hence the words *etheric*, meaning 'delicate spiritual substance', and *ether* meaning 'heavenly, or Cosmic, Light'. This 'Light' in the Centre was thus the Light out of which the Four Elements *came*

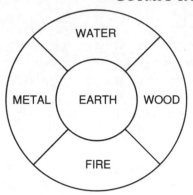

Figure 26. The Five Elements of Chinese tradition on a Medicine Wheel, with Earth at its centre as the uniting element

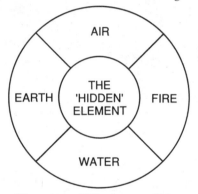

Figure 27. The Four Elements of Western tradition on a Medicine Wheel, with the 'missing' fifth element at the centre

in the process of manifestation. In the complementary Chinese system the Earth at the Centre is what the other four Elements *become* in the process of manifestation: two sides of the same 'coin', complementary aspects of a single reality.

Confirmation of these five phases of cyclic movement is provided by an American Indian numeric system called the Twenty Count, which makes use of the numbers 1–20 inclusive. When applied to the Medicine Wheel the fifth number of each sequence – 5, 10, 15, 20 – is positioned at the centre.

THE GENETIC ALPHABET

The patterns of existence within a multi-dimensional Reality, including everything in the manifest Universe, are set in

motion and kept in being through a Triad arising from the Unity of the Yin and Yang polarities and the creative and harmonic interplay provided by Four great powers that animate what is coming into form. Compare this most ancient understanding with the findings of modern-day genetic scientists who have discovered that each chromosome (a rod-like structure which carries the genes within a cell) is made up of the double spiral of DNA substance. A gene is composed of **four** bases – adenine, thymine, guanine and cytosine – which form the cross-links between the double spiral of the DNA molecule. The genetic alphabet comprises just **four** characters – A, T, G and C – the initial letters of the four bases. These letters form a genetic code in which any **three** form the template for the production of a basic building block of protein – an amino acid. There are only **twenty** amino acids but they can be arranged in an infinite number of diverse sequences, each with its own specialist and unique function. What is being hailed as the greatest discovery of all time is but a confirmation of ancient shamanic wisdom which was aware that what is coming into manifestation is a process of natural order directed by intelligence.

Before we undertake direct personal experience of relating with these Intelligences, we need first to consider the miraculous power that was understood by the Ancients to animate what is coming into form and which provides every living thing with its sense of *alive*-ness.

There exists a community of living Beings whose unique expressions create an orchestration of awesome beauty and whose inherent power manifests itself in what we call Nature.

7. 'That Without Which Nothing Can Exist'

THERE IS A POWER APPARENT in Nature all around us, although it goes unperceived by most people. It is unknown to materialistic science because it is not physical, but it has been recognized by shamans for thousands of years as an underlying essence that enables every living thing to experience 'alive-ness'.

An essence may be defined as a pure, unrefined primal energy from which something is derived. All things are enveloped and immersed in this essence and, indeed, are sustained within it. Everything in the physical Universe either vibrates or pulsates with it, and everything is kept in being because of it. Even the apparent inanimate nature of some things – rocks and stones, for instance – is an illusion for they, too, are 'alive' with it.

The essence of that 'aliveness' which generates activity in every living creature, from elementary amoeba to sophisticated human being, is a spiritual essence which was referred to by some shamans as 'That Without Which Nothing Can Exist'.

In Polynesia and parts of North America is was called *Mana* (Mah-nah), meaning 'miraculous power'. In China it was called *Chi* (Chee), meaning 'life force', and in Japan *Ki* (Kee) – 'vital essence'. In India it was known by the Sanskrit word *Prana* (Prah-na) – 'absolute energy' – and by shamans of the ancient Northern peoples by the Norse word *Megin* (May-gin), meaning 'inner power'. Each of these words refers to an *aspect* of the same primal power and indicates that among indigenous peoples in all parts of the world there was an understanding of an essence which pervades and activates all living forms yet

is itself *not* matter. That essence is in the air we breathe and in what we consume.

MANA

The Hawaiian word *Mana* was also understood by shamans throughout other Pacific islands and by some Native American tribes as simply 'the Life Force'. Hawaiian is a very ancient language with some unusual qualities. Words have a basic or 'surface' meaning, but by breaking them down into component units and root words they take on extended meanings. These meanings, which are 'hidden' within the word, provide a fuller understanding of what the word represents. Indeed, the closer a word is examined the more profoundly detailed it is, just like Nature itself! Mana is also the name given by kahuna shamans of Hawaii to describe a source of power that enabled them to perform apparently 'miraculous' deeds.

The word *kahuna*, in its general sense, means 'master' or 'expert'. *Huna* means 'secret' or 'hidden'. Kahuna shamans were known as 'the Keepers of the Secrets' because they were the guardians of an ancient but hidden knowledge of what lay behind the realm of appearances. So a kahuna shaman might be defined as a person who was a Master of the secrets of life that are hidden from view. The title 'Keeper', as with most mystical traditions, did not imply being kept out of reach, but rather implied being preserved. The kahunas preserved the integrity of an ancient wisdom with which they had been entrusted. In other cultures, tribal shamans guarded the knowledge that enabled them to have access to the forces of Nature and they shared it only with specially chosen initiates who were apprenticed to them and who would carry the work on into future generations. Only the 'travelling' shamans who journeyed from tribe to tribe or between communities, gathering new knowledge as they went and mixing what they learned with what they already knew, passed on any of the knowledge, and then only to those whose hearts were such that they would apply it in love and harmony. Indeed, this book is being written in accordance with the spirit of the 'travelling' shamans.

According to these oral teachings, the power behind this

'miraculous force' was a combination of four different aspects of power.

Power as an energizing and creative force.
Power as mastery and control.
Power as influence and authority.
Power as ability to perform specific work with confidence.

By combining all these facets, Mana can be understood as 'an energizing force with an inherent authority to bring into and maintain in being with confidence and control'.

Hawaiian dictionaries further define the word Mana as 'a power that *spreads'*. *Ma* is its prefix and *Na* its suffix. *Ma* can be understood as 'to entwine' and *Na* as 'belonging to'. So Mana can be regarded as 'an entwining power that belongs to whatever it clings to'. Let us go further: *Ma* also means 'by means of' and 'to make firm or solid'. So Mana has an ability to make things appear to be solid – in other words, to manifest! **Mana is a power that makes the invisible visible**!

Na means 'particle' as well as 'belonging to'. So Mana is a particle that belongs to something. Belongs to what? To its original source, of course. Mana comes direct from an Original Source!

The root word *Ana* means 'a pattern' and also 'balls of substance that satiate'. So Mana is a cluster of particles of a spiritual substance that satiates what it brings life to. The word *Maa* means 'breeze' or 'breath' and this carries our comprehension even further. **Mana is a spiritual substance that is carried in the air and may be likened to the soft breeze of breath.**

Kahuna shamans were aware that Mana *flows*. They likened it to a current of water, for in ancient times the Life Force was often symbolized as water – simply a wavy line. However, today its nature might be likened more to electricity with its different strengths or voltages. Mana has certain magnetic qualities for, as the breakdown of the word revealed, it clings, as grapes do to a vine. In ancient times the Life Force was often symbolized as a grapevine.

As Mana is thus a vital force that flows, so its primary function is *movement*. But that movement is not so much that which activates matter but rather that which becomes organized into matter. It *satiates*!

If life is considered basically to be movement, then it is Mana

that actually makes that movement possible. Without movement, vibration, vitality, activity, pulsation, circulation and flow, there is no life. No Mana!

It is in the atmosphere of Space that Mana is in its most free state, and it is from the air that it can be drawn in most easily – not through the lungs of the physical body, but through the chakras of the Energic Body. Though Mana is *in* the air it is not the air, nor is it a chemical constituent *of* air. And although Mana is taken in with the breath, it is not atmospheric substance, the oxygen contained in the air, or the breath itself. The air and the breath are merely *charged* with it.

Since scientists can find no chemical trace of Mana in atmospheric air, or discover it through the use of scientific instruments, they have either denied its existence or claimed that such a concept is unscientific and unprovable. Medical science, too, denies the existence of such a vital force because it cannot explain it. Yet many doctors recognize that there are locations – some coastal resorts or high places, for example – that have a more generous supply of a vital 'something' 'in the air' which helps to restore health and vitality. That 'something' is Mana.

Oxygen in the air, when taken into the lungs, is absorbed into the bloodstream and carried by the circulatory system to every cell and used for building, maintaining and replenishing the human body. Similarly, Mana is absorbed. When it is conveyed to the central nervous system it is used to power the thoughts that flow through the mind. Indeed, Mana is an energizing force that gives life to every creative thought and is also the power that enables such thoughts to manifest in physical reality. So Mana is not only the breath of life, it is the *power of thought* also.

Mana, then, is not a physical energy but a spiritual essence with a fluidity which likens it to electricity and, like an electric current, its flow is at different strengths or voltages. At a basic level it keeps the physical and Energic Bodies functioning. At a higher frequency it is the vitality that enables you to *think*. At a higher strength still, it is a power that restores to wholeness in all dimensions, for it is the power of healing or *whole*-ness.

Mana at its different 'strengths' thus enables all the 'bodies' that comprise our total being to function efficiently. The finer and more subtle the 'body' the stronger must be the Mana to power it.

Mana has also been likened to fine rain which causes shoots to burst forth from seed and grow into plants and trees and bear fruit – for Mana saturates substance, brings it to life, and then causes it to grow and develop in an organic way.

CHI

Among the Taoist shamans of China and Tibet, this same fundamental essence was known as *Chi*. The Chinese character for Chi embraces more than a name or even a concept. It is an expression of the very *being* of something that is universal, for Chi not only names the essence but expresses its nature and spirit, for Chi is also a sound. Chi is the whisper in a breeze. Chi is the song in sunlight and in moonlight. Chi is the sound of the gentle kiss of rain. Chi orchestrates the very patterns of energy on the Earth and in the Earth that cause plants and crops to grow and enable every creature that feeds from the Earth to thrive and develop. This is why I shall use the word Chi from now on rather than Mana, or Prana, or Megin. The word Chi produces a sound that not only flows more easily with the breath, but also harmonizes with the energies of Nature. For instance, by expressing the sound of Chi you can

Figure 28. The Chinese character for Chi has several meanings. It can mean 'air' or 'breath', but it also represents the concept of a vital essence, a fundamental energy of the Universe that sustains life and is present in the tiniest cell and the largest planet.

readily connect with the energy of the Wind, the Sun, the Earth, the Moon, and even the stars.

The sound of Chi reaches beyond the range of audible frequencies for it penetrates *within* and reverberates through all dimensions of existence. This is because Chi is the sound of the harmonious vibration of the Universe. It is the Life-energy of harmony. Harmony is what creates beauty. Love is what creates harmony. So Chi is also a power of Love. The spirit of Chi is continuity of life in a process of immortality. I shall repeat that for it is very important: **The spirit of Chi is continuity of life in a process of immortality**.

Chi is thus the motivating essence that breathes life into *all* things. Without Chi, the Sun would not shine, mountains would not have form, rivers would not flow, trees would not grow, and humankind would not be. Chi is what *links* spirit with substance. Chi is what generates awareness from within because life itself is manifested outwards from within. Everything is created not by some *outside* source, as commonly assumed, but from *within*. Spirit is the essence that generates movement and Chi is a power that makes movement possible.

Although Chi is taken in mostly with the breath, it is absorbed also through food and drink and from contact with the Earth, the Sun, the Moon and the stars. The continuous flow of Chi along the intricate network of nadis and meridians, links the bone structure and the soft tissues with the vital organs and the brain and enables the physical body to function as a unified whole. Diffused through the body, Chi provides its protective and defensive energy also. Indeed, fatigue, lack of vitality, and sickness are the results of diminishing Chi or an obstruction in its flow.

CHI DYNAMICS

The original shamanic techniques for generating Chi and connecting with the Life-energies of Nature have remained largely hidden until this present time in human history when, with the dawning of a new millennium, an opportunity for an expansion of human consciousness to an awareness of multidimensional reality becomes possible. In ancient China,

exercises to stimulate and channel the internal flow of Chi developed out of the original shamanic wisdom to become an inner teaching of both religious and mystical systems. In this context they became known as *Chi Kung* (Chee Gung) which means 'life-energy exercises'. These exercises were not taught openly but kept within the confines of restricted groups of dedicated students who were supervised by a Chi Kung Master. Different systems of Chi Kung arose because of this, depending upon whether it was being employed primarily for health, for martial arts, or for personal and spiritual development. Today, all these systems are openly available.

The original shamanic techniques, however, are now being rediscovered and adapted to modern times and made suitable for people of all ages and all walks of life, through the Shamanics and research work of Australian channeller, Gaye Wright, and her partner, Rod Nicholson, himself a Chi Kung Master, who call this modern-day adaptation of the ancient wisdom, *Chi Dynamics*.

The changes which Chi Dynamics can bring about in the breathing, the absorption of higher levels of oxygen, and the circulation of a greater flow of Chi throughout the entire energy-system, combine together to change the metabolic rate, improve the body's natural defence mechanisms, and invigorate and regenerate the body and mind and enliven the Soul. Taking in an increased supply of Chi and accumulating it within the body is a basic movement of Chi Dynamics and becomes our next Experience of Shamanics.

Experience 13: The Circular Chi Breath

Stand with your feet shoulder-width apart, back straight, and knees slightly bent in the horse-riding stance described in Experience No 7. The arms should hang freely by your sides with your hands held with the palms cupped upwards around the navel area with the fingertips just touching (Fig. 29A).

Inhale by sucking air through the mouth, and at the same time lift the arms outwards and upwards in a circular movement so the fingertips meet again at a point about half a metre or 18 inches above the head. This upward movement should be slow and in keeping with the intake of air (Fig. 29 B and C).

Hold the breath for a few seconds whilst you are in this position, but do not strain in any way.

Figure 29. The sequence of movements for performing the Circular Chi Breath

Figure 30. Breathing in Chi by sucking in air through the mouth

Figure 31. Exhaling is done through a smile as air is pushed out through the mouth with a 'sheee' sound.

Exhale slowly. Smile as you expel the air audibly through your slightly-open mouth, making a 'sheee' sound. The hands – palms down and with middle fingers touching – should press gently downwards in a vertical movement like pushing air out of an air cushion. The downward movement of the hands should be in unison with the slow expelling of the breath (Fig. 29 D and E).

Pause when the hands reach the navel area and turn the palms upward in a gesture of containing the Chi. Visualize the Chi settling in a location about two finger-widths below the belly button and about 5 centimetres (2 inches) beneath the surface (Fig. 29F). The Chinese called this the *tan-tien* – a focal point where the Chi is stored and from where it may be networked throughout the body through

electromagnetic and biochemical essences and body fluids. The surface meaning of the Chinese word tan-tien is 'energy-field'. *Tien* means 'heaven' or 'Cosmic elixir'. *Tan* means 'lake', 'reservoir' or 'container'. So tan-tien is like a lake or reservoir that contains an elixir which comes from heaven, or the Universe – a 'heavenly place'.

Repeat the entire sequence, sucking in air as you raise your arms in a sweeping motion, and as you do so visualize 'collecting' in Chi from the atmosphere that surrounds you. As your fingers touch above your head, imagine the Chi collected there. Then, as you exhale, visualize the Chi being pushed down a vertical channel in the centre of your body and through the chakras until it reaches the storage area of the tan-tien. Let the expelled air make a 'sheeee' sound through your teeth as you smile on the out-breath.

Turn the palms upwards whilst you pause before the next in-breath and visualize the Chi settling in the tan-tien like little white granules descending in a snow-scene globe and settling in the lower portion after it has been upturned.

Repeat this sequence several times.

At the end of this session – which will take only a few minutes – you will not only have increased your supply of Chi but also stored some in your tan-tien for future use.

You can check the input of Chi quite simply by performing the following exercise.

Experience 14: Checking the Input of Chi

Open and close your hands as rapidly as possible – from open hand to closed fist – and keep this up until the hands tire. Then raise the hands chest high and massage them briskly, one with the other, in a gesture similar to washing the hands vigorously.

Shake the fingers as if flicking drops of water onto the ground.

Now put your hands together in an attitude of prayer so the fingertips are just touching but leaving a hollow between the palms. Focus your awareness on the space between the palms and check for any sensation, however gentle.

What are you experiencing in the palms of your hands and in your fingertips? Is there warmth or coolness? Is there a tingling sensation? Or a pulsation?

Separate your hands so the fingers are 12–15 centimetres apart (about 5–6 inches). Move them slowly towards each other until they are almost touching, then move them apart again. This movement should be like compressing a small balloon between the palms. As

you repeat this movement of pressing and relaxing, be aware of any sensations you are experiencing in your hands. A prickly sensation, perhaps? Or a pulling feeling between the palms like magnets coming together or being moved apart?

Whatever the sensation and however sensitive your perception, what you are experiencing is a field of Chi energy you have absorbed. Your hands are instruments of touch, and what you are touching are particles of life-energy like fine globules of gentle rain.

Chi is intangible and invisible. It has no weight, yet it cannot be lifted. It is unresisting, yet it can be pliable. Although it has no form, it can be held. Although it is something you have always had, it has been unnoticed. This 'stuff' of Life is in you. It is part of you. It enables you to *be* you. It enables you to *be*! And this same 'stuff' of Life is in everyone and everything. Not just humans, but animals and birds and creatures that swim and crawl. It is in trees and plants, rocks and stones. It is in the Sun and the Moon and the stars.

Everything has its own Chi, which is the Life Force that is absorbed *into* it. So there is Chi of the Earth, and Chi of the Sun. There is Chi of the Moon, and Chi of the stars and planets. Trees and plants have their own Chi, as do all creatures that walk, run, crawl, fly or swim, and even the rocks and mountains that stand still. Chi is your connection with everything. As a multi-dimensional being, you become connected with all things and with all dimensions when you *honour* the Life Force that is in all things.

SHAMANIC TOOLS

I mentioned earlier in this chapter that the Life Force has a sound (though ordinarily it is inaudible) because it is essentially movement and movement is what produces sound. The Life Force *pulsates* like a heart-beat or the regular, monotonous rhythm of a drum, and it also *vibrates*, swirling and spiralling in flowing, circular motions like seeds swishing in a rattle when it is shaken. So a drum and a rattle in the hands of a shamanist are not simply means of making a noise, however joyful, but also means of simulating the sound and movement of the Life

Force. This is why the drum and the rattle are principal tools of the shaman.

A shamanic tool is an extension of the person using it, and its purpose is to perform *work*. Its power and effectiveness are derived directly from the skill and intention of the person using it and from their motive for needing to do so. A drum and a rattle in the hands of a shamanist are conditioned by his or her motive and directed by their intention.

Motive is an expression of the desire and generates activity. Intention is an act of the Will towards a specific purpose, and channels its use. In Shamanics, the motive is always the same – Love and Harmony. Only the intention changes. In Shamanics, whatever is done is performed out of loving service and in order to restore or retain harmony through co-operation with the natural forces. It is motive that separates the shamanist from the sorcerer. A sorcerer endeavours to manipulate and exert control over natural forces for selfish purposes. When manipulation and exploitation of natural forces is motivated by self-interest, greed and egotism, it creates stress, and at some level causes pain. It is the cause, too, of much of the misery, unhappiness, confusion and division in the world, for it sets negative energies in motion.

An intention is a positive affirmation that prepares a channel through substance along which energy may flow unimpeded. The intention is what connects the rattle to the rattler and may differ with each 'working', and may even change within a working. It specifies not only the *aim* but the *outcome* and must always be clear and precise if it is to be effective. For instance, the intention of a simple working may be to disperse stressful energies and to restore harmony to a person's body and mind. That intention would need to be repeated silently by the rattler whose attention would be focused upon it. The rattling sound itself, once started, will then free any congestion that has built up in the receiver's energy-system and smooth out the fibres of the Energic Body, much as a gentle brushing revitalizes and conditions the hair. The pleasant sound relaxes the mind also, as the receiver undergoes what could be described as a sonic massage.

The Rattle

Shamanists will tell you that the rattle 'speaks' to them. How? By subtle sound and movement changes as it is lightly held in the hand, its movement and sound respond to the wave pattern of energies. The rattle's use is connected to the rattler's intent and is conditioned by the motive. As a result the rattler is sensitive to the most subtle changes in sound, intensity and movement.

A rattle should not be gripped too firmly or shaken vigorously just to produce a noise. It should be held lightly by the thumb and forefinger at the point of balance in the handle. The palm of the hand and the little finger serve as a guard to protect it from being dropped. Before starting to rattle, the rattler should focus on the intention and repeat it silently several times. Then, with a gentle movement of the wrist, the rattle is given an initial impetus to activate it. Once 'primed' in this way it should be allowed to take on its own movement as it responds to the energy-field which surrounds it. The skilled rattler allows the rattle to move with the flow of subtle energies rather than wilfully directing it.

The rattle is also a *transformational* tool. It enables a gentle

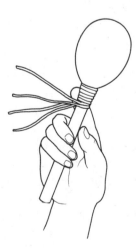

Figure 32. The rattle should be held lightly by the thumb and forefinger at the point of balance in the handle and with the little finger serving as a 'guard'.

change of frequency levels to take place as a preliminary to a shift in awareness into an altered state of consciousness. This is important because sudden change could cause a shock – like being awakened suddenly from a vivid dream – or disorientation, which results in a feeling of being 'spaced out'.

The rattling sound relaxes the mind and effects a slight change in brain-wave patterns so there is a transition from Beta brain-wave activity, which is normal waking consciousness, into the slower Alpha state which occurs just before the body normally moves into sleep. It is the drum that then takes over to carry the awareness into a Theta brain-wave state and an experience that might be likened to a waking dream which shamanists call a shamanic 'journey', which is movement into another perception of awareness.

Rattling and drumming techniques cannot be learned just from the printed word. They need to be demonstrated visually and sonically and practised under supervision until skill is acquired.

Shamanists are men and women whose vision and experience of reality transcends that of 'ordinary' mundane activity. They not only understand that there are many dimensions to our being, but are able to enter into these other realities and experience them. Gaye Wright emphasizes: 'Chi Dynamics is supportive to anyone sincerely seeking experience of other realities, whatever shamanic tradition they are pursuing, provided that tradition is one that works towards harmony.'

Chi is thus fundamental to the very purpose of life, which is to cultivate our Spirit – our inherent immortality. Immortality is an experience of the ever-present Now and is itself a Reality we can be aware of in the process of ordinary everyday living.

That which is immortal exists in another dimension and is enabled to take in Chi from the Universe – from the stars and planets and Cosmic particles – and absorbs it directly without the need to be nourished by an intake of minerals, vegetation or animal flesh as food.

The essence of Chi is closer to our needs than the breath we take that conveys it, for it provides us with our very aliveness, which it sustains and maintains through its mighty power.

8. Working with the Elements

IN THE UNSPOILED ENVIRONMENT of hills and mountains, lakes and valleys, rivers and streams, open countryside or coastal region, there is a reality that exists behind the external appearance of natural beauty. We might call this *hidden* reality the **Spiritual Ecology** because it is where the non-material nature of life-forms find expression and share relationships. The natural environment *affects* us as human beings from **outside** ourselves. The spiritual ecology *supports* us from **within**.

The Medicine Wheel enables us to find ways of access into this hidden reality and is a symbolic device which not only serves as a means of establishing relationships with other life forms but functions also as a direction-finder to help us find our way about a multi-dimensional Universe.

WORKING WITH THE MEDICINE WHEEL

The word 'medicine' in a shamanic context means inherent power – the drive for completeness that comes from within. The word 'wheel' means a hoop or container in which inter-related and interdependent energies pulsate and flow in circular, cyclical and spiralling movements. The Medicine Wheel encompasses the whole Universe and represents also the totality of our own personal 'space', for we are each a miniaturization of a greater universe and function in accordance with similar laws. The Medicine Wheel is not confined to Native American traditions for it is a universal symbol and a catalyst for effecting change. It operates as a process of integration.

127

Integration might be defined as a bringing together of fragmented portions into a harmonious whole so they may function together in harmony and thus create beauty. It can be represented as an encircled cross or an eight-spoked wheel – a circle within which are directional indicators. Native peoples used circles, spirals and labyrinths as a means of coming to an understanding of the Universe and themselves, because Nature itself was perceived as working in circles, cycles and spirals, and the Life Force itself moved in a similar way. When humans come into balance with Nature we come into harmony with the rhythm, vibration and pulsation of Life itself with the result that we, too, become vibrant, joyful and harmonious beings.

There is no beginning or end to a circle. Any place on a circle is both a starting and a finishing point. Beginnings and endings are thus wherever we are on a circle. The 'Wise Ones' understood the implications of this. Even Life and Death were not regarded as a beginning and ending, only *changes* – a transition from one plane of existence to another. A change in the way alive-ness is experienced. A move from one ring of a spiral to another. Shamanic understanding of human life is that we are each a Spirit with a body, not a body with a Spirit. Since Spirit is eternally alive, one's birthplace on the Circle or Cycle of Life is but a perception point from which Spirit is enabled to experience its aliveness in physical reality.

When shamanists sit in a circle they indicate that no one is more important than anyone else. No one has predominance. Each person is a circle of awareness contributing his or her individual energy-expression to the well-being of the whole group and in furtherance of the development of each and all. Each is an energy-system touching and being touched by other energy-systems, all connected by the circle for the benefit of each and all.

A circle establishes a position in Time and Space and a means of 'belonging'. It provides, too, a sense of direction, for from the centre of our own individual 'circle of awareness' there is that which is in front of us, that which is behind, that to our left, and that to our right. There is an above and a below also, for the Medicine Wheel is not a two-dimensional flatness but is spherical and has a centre. The circle can thus be perceived as having four segments – one in front, one behind, one to the

left, and another to the right. North, South, West and East. Sky above, Earth beneath. The point of balance and equilibrium in the centre leads also to the discovery of the 'within'. This directional awareness and a coming into attunement with the circular and cyclical nature of Reality was part of a very ancient art of Directionology. In ancient times and among some indigenous peoples, the direction in which things were located, or moved to and from, was given significance, whether it was the direction of winds that signalled weather changes, or the Sun which determined the time of day, or the comings and goings of people and events. Each direction was associated with features of the spiritual ecology and the way energies *moved*, with the Elements which affected the way things were *formed*, and with relationships between living beings who shared the Earth's environment. Each provided a means of access into the spiritual ecology and direct contact with the powers of Nature, making it possible to acquire personal understanding of aspects of one's own composite being which might otherwise remain hidden.

A reason the Medicine Wheel is a catalyst of ancient wisdom is that it is aligned towards *harmony* and indicates the most balanced way a human being can relate to the ecology and make use of his or her energies and develop the potentials that lie within. Its alignments enable us to discover our own unique individuality and provide us with a connectedness to all things which can empower us to express more fully what we are. The Medicine Wheel is aligned to allow the Spirit to have pre-eminence, with the *support* of the mind. Sorcerers, mind manipulators, exploiters, and others seeking power for selfish ends, either knowingly or unwittingly, apply methods which switch these alignments and put the intellect in control in the belief that knowledge is derived through reason and results obtained by mental power alone. We have all inherited this conditioning and as a result have so elevated the mind that the Spirit has become either forgotten or ignored.

Applied to us as individuals, the Medicine Wheel aligns the Will to the Spirit to provide the power to 'give what I am', and is in harmony with the Universe. Methods that align the Will with the Ego generate the power to 'get what I want' – in other words, to attempt to satisfy the insatiable, selfish and self-centred desires of the Ego. That is the essential difference. The

consequences of people following the 'misaligned' way are in evidence in the world all around us.

In Chapter 6 I indicated that the Elements are intelligences that originated from an unmanifest Source, and that the Elements have expression in the way energies come into formation. In order that these intangible Powers might be comprehended by the human mind, they were likened to something tangible that has similar characteristics so that their abstract qualities might be better understood – Air, Fire, Water and Earth (and in Taoist understanding, there is Wood and Metal also).

However, before attempting such connections, let us first familiarize ourselves with a method of engaging the Spirit, for in the spiritual ecology communication is with the Spirit rather than the mind. Our first practical assignment in this sequence of Experiences is thus to go out into the natural environment and make contact with Nature in a rather different way than we may have done before, and through this new approach obtain personal teaching from Nature in return. The series of Experiences which follow should be undertaken over a period of several days or even weeks for their full benefit to be obtained. They may also be repeated, for the benefits to be gained from them are inexhaustible. The first in this sequence is a 'getting to know you' approach. So if you want to get to know Nature better, you need to treat her as a friend and communicate with her, and listen also. Choose a day when you can go out into the natural environment and without any need for hurry, just enjoy being there. Take a notebook and pen so you can record your experiences immediately, and if you have a rattle or can make or acquire one, take that, too, and a small pocket compass.

Experience 15: Making Friends with Nature

When you arrive at your Nature spot, be it a park, woodland or open countryside, just walk around unhurriedly and absorb the beauty all around you and send out loving thoughts towards it. You are saying 'Hello' to Nature.

In a natural environment it isn't too difficult to express appreciation of trees and flowers and grass beneath your feet, if only to yourself. Seeing birds and animals, feeling a breeze on your face, hearing the gentle murmur of flowing water – each of these things stimulates

both the mind and the Spirit. But if you truly want your contact to be effective you need to speak your thoughts from the *heart*, as you would if confiding in a trusted friend.

So speak your feelings. There is no need to be embarrassed. No one will hear you, only Nature herself, and the trees, flowers, birds and animals. And they will welcome what you have to say because so very few humans say such things any more. Humans have forgotten how to open their hearts to Mother Nature and to speak to her as one of her children. We humans have forgotten how to give *ourselves*. We have lost the knowledge even of what *Love* is. So ask Mother Nature to help you to come closer to her and to know her. Ask her to open your heart to her Love and *to* love.

Enjoy the beauty all around you. Use all your senses to really experience it. Don't just *see* it. *Hear* it. *Feel* it. *Smell* it. *Taste* it. When you then sense that you are in contact with Nature, start rattling.

Move around slowly, eyes half closed, rattling gently as you go. After a little while the rattling may seem to be leading you towards a particular tree, or drawing your attention to a stone on the ground, perhaps, or a twig, a feather, or some other small object. Stop your rattling, and if it is a small object pick it up and hold it in your left hand – your receiving hand. If it is a large object – a tree or bush or rock, perhaps, go and sit beside it.

Close your eyes and ask for advice on what attribute you need to find meaning and purpose in your own life. What quality is it that you need to acquire and make your own? Open your eyes and wait for a response. Is the object you have picked up or are sitting nearby attempting in some non-verbal way to impart understanding to you? Is Nature that is around you in some way indicating something that has not been obvious to you in the past?

Is your attention being drawn to a particular feature in your surroundings that in some way has a message for you contained within itself? Don't try to intellectualize. Just be relaxed, open and receptive, and a teaching will come to you. When you have an answer, write it in your notebook immediately, together with a brief account of what you have just experienced.

Then pick up the rattle and rattle around the area again, this time in a gesture of gratitude and love. With your rattle, which is stimulating the sound of the Life Force, you are saturating the area with the harmonic vibrations of love and gratitude.

Now contact the Four Directions.

If you have brought a compass with you, find East. If not, work this out for yourself. East is the direction in which the Sun rises, so depending on the season of the year and the time of day it will now be to the left of the Sun.

Spend a few minutes facing East, just with the intention of connecting with the Spirit of the East. Be aware of any intuitive feeling you may experience, of any inspirational thoughts that come into your head; and contemplate on anything in the environment to which your attention may in some way be directed. Make a note of your experiences.

Then turn to your right and face South. Follow the same procedure as with East. Again, make a note of what you experience.

Then further to your right and do the same as you face West.

Turn to your right again and face North and repeat the sequence.

Finally, a sequence to help you recognize the Elements in their mode of balance and equilibrium – Fire, Air, Water and Earth.

Face in the direction of the Sun. The Sun helps us readily to link with the Element of **Fire**. So send out loving greetings to the Sun, rattling as you do. Then stop your rattling and wait for a response. Make a note of what comes to you.

Next, **Air**. Take a few deep breaths and experience how Air penetrates every part of your being. Consider how Air feeds and supports Nature all around you. Thank Air for bringing the breath of Life. Rattle to the Air. Stop, and wait for a response.

Then, **Water**. Consider the beauty of Water and the qualities that water brings – how it refreshes and soothes, disperses and dilutes. If you are near water, face it and send out loving greetings to it. Rattle to Water, and make a note of the response.

Finally, **Earth**. Consider the stability of earth beneath your feet. Look around at the beauty which clothes the Earth. Your physical body is composed of substances of the Earth, so thank Earth for nourishing and sustaining you in physical existence. Rattle to the Element of Earth, and wait for a response.

You have now completed this first familiarization Experience, so you may say farewell to your Nature spot, with a promise to return shortly.

Consider carefully all of your notes once you arrive home.

GIVING AND RECEIVING

This Experience will have demonstrated to you another important principle – that of *giving* and *receiving* – and that there is a significant difference between the giving and receiving inherent in the Way of Harmony and the taking and getting that is pronounced on the Path of Self-will.

Since everything flows and vibrates and has its polarity, there needs to be both a giving and a receiving in order for

balance to be maintained and further receiving to take place. So, when we *receive* a benefit from Nature, as we have in Experience 15, we have a responsibility to *give* something in return – a tangible gesture of our appreciation and our willingness to exchange something of our energies so that Nature herself may benefit also. This exchange of energies is called by Native Americans the 'Give-Away'.

From now on, every time you go out into Nature, take with you a pouch containing mixed herbs, dried lavender, tobacco or cornmeal as your 'Give-Away'. Sprinkle a little around the place where you have been and give thanks for the teachings you received. You may even leave a part of yourself there – strands of hair, saliva rubbed into the bark of a tree, or perhaps the moisture of your tears on occasion. Enter the real spirit of the 'Give-Away' as you perform it and you will receive a further blessing. Now for our next excursion into Nature.

THE STANDING PEOPLE

Native Americans call trees 'the Standing People', for although trees are alive and aware of their own existence just as surely as we are – though in a differently-organized way – they are immobile and stay rooted where they are. A tree is nurtured by the Earth, who is its 'mother', and energized by the Sun – the 'father' to whom it lifts its branches and leaves in recognition. So a tree is a 'link' between Heaven and Earth as well as a 'guardian' of our Earth environment, purifying the atmosphere with the oxygen it breathes out and absorbing the carbon dioxide we exhale. Trees are sensitive to their surroundings and have much wisdom to impart – if we are humble enough to accept teaching from them. Having now made contact with Nature, you are ready to return to obtain further teaching about communicating with Nature and the natural powers. A tree can show you how.

Again, choose a day when you can spend time in an unhurried way in Nature. You will need to go to a place where there are trees and where you are unlikely to be distracted by the presence of other people. Take a notebook and pen with you, a pouch containing materials for your 'Give-Away', and a rattle if you have one.

Experience 16: Learning Spiritual Communication

Find a place among trees where you can rattle gently without distraction or disturbance. Consider your motive – which is Love and Harmony – and your intention, which is to receive a teaching on communicating with Nature. Allow yourself to be drawn towards a particular tree. Stop your rattling and admire the tree's form and beauty. Tell it how beautiful it is. Ask it to share its energy with you.

Place your left hand, palm forward, against the trunk at forehead height, place your right hand on top of that, and then rest your forehead against the back of your right hand. Close your eyes, relax, and clear your mind. Breathe slowly and deeply and allow your awareness to be in the tree. Feel energy from the Earth being drawn up through your body from your feet, just as sap rises in the tree. As you breathe out slowly, sense the warm glow of radiance from the Sun move down from the top of your head to the soles of your feet and into the earth. Continue this in- and out-breathing for a while and experience what it is like to be a tree. Allow it to impart its stability and strength to you.

Now allow the spirit intelligence of the tree to communicate with you. This is not done with the mind. There is no need to 'think' about it, meditate upon it, or contemplate on its rationality or otherwise. It can be done only by your Spirit being in contact with the tree's spirit, and this is attained by having your awareness in the tree. You had little difficulty in moving your awareness into your hand in Experience 3, and this is but an extension of that technique. Then ask the tree to give you a personal teaching about communicating with Nature, and wait for a response.

Check on any sensations you may experience in your physical body. A tingling, perhaps, or a feeling of warmth or coolness. What impressions come into your mind? You may become aware of visual images, or words may come into your mind. Become aware of any inner feeling – joy, gladness, love, gratitude, elation, invigoration, perhaps. Identify each experience and enjoy it, for it will not be unpleasant. You will know instinctively when·communication has finished. Then give the tree a hug, sit down with your back resting against its trunk and write notes on what you experienced. You may not understand the full meaning of the 'message' right away. That may come later when you review your notes or at some unexpected time. Finally, get up, thank the tree, and perform your 'Give-Away'. Finish by rattling around the tree.

CONNECTING WITH THE FOUR ELEMENTS

We are now ready to establish a connectedness with the Four Elements. We will begin with **Air**, because on the Medicine Wheel Air is associates with **North** and the qualities of clarity and renewal which we are in the process of establishing within ourselves.

North on the Medicine Wheel is sometimes referred to as 'the Place of Renewal', for the Power of the North is an ability to make fresh new beginnings through the wisdom gained by seeing more clearly what in the past has not been perceived and understood. Air is an Element of constant activity and variety of movement. Invigorating and stimulating, Air is also unpredictable and has a quality of unexpectedness. It is likened to the mind and to thoughts, which have similar characteristics.

For this Experience you will need to return to a familiar Nature spot and again to take with you a notebook and pen, a rattle, and a 'Give-Away'.

Experience 17: Connecting with the Element of Air

When you arrive at your Nature spot, rattle around for a while and be led to a place where you can make your connection with **Air**. On the way look for a token from the Animal Kingdom which is related to **North** on the Medicine Wheel – and with the mode of receiving. A bird's feather, perhaps, a tuft of fur or horse hair, an acorn dropped by a squirrel, and so on. This will be a 'Helper' in aiding you to recognize your own need to receive what the Universe has to offer you.

You are now seeking to renew your entire life and to enter a new and exciting phase of self-realization and transformation.

Stop rattling, sit down, and hold the animal token in your left hand and place your hand over your navel. Put your right hand on top of your left; this connects the token to the centre of your energy-system and your connection to all things. Seek to be given the wisdom to understand the true nature of receiving, which is an attribute of North on the Medicine Wheel. Receiving should not be confused with getting or with taking. Be alert and observant as you wait for a response. It may come in the shape and form of passing clouds, in the movement of the wind, in the flight of birds in the sky, or in some other way. Write down the teaching you receive.

Now to connect more closely with the Element of Air. Remind

yourself that your motive is that of Love and Harmony and that the contact to be made is between your Spirit and the Spirit of the Element.

Allow your senses to experience what it must be like to *be* Air. *Sense* the unimpeded freedom of movement. *Feel* the gentle touch of Air in the breeze, yet its enormous strength in being able to hold aloft a giant airliner. *Listen* to the sound of Air in the wind. *Smell* its pure freshness. *Taste* it. *Absorb* it. Be *invigorated* by it. Be *stimulated* by it.

Now, ask the Spirit of the Element of Air to give you a personal teaching about your own concept of yourself. That's right, ask Air to clarify the thoughts you have about yourself that are strictly not true because they are not about the *real* 'You', only what you have *thought* about yourself. They are thoughts that have held you back and prevented you from realizing your true potential because they have been debilitating, lowering your self-esteem, minimizing your worth, and depriving you of inner strength. Then, when they are recognized for what they are – mental conditioning – that concept of yourself that has been limiting and restrictive can be released so you can renew your life with a fresh impetus.

Be relaxed but alert, and watch carefully for what Air is endeavouring to reveal to you. Listen intently for the whisper in the wind. What is Air *saying*? Look for the way Air is *moving*. Which Direction is it moving from and moving to? What is Air endeavouring to *show* you in a non-verbal way?

Make notes of your experience and consider them carefully. Then sprinkle an offering to the wind and the Power of the North in a gesture of appreciation for what has been revealed to you. Then look to the far North and repeat this question four times: **'How am I a greater being than I *think* I am?'**

Record the response in your notebook. Then sprinkle an offering around the area as a 'thank you' gesture to the Element of Air and the Spirit of the North.

We now move across to **West** on the Medicine Wheel to activate the power of transformation, which is an ability to change from what has been to what can be. It is a process of *becoming*, of developing potential.

The West is associated with the physical body and the material things of life. It is related to the Mineral Kingdom and with the *holding* of energy. West on the Medicine Wheel is sometimes referred to as 'the Place of Introspection' where can be found the strength that comes from within.

In the West we can connect with the Element of **Earth**, whose

qualities include stability, solidity, nurturing, and the power of manifestation. So the Element of Earth can help us to bring into existence what is needed for our own self-development, security and well-being.

For this Experience, you may return to a Nature spot you have visited before where there is an abundance of trees. Again, take with you a notebook and pen, a rattle and a 'Give-Away'.

Experience 18: Connecting with the Element of Earth

During your walk to a sitting place among the trees, rattle gently and be on the look-out for a small stone or pebble which you can hold. Pick up a stone that attracts you and ask it if it is to be your helper. If intuitively you feel a positive response, carry it with you in your left hand as you continue to rattle. If not, put the stone down where you found it and continue looking until you obtain a stone that gives you a positive response. This is your helper from the Mineral Kingdom on your journey to the **West**.

Allow a power spot to draw you near or beside a tree. Rather than be looking for it, let it *call* **you**. When you intuitively feel you have located the right place, rattle around the area for a while in order to 'tune in' to it. Then stop your rattling and sit down on the ground facing West. Keep the stone firmly grasped in your left hand.

Now make direct personal contact with the Spirit of the Element of **Earth** simply by *intending* to do so. And remember, your motive for making the connection is Love and Harmony. The connection is made between *your* Spirit and the Spirit of the Element of Earth and has nothing to do with the mind or mental powers. Connection can be made firm by engaging your senses and allowing them to experience what it is like to be as Earth is. What kind of *sensations* are you experiencing? What *feelings* do you have being like Earth? What *impressions* come into your mind? What does Earth *sound* like, *taste* like, *smell* like? Make a note of these experiences.

Examine the stone you have been holding. The emphasis of the West is on *holding* – retaining what is essential whilst changing what is necessary for further development. Seek to be shown what you are holding onto in your life that is preventing you from moving forward and making real progress in all aspects of your life. Identify what it is that has you in the grip of inertia and keeps you stuck in a continual repetition of the same old problem even though it may sometimes re-appear in a different guise. It is attached to you and you to it and so nothing appears to change and set you free.

Look at the stone in your hand. Examine carefully its shape. Ask the stone to help you to recognize what change you need to make in your life to enable you to become more of what you truly are *inside*. Examine its marks, shapes and impressions. What do they remind you of? What meaning do they convey to you? Relate them to yourself and to the circumstances of your life now. Write your findings in your notebook.

Hold the stone to your navel, with the right hand on top of the left hand. Close your eyes and 'see' those circumstances as an energy – an almost 'solid' energy that has been a burden weighing you down. Allow that energy to move into the stone and be absorbed by it – *held* by it. You will know when that has happened for it will be as if a weight has been removed from your shoulders and you experience a sense of freedom and relief. Now bury the stone in soft earth near where you have been sitting. The Earth itself will absorb and dispel that negative energy – recycle it so it can do no harm.

You are now ready to receive a direct teaching from Earth. Sit with your feet about shoulder-width apart, your back against a tree, and facing West, so there is a small area of ground between your legs and feet. Focus your attention on that portion of ground and ask the Element of Earth to give you a personal teaching that is relevant to your current needs and circumstances. How can the qualities of the Element of Earth assist you? Remind yourself that your motive is Love and Harmony and your intention is to receive a teaching that will help you to be more settled and secure within yourself.

Write the 'message' you receive in your notebook and consider it carefully.

Then look to the horizon in the West and put this question four times: **'In what way can I best manifest what I *am*?'** Record the response in your notebook.

Finally, sprinkle an offering around the area as a 'thank you' gesture to the Element of Earth and the Spirit of the West, and then rattle around before you depart.

The next stage in our 'working' of the Medicine Wheel is to move to the Centre on our way to the East, for the Centre is where energies can be brought into balance and harmony. We do not need to go outside to make our connections with the Centre for we can do it in our own personal Quiet Place indoors. But before we undertake this I want to introduce another shamanic teaching of some importance. It has to do with cleansing.

Smudging

Before undertaking shamanic work, shamanists consider it essential to disperse negative vibrations in the immediate area and from themselves. It is as essential as washing before preparing or eating a meal. Native Americans were familiar with plants that grew in the environment in which they lived, and had an understanding of their special qualities which could aid and support humans. Sage was a plant they regarded highly because it contained certain cleansing qualities and, when burned in a particular way, its smoke purified the atmosphere and even the fibres of the human aura. The act of cleansing with the smoke of smouldering sage is called 'smudging'.

A bundle of dried sage, sometimes mixed with sweetgrass – a North American plant which when similarly burned, refreshes and exudes positive energies – or lavender, which has similar properties, is tied together to form a stick and its end lit to produce smoke as it smoulders. Smudge bundles, or smudge 'sticks', can be purchased today from specialist shops that sell native-made products. Alternatively, a smudge 'mix' can be made simply by mixing a portion of dried sage – readily obtainable in most grocery shops and supermarkets – with a sprinkle of dried lavender. By placing the mix in a shallow earthenware dish or bowl it can then be lit and fanned to produce smoke which has a pleasant and gentle aroma. The smudge mix or bundle may need to be fanned vigorously to keep it smouldering. The smoke is then dispersed by fanning it around the room or working area and towards yourself. When drawing the smoke to yourself, fan it first to the chest area, then up above the head, then down the body towards the feet so that the whole of the Energic Body is covered. Take one or two deeper breaths as you fan in order to inhale some of the smoke. The smoke is in no way addictive, and smudging has beneficial effects which will become apparent to you through the experience of smudging.

So, obtain for yourself a smudge-stick or bundle, or make your own smudge mix with dried sage and lavender before going on to perform Experience 19. If you are to use a smudge-stick or bundle you will need a smudge 'pot' – a small earthenware jar containing a little sand or earth into which the lighted

end of the bundle of herbs can be plunged after use in order to extinguish it. A lighted smudge mix will usually go out unless it is continuously fanned, whereas a lighted bundle is likely to continue burning.

For the next Experience, choose a time when you can go to your indoor Quiet Place and be left undisturbed for about an hour. You will need a candle and candle-holder, a smudge bundle, or smudge mix and smudge pot, a small fan or a piece of folded card, long matches, a rattle, and your notebook and pen. Have something suitable for the candle-holder to stand on in the centre of the room so it does not constitute a fire hazard, and place your smudging equipment where it will be handy.

Experience 19: Connecting with the Centre

Light your smudge-stick or smudge mix and fan the smoke all around you. Then smudge yourself. As you are doing so, have in mind its purifying and cleansing purpose and the motive behind what you are engaged in, which is Love and Harmony. After use, stub out the lighted end of the smudge-stick into its pot or check that the smudge mix is no longer smouldering. Then light your candle.

Sit comfortably on the floor or on a chair within reach of the candle. Now rattle around yourself from your sitting position and concentrate on your intention that the purpose of this Experience is to connect with your own Centre.

Put down your rattle and focus your attention on the candle flame, which is a symbol of your own Centre. What you have manifested by lighting the candle and producing a flame is a symbolic representation of the 'Light' that is at your Centre within you.

By this Inner Light you are enabled to perceive what was previously hidden. The unseen is *there* all the time, but hidden in darkness until spiritual Light provides illumination for things to be seen as they really are rather than as they are assumed, imagined, or believed to be in accordance with the limited vision of physical eyes.

The Centre is 'the Place of Harmonious Being' on the Medicine Wheel. It is where all energies may be brought together and balanced. It is where your own Source may be contacted, for it was at this, the very core, that you first began to be knitted together as a physical being in your mother's womb to become an individual human being.

The word 'individual' is derived from the Latin *individuus*, which means 'without division'. So true individuality means being brought

into harmony with everything else, and not being **separate** from it as we have been led to assume. It entails a bringing together of our *inner* and *outer* selves in harmony with the entirety of our being.

Contemplate for a while on the candle flame as a symbol of an Inner Light that goes everywhere with you. It is always present – always *there* with you in an ever-present *Now*. All that has ever been is here also at the Centre, and all that will ever be is generated from the Centre within, which is its Source.

Now bring to light a problem, situation or condition that has kept on recurring in your life to throw you off balance and cause you confusion. Identify it. Consider how it has come about. Is it through someone else's expectations of you? Is it because of an 'attachment' of some kind? A demand that has been put upon you by another person? The result of something you have done or omitted to do? Find a key word or words to identify it and write the word or words on a small slip of paper torn from your notebook.

You are now going to release that condition through seeing it in a new light – no longer as an obstacle that obstructs and hampers you and weighs you down with its burden, but as an opportunity for making new progress and the beginning of taking responsibility for your own life and your own destiny.

Commit that problem to your Inner Light. Since it has been recurring in your life, although perhaps in different guises, it has been endeavouring to teach you something important. What has it been trying to teach you? What lesson for your ultimate good and well-being has it been attempting to impart? What kind of *challenge* has it been presenting to you? Allow your own Inner Light to shed *new* light on it so you can now perceive it as a window of opportunity. Write down this new understanding when it comes.

You are now going to let go of any resentment, fear or guilt that has accompanied that condition. **Forgive** whoever may have caused what hurt has come to you – for what they may have done or neglected to do. And that includes *yourself*. Forgive *yourself* also for whatever feelings of resentment, frustration, injustice, and even guilt, you have experienced and nurtured. Let them now vanish away as you commit that slip of paper to the candle flame. Watch them being consumed and transmuted into new inner strengths. Drop the remains of the paper into a smudge pot.

Make a note of what understanding comes to you.

Now put this question four times as you stare into the candle flame: **'When I am at the centre of my own being, am I the creator of my own reality?'**

Again, record in your notebook what response you obtain. Then snuff out the candle and pack away the items you have used.

Our next Experience is to connect with the Element of **Fire**, which is approached in the **East** on the Medicine Wheel and is associated with the Human Kingdom. The Power of the East is enlightenment – an ability that enables us to perceive things from a 'higher' perspective, for the East is where the light of the Sun first comes to us at the dawning of each new day to disperse the darkness that blocks our vision. The East is related to the Spirit and its mode of emphasis is on determining the direction in which our energies are exerted.

Decide on a place in Nature where there is a hill or sloping ground where you can look down onto natural countryside below. Choose a time when the Sun is shining. Take with you your notebook and pen and rattle.

Experience 20: Connecting with the Element of Fire

When you have found a power spot where you can look to the East above the level of much of the land in the immediate vicinity, rattle around the area with the intention of connecting with the Element of **Fire** and to learning how your life can come more in harmony with your Spirit.

Look towards the distant sky in the **East** and ask the Spirit of the East to bring enlightenment into an aspect of your life which has been unclear to you and in which you have not been able to see which way to turn. Enlightenment enables us to perceive things as they *are* and is thus also a power of discernment. As in previous Experiences, be alert and watchful but without any predetermined ideas, for understanding is likely to come to you in an unexpected way, perhaps through a movement or a sudden flash of illumination. When it comes, make a note of it.

Now face in the direction of the Sun, but don't look directly at it. The Sun is a great ball of Fire and the source of light and radiance which enables all living things in our solar system to have their existence. Connect with the Element of Fire through the Sun. *Breathe* in that glowing solar energy. *Feel* its radiance and expansiveness. *Feel* the touch of its warm rays on your face. Experience the clarity of **vision** that the light of the Sun enables you to have so you can perceive things in the distance. Smell the *aroma* which the heart of the Sun has released from Nature all around you *Taste* it in your mouth. Sense the *transmuting* power of the Sun – of Fire. What must it *be* like to **be** a Sun and to generate such power? To **be** Fire? Experience the *fire* of your Spirit!

Now ask the Element of Fire to enlighten you by imparting a

personal teaching on how to make choices with your Spirit rather than through your Ego, so that your life can come more in harmony with your Soul's purpose.

Make a note of whatever comes to you in whatever way and consider it carefully.

Recognize now that you also are a 'Sun'. A 'Sun' at the centre of your own 'universe' of awareness. And you are now coming into the light of recognition of what you truly are. So now put this question four times: **'Why have I not yet discovered what I have chosen to be?'**

Make a note of whatever response you receive.

Your 'Give-Away' this time should be something of *yourself*: a few strands of hair, or spittle, perhaps.

Give thanks to the Power of the East and the Element of Fire by rattling around the area before you leave.

Again, during the next few days meditate on the personal teachings you have received.

Teachability is an attribute that can be acquired through connectedness with the Power of the **South**. It is a quality of willingness to learn new things. It is having an open mind to receive fresh ideas – an almost child-like attitude of treating every new experience as an exciting adventure of discovery. It is living life close to the Soul and is why the South direction on the Medicine Wheel is often referred to as 'the Close-to Place'.

For your next Experience you will need to find a place in Nature where you can be beside water – a lake, river or stream. Take with you a rattle and your notebook and pen.

Experience 21: Connecting with the Element of Water

Allow yourself to be drawn to a place where you can be beside the water and facing **South**. Rattle gently around the area with the intention of attaining through the Power of the South an open-mindedness that will enable you to comprehend a truth about your own identity. South on the Medicine Wheel is associated with the Element of **Water** and its area of greatest influence is with the Energic Body and the emotions. It is associated with the Plant Kingdom and its mode of emphasis is on *giving*.

Sit facing the water and become aware of how water *flows*. Watch its movement carefully and become attuned to it. Notice how it *adapts* itself to its environment. Consider the shape it makes with the land that contains it. Listen for the healing *sound* of water and its soothing

rhythm. Get up and put your hands in the water. Sense its *fluidity* and feel its *texture*. Consider how refreshing it is to be in the *presence* of water.

Now ask the Spirit of the Element of Water to give you a personal teaching about how you may *give* of yourself without being vulnerable – how best you can express your True Self? And ask for an insight into coping with your emotions in a more balanced and harmonious way. Allow Water to bring you a teaching in whatever way is appropriate and necessary.

Write the response in your notebook.

Now kneel beside the water's edge and look at your own reflection in the water. Put this question to Water four times, each with a different emphasis, and consider carefully the response you get from each before proceeding to the next, and make a note of it in your notebook.

'Who am I?' '*Who* am I?' 'Who *am* I?' 'Who am *I?*'

After you have made notes of all the responses, sprinkle a 'Give-Away' offering into the water and rattle gently to the Element of Water in appreciation before departing.

We have traversed the Four Directions, and it is necessary now to return to the Centre in order to make contact with the Within. The final Experience in this sequence should be performed in your own indoor Quiet Place at a time when you can be undisturbed for an hour or so. You will need a candle and candle-holder, smudging equipment and matches, a rattle, and notebook and pen.

Experience 22: Connecting with the Centre Within

Set out your candle and smudging equipment on a table or flat surface in front of you. Light the candle to indicate that you have switched from mundane to shamanic activity, and smudge yourself and the area around you. Then rattle around yourself and the surface in front of you.

The inner flame around the wick within the 'outer' flame is symbolic of the Spirit which is at the core of your being – the essence at the very *heart* of the Flame Within. The Spirit might be described as an *inner* mind whose understanding is not obtained through a process of deduction and reasoning, but functions from a *knowingness* because it has existed longer than your mind and its awareness extends beyond rationality. Meditate on this for a while.

Review now all the personal teachings you have been given during

your working of the Medicine Wheel and this sequence of Experiences and consider their implications. Make a note of further understandings that may come to you.

Rattle around yourself and give thanks for the new understandings you have acquired. Before extinguishing the candle, recognize that its flame is a representation of your own inner reality, but your own Inner Light never goes out.

Your journey round the Medicine Wheel has taken you from the North to the West, across the Centre to the East and then to the South, and so traced the Wakan-Tanka symbol which represents energy being manifested into form, and the invisible reality that is *within* becoming physical reality *without*. By then connecting to the *inner* Centre and to your starting point you have traced a figure of eight pattern – a symbol of infinite possibilities.

You have now established that your future is full of infinite possibilities!

My Soul

I have a body, as you can see
But did you know there's more to me?
I'm not just bone and blood and skin
There's something more special deep within
There's more to me than meets the eye
Something that makes me laugh and cry
This special 'feeling' is my Soul
It gives my body life and control
What you see
On the outside of me
Is just
A plain old mask!

Written by my granddaughter, Angela,
at the age of twelve

9. The Reality of the Soul

THE SOUL RARELY EXERCISES the attention of most people. Little or nothing is known about what it is, why it exists, and what its purpose is. To many, the Soul is an intangible 'something' that figures in religious belief. In other words, it is something to be believed in rather than known about! Materialistic science has no conception of the Soul either, because the activities of science are limited to physical reality. Dictionaries define the Soul as a nebulous 'immaterial part of man' and as 'an entity distinct from the body'.

Speculation about the existence of the Soul and its nature and purpose has occupied the minds of the world's leading thinkers throughout recorded history. The Greek philosopher Plato (429–347 BC), for instance, argued that the Soul is not the flesh-and-blood person but the 'true' individual. Socrates, the Athenian philosopher (469–399 BC) reasoned that the Soul is an unseen intelligence that provides the body with its sense of 'aliveness' and existed before coming into the form of a human being.

The idea of the Soul as a deathless entity that experienced successive lives was part of early-Christian belief. It was not until AD 553 that this belief was declared as anathema by the Second Council of Constantinople; and those who subsequently held on to such a belief were denounced as heretics! The word *reincarnation* was not coined until the mid-nineteenth-century spiritualist revival. Theological opinion advanced the view that an outside deity created the Soul, that the Soul brought into being the mind, and the mind fashioned the physical body. According to this assumption, the 'lusts of the flesh' and the

desires of the physical body were impediments to the Soul's need to return to its Source – to the Godhead. Western mystical tradition is based upon a similar belief about the Soul.

The French philosopher René Descartes (1596–1650), considered by some to be one of the most original thinkers of all time, equated the mind with the Soul. His postulation, 'I think, therefore I am', indicated that to think is to exist. He concluded that the entire nature of a human being is to *think*. In other words, a human being is essentially a *thinking* being! Near the end of his life, Descartes suggested that the seat of the Soul is in the pineal gland located in the brain. From this speculation there has arisen an assumption that we are beings with a mind and inside us is a Soul, and that it is the mind that influences and controls us. As a result of this concept, the Soul has become a slave to the mind!

So what is the Soul? Is it separate from the physical body and the mind? Or is it an integral part of one or the other, or both? Is it, as some have speculated, a sort of invisible vapour, like a puff of smoke, or a 'ghost' that is in some way 'attached' to us?

Quite simply, your Soul is your *internal* being. It is what houses your own inexhaustible creative Source. The Soul is to the Spirit what the bones are to the physical body. It is the *supportive* structure at the spiritual level. Creativity is an activity of the Soul, not the mind. The mind is a *process* the Soul *uses* in order for its creativity to find expression in physical form. When you are being *creative* you are coming into harmony with your Soul and your own spiritual Source.

Far from being a nebulous 'entity' that is beyond comprehension and out of reach, your Soul is very close to you because it is your internal being. It has *feelings*. It experiences joy and sorrow, ecstasy and depression, excitement and trauma, for it is the source of your true feelings. Not your emotions – which, as I indicated earlier, are attachments to thoughts – but your feelings. The mind is the source of your emotions, because emotions are movements in the mental body. But pure feeling is a quality of Soul awareness, not of a mental condition, and it has a constancy that emotion lacks. Nor is a true feeling a belief. A belief is an intellectual conviction – an attitude of mind – whereas a feeling is an experience of the 'heart' and a response of the Soul. A belief can be firmly held, even rigidly

maintained, through exercise of the mind. A feeling is more spontaneous, more fluid and less tangible and describable. When what is held as a belief is challenged by a feeling that it is not quite *right*, a Soul response is conflicting with a mental acceptance that does not harmonize with the Soul's perception of reality.

Shamanics is a modern-day equivalent of what Native American shamans called 'the Way with Heart', which is the direction in which the Soul yearns to go. The heart referred to is not, of course, the physical heart that pumps blood to the cells of the physical body, but the heart of the Soul which circulates spirit essence throughout the total being. The physical heart is at the centre of your manifest *mortality*. The heart of the Soul is at the centre of your potential *immortality*.

The Soul has identity and it has intelligence – an awareness of its own self-hood. It is the *You* that is the intelligence of your Soul, so you might call it your 'Soul Self' because it is the highest, most noble, most evolved, most spiritual aspect of your total being. It is sometimes referred to as the *High* Self, not only because of its heightened awareness, but because in relation to the physical body its centre of awareness is located above the head.

Your Soul is involved in the direction of your life and in your day-to-day activities. Few people examine how the Soul feels about a situation or concern in their life, or about the kind of work they are engaged in. So let us look at one way of sensing your Soul's response to any aspect of your life. For the purpose of this example, let us consider your job or the sort of work you should be doing in order to find job satisfaction.

Experience 23: Sensing Soul Response

Go to your indoor Quiet Place and light a candle as a focus of attention, and have with you a notebook and pen.

For this Experience you are going to contemplate your work situation. If you are unemployed, think about the sort of work that would harmonize with your Soul. This same technique may be used for any other aspect of your life.

Contemplation is different from meditation. Meditation is a reflective method of calming the mind and slowing the thoughts and is a preliminary to action. The word meditation is derived from the Latin *meditare* which means 'to think effectively'. Contemplation is derived

from the Latin *contemplare* which means 'to look with attention' or 'to look with insight'. The insight you are after in this Experience is an insight into the Soul about one aspect of your life.

Stare into the candle flame and simply concentrate on how you feel about your job. Or how you feel about the sort of job you consider yourself capable of doing.

Focus on the nature of the work and the kind of effort and application it entails. What kind of *feelings* are generated within you as you contemplate that work? Are they feelings of joy, excitement, warmth, aliveness, achievement? Or sadness, disappointment, resentment and gloom? Identify each feeling. Put a name to it and write it in your notebook. Don't reflect on it now. That can be done later. The point of this exercise is to identify what feelings are generated through contemplation on a particular aspect of your life.

Though certain kinds of work may not be what the mind might prefer, the Soul response may be quite different. There are many jobs which to some people may appear to be menial and unattractive but which are vital contributions to the well-being of an organization or even a whole community. Such jobs are not only worthwhile but can be 'good for the Soul', and the Soul will recognize their value to the Spirit.

I write here from personal experience, for at one period in my life the most menial work I have ever done, and which at a time when my Ego had charge of my life I would have considered to be beneath my 'dignity', turned out to be the most appreciated, and though the least financially rewarding, was perhaps among the most satisfying. This book could not have been written without its lesson in humility.

When you have contemplated various aspects of a job situation in this way and have listed the feelings that have been generated, meditate on each of those feelings in turn and collectively. What is the Soul response telling you about the suitability of that work situation? Is the work compatible with those inner feelings? Is it the kind of work that is aligned with your true development?

This same technique can be applied to other aspects of your life.

THE SOUL BODY

The Soul is a 'body' which serves as a vehicle to enable it to function in the parallel universe of the Soul and experience its individual existence there, just as your physical body enables you to experience physical existence in the realm of matter. The Soul body can be hurt, too, and suffer the loss of particles of

itself! The Soul body is a shimmering, vibrating hologram of pure energy. A hologram is a three-dimensional image within which energy-waves cross each other and cause an interference pattern which stores information about the complete movement and interplay of energy. Indeed, the Soul is not just an energy-system but an information data bank containing the accumulated memories of all that has been experienced to advance its development. The Soul body functions like a vast hologram – and so does the multi-dimensional Universe – which means that within each of us as multi-dimensional beings is the truth of the entire Universe!

The Soul body is composed of substance that was understood by shamans of all cultures as a miraculous inner power that in some way provides every living being with its ability to exist. The substance of the Soul body is the very energy of the Life Force itself. In the physical body it is the life blood that flows and circulates and carries sustenance to every cell. In the mental body it is thought that flows and keeps the mind 'alive'. At Soul level it is the movement of Chi that constitutes the substance of the Soul. And it is the movement of Chi that creates non-physical Light. **So the Soul is a body of light!**

The Soul body is thus a dynamic energy-field which conveys within it the intelligence of the Soul Self in a parallel universe that is the Soul realm of existence. The substance of the Soul body in its dimension has *radiance*. Indeed, when on the physical plane someone compliments another person for looking 'radiant', or 'glowing', or being 'bright', they are sensing the substance of that individual's Soul body. The 'shape' of the Soul body might be described as ovoid, but where integration with the Soul Self is in process it is more like the shape of a candle flame than, say, an egg – another reason why candles have figured so prominently in religious and mystical practices, for they are 'reminders' of the need for Soul's body of light to be congruent with the Soul Self! Where an individual is out of contact with the Soul 'consciousness' (and so lacks 'conscience' and other spiritual qualities), the Soul Self is disconnected, though not detached.

Since the Soul body is composed of 'Light' it can expand as its light intensifies, or contract when its radiance is dimmed, and forms a cocoon in which the physical and Energic Bodies are contained until they are jettisoned when the Spirit with-

draws its life from them at death. The 'light' of the Soul body is multi-coloured with 'positive' attributes generating lighter or brighter colours and 'negative' tendencies being expressed in murky hues.

Although the Soul body is non-physical, an idea of its 'spatial' extent in relation to the physical body can be obtained. Here's how:

Experience 24: Exploring Your Soul Body

Stand upright, feet slightly apart so you are comfortably balanced, with arms hanging loosely by your sides. Stretch your arms outwards and upwards with the palms of the hands facing downwards until the middle fingers just touch about half a metre above your head. This point marks approximately the upper reaches of your Soul body – the 'tip' of its flame 'shape'.

Now move your arms outwards and downwards until they reach shoulder level and are parallel to the ground. Your fingertips are now at the perimeter of your Soul body.

Stretch your arms out in front of you, still keeping them parallel to the ground, and your fingers will be more or less at the frontal reaches of your Soul body.

Move your arms in a backward arc until they are again horizontal to your body and you will have traced a semi-circle in front of you. Visualize a similar semi-circle extending out behind you and beneath your feet and you will have an approximate idea of the extent of your Soul body.

I have stressed 'approximate' because this exercise is simply to provide you with a general idea that is in accordance with kahuna understanding, but it is in no way precise because the Soul body itself is flexible and expands and contracts in accordance with the quality of Life-energy from which it is composed, and the 'Light' it emits may similarly vary in intensity.

Shamans of all cultures have been able to attain direct personal contact with the Soul body as do shamanists today, through a shift in their awareness. This altered state of awareness is not of the mind or a figment of the imagination, but an experience of another reality made possible through a change in conscious awareness aided usually by drumming or rattling. The rhythm of rattling or the precise and monotonous beating of a drum induces a relaxed and tranquil state which is essential if a switch in awareness is to take place. My book *Shamanic Experi-*

ence provides detailed guidance on shamanic journeying technique. A shaman or shamanist is thus a kind of space traveller who is enabled to traverse 'inner' space and to experience awareness there.

SOUL RETRIEVAL

Among the skills attributed to shamans is a technique that has been described as Soul Retrieval which is based upon an understanding that the Soul can suffer depletion as a result of a physical, mental or emotional traumas and that a 'fragment' of it can in some way become detached, leaving the individual with a sense of loss. Traumas such as separation, bereavement, rape, sexual abuse, a bad accident, war experience, severe shock, and constant frustration and failure are said to be common causes of this kind of loss. Through an altered state of awareness, the shaman is enabled to locate and retrieve the disconnected 'fragment' and restore it to the client. In Shamanics this technique is more appropriately called 'Life-energy Restoral' since experience over a prolonged period has demonstrated that the loss that is suffered is Life-energy. The Life-energy is that generated by the movement of life – by the experience of living. The Soul is comprised of movement of Life-energy which generates the 'Light' of the Soul. In other words, the individual has actually lost a relevant part of his or her life, resulting in a sense of incompleteness and a loss of Soul radiance. Again, experience has demonstrated that it is not sufficient for that particle of the individual's life to be located and retrieved. It requires to be *restored* to the person and *accepted* fully and lovingly so that it can be fully integrated. Symptoms of loss of Life-energy include chronic depression, loss of memory, illness or pain that defies medical diagnosis, debility, emotional turmoil and a sense of being 'incomplete' – of being 'dis-spirited'.

To perform Life-energy Restoral the shamanist must venture into non-ordinary reality to locate the 'experience' during which Life-energy was lost, retrieve the Life-energy, restore it to the individual and provide the person with the opportunity to integrate it within the totality of their being. In such work the intellect is not engaged. It is not the mind but the awareness that 'journeys' into the non-ordinary reality of the Soul to

search for, then identify, communicate with, and retrieve, that particle of Life and restore it to the individual. This particle of the 'light' of the Soul contains the appearance of the individual at the time in ordinary reality that loss of Life-energy occurred. It is 'captured' in time like a video sequence recorded on a camcorder. That may have been several months or even many years ago. So the shamanist could be confronted not with the appearance of an adult, but of a child or infant. Once identified and communicated with, it is then invited to return with the shamanist to be restored. Shamanists on the Path of Love and Harmony do not resort to forceful or manipulative methods. There is no persuasion. Over a period of several years, my wife and I have participated in or supervised scores of such restorals and in all cases that 'particle' of Life has not only wanted to be restored but appears to have been waiting for it to happen. It is as if there is knowledge in advance that the opportunity for restoral and integration has arrived.

Although in this Chapter I have touched upon the fundamental principles of Life-energy Restoral, I must stress that I consider it unwise to attempt to teach the technique in a book. In my considered opinion this kind of work should not be undertaken by anyone before considerable experience of non-ordinary realities has been gained. Even then it should be under the careful guidance and supervision of a trained shamanist. Nor is it work that should be entered into lightly or undertaken out of curiosity and just for the experience of trying it.

It is appropriate, however, that I should outline some examples so that you are better able to grasp something of its nature and recognize how different it is from other 'therapies'. The examples I am going to relate here were each conducted in a workshop environment with several people present to observe the technique being demonstrated and to witness the authenticity of the experience. Usually, of course, this kind of work is performed on a one-to-one basis and under conditions of strict confidentiality.

The cases outlined here were conducted at different times over a three-year period and before different groups of people. At each event volunteers were invited from the group to be the 'client' for Life-energy restoral. The only proviso was that they should each feel that something was 'missing' in their life

which they could not identify. No preliminary consultation took place, and no analytical work was done beforehand in order to identify a missing element. In each case my wife Beryl was to be the shamanist who performed the retrieval and restoral work and I was to supervise the proceedings. In each case neither of us had solicited any information from the volunteers regarding their personal lives. I must make it clear also that the work is not clairvoyance or a form of hypnotism. The shamanist performing the work is in full control of their own Will at all times and is fully aware of what is going on. So is the client. There is no question, either, of control by an intermediary. As I have stressed earlier, much shamanic work is essentially spiritual but not mediumistic. Only the awareness of the shamanist is activated – the mind is put into a mode of passive neutrality.

Usually there are a number of volunteers and Beryl's selection of an individual is strictly intuitive and often takes place only moments before the work is to begin.

In a workshop environment, the rest of the group is invited to be supportive of the one performing the work, as was the case in tribal groups when the shaman was supported by the family of a 'client', and in certain cases by the whole community. Physical support is given by rattling and drumming, under my supervision and during which it becomes clear to Beryl where her journey in non-ordinary reality is to begin. She and the 'client' lie down side by side in the centre of the circle of participants with shoulders, hips and ankles touching. There needs to be physical contact since the physical body, as I have previously explained, serves as a transformer. It is essential, too, that both are completely relaxed and at ease. Each wears an eye-shield to screen out any visual distractions. Drumming and rattling provides the sonic means of taking her awareness into another reality where the journey is to start. This may take just a few minutes of group rattling and drumming or it may take some time.

Beryl's technique is to speak aloud what she is experiencing so the 'client' is able to 'share' the 'journey' with her, and so that in a workshop situation participants are aware also of what is happening *as* it is happening. She signals to me when it becomes clear to her where the 'journey' is to begin in non-ordinary reality. Beryl then sits up and describes the starting

location before continuing the journey alongside the 'client' using recorded drumming on a personal stereo. In the cases that follow the names have been changed to protect identity.

CASE 1: Sandra: a young woman in her mid-twenties

Beryl became aware of being in a country lane with the sound of horses trotting towards a field where a gymkhana was in preparation, and this is where she was to begin her shamanic journey.

As her 'journey' began, Beryl's attention was drawn to a family who were involved in the gymkhana events. As they busied themselves with grooming the ponies she saw that a little girl aged three or four had wandered off towards the left of the field and away from where the events were taking place. She described the girl as a happy and confident little child, not at all worried at being alone.

Then Beryl became aware of the sound of flowing water. She described a river and a lock and sensed that the child had fallen into the water and had been pulled out. Beryl spoke to the child and asked her if her name was Sandra, and told her that Sandra was now grown up and wanted her back.

At that point the little girl vaporized and Beryl brought her back on the breath and restored her to her client in accordance with a shamanic technique which enables this to happen.

Sandra herself was very moved by the experience and said she wanted to share a personal matter with everyone. Her family were horse-riding enthusiasts and had attended gymkhana events during her upbringing, and she did have a vague memory of having fallen into some water at an early age. But what impressed her most was that Beryl had said the child had such confidence and was happy to be on her own, whereas she, Sandra, had for many years suffered from agrophobia and had an acute fear of being alone. She realized that what had now happened was that a 'part' of her which had no fear of being alone and no fear of open spaces had been restored to her.

Days later, Sandra's mother contacted us and told us what an improvement there had been in her daughter's condition, and confirmed that a near-drowning incident had taken place near a gymkhana event when Sandra was a small child.

Sandra's mother later became one of our students, and

Sandra no longer suffers from the condition that caused her so much anguish.

This example helps to demonstrate that what is restored to the individual is a quality, or qualities, that had been present or prevalent at one time, but had disappeared as a result of 'loss' of Life-energy – in this case a near-death experience.

CASE 2: Trevor, a man in his forties

During the initial rattling and drumming Beryl became aware of a five-bar gate leading into a field which sloped down towards a lake, and that she was to start her journey by going through this gate.

It was a sunny day with the Sun almost directly above, and as Beryl neared the lake she was aware of something unusual. There was a shadow across the right-hand side of the lake yet nothing around the lake on that side to indicate how such a shadow could be cast.

As she walked nearer to the lake she looked down and saw the end of a piece of white string. She picked it up with her right hand and began winding it into a ball around the fingers of her left hand whilst walking along in the direction the string was leading her.

She continued walking, puzzled about the string, which eventually led her to a crevice near the edge of the lake. Inside was a boy, about five years of age, holding the other end of the string. He was wearing a knitted grey-blue jumper which was ripped from the neck down.

Beryl had a conversation with the boy who confirmed that his name was Trevor, but he was reluctant to explain how his jumper became torn. So Beryl explained that Trevor was now grown-up and wanted him back. He walked away, indicating that he wanted Beryl to follow him as there was another experience to be 'found'.

The two walked hand in hand and Beryl was led over a hill to where there was a large house that looked more like a country mansion. It had unusual windows which appeared to be black and reflected the light like mirrors. She described their shape and the features of the building in some detail.

The boy led her to the front door and through the house to

a room at the rear which appeared to be a sort of store-room. Standing by a wall was a youth of about seventeen years of age. Beryl talked with him for a while and he confirmed he was Trevor also, at that later age, and was willing to return. Youth and boy both vaporized and Beryl brought them back on the breath and restored them to her 'client'.

In the conversation that then took place between Beryl and Trevor, which we were all able to share, Trevor explained that he knew the place she had described. It was in Ireland. He knew the area which Beryl had described for he had spent years of his younger life there. The lake had the strange phenomenon Beryl had described. He also recognized the big house from her description. He had visited it many times when he was an apprentice and had always been shown great courtesy by the lady of the house. It was a place where he had always liked to be and so could not understand how it was possible to have lost a part of his Life there since it held so many happy memories for him.

Beryl, who had never been to Ireland, explained that such a loss was not always the result of a trauma. There was an old saying about leaving the heart in a place that means much to us, and clearly this was the case with Trevor. When the time came that he could no longer visit that house he left part of his Soul (heart) there as a young man.

Trevor, however, had no recollection of anything happening at around the age of five or six. At that time, he said, he lived with his grandparents. We explained that the memory of an incident that happened during early childhood may have been long forgotten, but when a restoral takes place memory of it returns, sometimes immediately, sometimes in a few hours, sometimes in a few days.

Since the whole episode seemed to be quite overwhelming to Trevor we suggested that we broke for a cup of tea and that he go for a walk in the grounds for a while and return to the workshop when he felt fully grounded.

He returned about half an hour later bubbling with excitement. He described it as incredible, but a memory had returned to him of an incident that happened at his grandparents' home when he was about five years of age.

During his walk he had a vivid recollection of sitting in front of the fire in their home, and whilst the adults were talking he

played with a long white silk scarf that belonged to his grandfather. He wrapped the scarf round his neck several times just
as his grandfather used to do when he wore it. But one end of
the scarf became trapped under his grandfather's chair. Someone else came into the room, saw the other end of the scarf,
picked it up, and began idly wrapping it around his hand as
he stood by the fire talking to his family.

The scarf tightened around little Trevor's neck but he could
not cry out because it was choking him. Next thing he knew
he was lying on a bed with people standing over him, and the
knitted jumper he wore had been ripped apart during the
resuscitation.

It explained graphically the white string which had led Beryl
to the little boy during the first stage of the shamanic journey.

There was little more that needed to be said. Trevor had clearly
lost Life-energy at the age of five during a near-death experience.

Incidentally, it is not unusual for more than one particle of a
Life-energy to be restored on a single 'journey'. In this case
there were two, and we have experienced instances of as many
as three.

CASE 3: Richard, a man in his late fifties

During the initial rattling and drumming, Beryl was shown that
the 'journey' was to start at the brow of a hill.

Beryl found herself walking down the hill in a peaceful countryside location to a single-track railway. She looked both ways
to make sure there was no sign of a train, and stepped onto
the track. Then she found herself stepping over the sleepers –
jumping from one to another – and she continued running in
this way, enjoying every moment, though she knew she had
to listen for something. Then came an intense feeling that she
shouldn't be there and she kept repeating, 'I shouldn't be here;
I have this terrible feeling that I should *not* be here.' The feeling
was so intense that Beryl almost abandoned the 'journey'. She
felt that perhaps she had misread her intuition and should not
be doing this demonstration. Yet she still went on jumping the
sleepers.

The railway track took her under a bridge and then suddenly
she was confronted with a solid brick wall. In the non-ordinary

reality which she was experiencing, physical laws do not apply and she was able to simply pass through the wall, where she was confronted with a different scene.

A boy of about five or six years of age was playing with a rabbit in a field by a hedge. She engaged him in conversation and confirmed that he was Richard and wanted to come back with Beryl. The little boy vaporized and Beryl brought him back.

The subsequent conversation between Richard and Beryl was amazing. Richard said Beryl had described accurately the location where he lived as a small boy. There was a single-track railway line beyond the bottom of the garden where he lived, and he used to play on this line although his parents warned him never go on it. Hence he should not have been there. He used to do precisely what Beryl found herself doing – jumping the sleepers, and listening – listening intently all the time as a train could come from either direction.

His childhood was during the Second World War. He re-membered 'hiding' rabbits to prevent them being caught be-cause they were hunted to provide the family with a Sunday meal.

The brick wall was significant to him because around that age he was admitted to an isolation hospital with scarlet fever. In those days no visitors were allowed in an isolation ward and he remembered how abandoned he felt not seeing his parents. He did not know why he was there and felt that they had just left him there.

To a small child a sense of abandonment is very traumatic and sufficient for Life-energy to be lost.

As a result of this experience, Richard became more light-hearted and his life took on a quality of wonder that put more 'fun' into everyday living. His life now rings with the laughter of childhood.

THE SOUL AND LIFE EXPERIENCE

The Soul is another means by which we are enabled to experi-ence life as individuals. The physical body enables us to experi-ence life through what we see, hear, touch, taste and smell. The mental body enables us to experience life through what we

think, and through the ideas we have, the opinions we express, the comparisons and judgements we make, and the conclusions we arrive at – each and all of which colour our perspective of life. The Soul enables us to experience life through what we *create* for ourselves with our Life-energy. So the natural cycle is:

Soul *creates* and 'knows'.
Mind *thinks* and produces shapes and patterns from the knowledge it receives.
Body *forms*.
Spirit *chooses* as a result of what is experienced and learned from what is created, shaped and formed.

Your Soul is your contact with the multi-dimensional Universe and with Cosmic laws and Universal truths – principles which direct the way the Universe functions – and with a higher Intelligence and wisdom. The Universe and each individual are reflections of one another. We are each a little Universe – a microcosm that functions in a similar way as the macrocosm that is the Universe.

There is, however, a random factor that operates in our lives, just as there is a random Force that functions in Nature and throughout the Universe and is always *there*. In other words, uncertainty is a *fact* of life. It is a factor in one's alive-ness. So we must expect the unexpected as an essential feature of life, for it is how we react to that random factor that helps to develop strength of character and brings out the best or worst in us. That random Force is like the forge that tempers steel in order that it can have inner strength.

The Universe is abundance itself. It might also be described as the 'Place of Fulfilment' because every possibility is contained within it. That is so with us, too, except that our conditioning has convinced us that we are surrounded by limitations which deny us the abundance and fulfilment we crave. That same conditioning has made us believe that whatever is achieved can come only through struggle and competitiveness, plus a fair measure of luck and good fortune. That conditioning is based on beliefs that have been fashioned out of our own fears, vulnerability and frustrations, and by the manipulations, divisiveness and superstitious dogmas imposed on us by others.

Sometimes your Soul Self makes itself known to you through a 'still, small voice within' which some people call 'conscience'. Conscience is only active in people who have Soul contact occasionally for it is only the *Soul* that imparts concern about the possible effects of decisions and actions on others. Those who appear to have no conscience about their actions have lost contact with their Soul. This is the true meaning of a 'lost Soul' – the channels to it are obstructed, but not severed, otherwise the human life could not go on. There is simply a one-way impediment in communication flow so the people affected are unaware that they *have* a Soul.

It is possible to make conscious contact with the Soul aspect of your total being and actively to involve it in your everyday life. When conscious contact is established, the mind-patterns formed from beliefs that have been assumed to be true begin to disperse and are replaced by Soul-patterns which are free from mind-conditioning and are impressions of wholeness, well-being, balance and harmony. One way of doing this is to receive direct personal teaching from the Soul Self – through shamanic journeys – but this requires some familiarity with non-ordinary realities and previous experience in attaining altered states of awareness. Another is to awaken the Soul potential within. Since you are a unique reflection of the Universe – an individuated expression of a greater Whole – the Force that empowers the Universe and keeps it in being sustains you also. And since the Universe is empowered to create from *within itself* everything in abundance that is essential to its well-being, so you too, by awakening your Soul potential, can be enabled to express it in physical reality because those same Powers that are in the Universe are within *you*!

The meditative exercise that follows will enable you to look into your own Soul and obtain a personal teaching. It was taught to me by Suzanne Beflerive of Woodland Park, Colorado, USA, who has given me permission to pass it on to you. All you need is a small hand-mirror, a notebook and pen, and to be undisturbed for half an hour or so.

Experience 25: Looking into Your Soul

Look into the mirror. What do you see? Mirror reflecting mirror. Particles reflecting light. Light reflecting colours. Colours reflecting

sounds. Sounds becoming objects. Objects becoming mirrored . . . becoming dusty . . . becoming dust . . . dust reflecting light . . .

Look into your own eyes in the mirror. Look at the eyes in the mirror looking at you. You see the eyes. But what are the eyes seeing? Write down what they see.

Touch your own hand. Feel your hand touching your hand. Experience what the hand being touched is feeling. What is that hand feeling? Describe that feeling in your notebook.

Lick your own lips. Feel your tongue on your lips. What are you tasting? Describe that taste in your notebook.

Take a deep breath. The air brings in your own aroma every time you breathe. What are you smelling? Give it a name. Write that name in your notebook.

Whisper softly your own name. Listen to the sound of the letters of your name. Hear your voice saying them. What are you hearing? What is your name telling you about yourself? Write that in your notebook.

Look back into the mirror. Look into the eyes – your eyes. Touch your hand. Taste your lips. Smell your scent. Sound your name.

You are the sight, touch, taste, smell and sound of the Universe when you use your All. Observe your All carefully, for when you use your All you will find The All and come to know the All That Is.

The Soul expresses its nature through the physical body and through the mind, and as a result of the Earth-life experiences received back into itself through the body and mind the Soul receives impressions that will further its own individual nature. What is learned from Earth experience thus makes an impression on the Soul and is imprinted on the Spirit.

DISCOVERING YOUR SOUL'S PURPOSE

A fundamental purpose of life is to thrive and endure – that is, to grow and develop and to go on experiencing individual alive-ness. Growth and development are organic – that is, *natural* – and are for the purpose of perceiving the reality that exists beyond appearances and learning to make wise choices. There is also a *specific* purpose for your present life – a particular reason for being here at this period of time, in the place where you are and in the circumstances you find yourself. Once discovered it will make your life more meaningful and

fruitful and you will be able to make sense of much of what perplexes you at present.

To discover the specific mission of life was a reason some Native Americans underwent what they called a Vision Quest. By going out alone into Nature for three or four days and fasting for all that time, they hoped to be shown, through their contact with Nature and closeness to their own Soul, a vision that would enable them to glimpse what they were intended to attain in this present life. A Vision Quest, however, is not the only way of receiving such enlightenment. It can be received through shamanic journeys that give direct personal access to the Soul; the Soul Self will then tell or reveal what that purpose is. The Soul Self knows this because it was the Soul Self which existed in the Soul dimension before the physical 'you' was born. It determined the qualities the physical 'you' would be equipped with for this particular Earth 'mission', the perception point that would be in accordance with your birth on the Wheel of the Year, and the mode you would function in – male or female. Your parents provided the basis for your physical form. A shamanist experienced in shamanic journeying would obtain guidance on his or her own Soul's purpose from Upper World 'visitations'. A method of obtaining an indication can be obtained through the following Experience, which should be conducted in your usual Quiet Place at home. I must stress, however, that the results obtained are only an *indication*. All you will need is a candle and candle-holder, matches, your smudge-stick or smudge mix and smudge pot, and notebook and pen.

Experience 26: An Indication of Your Soul's Purpose

First smudge the room and yourself. Then sit comfortably at a desk or flat surface, on which you have your candle in its holder and your notebook and pen.

Light the candle and use the flame as your focal point and as a symbol of looking into the light of your Spirit. Reflect on your life up until now. What talents and skills have become apparent? List them in your notebook.

What activities have given you the greatest satisfaction? List them also.

What experiences in your life have brought you the greatest joy? Describe them in your notebook.

Now examine objectively all the answers you have written, as if analysing them from the perspective of someone who doesn't know you. What pattern is there? If what has been written was about someone else, what would you consider that person is best equipped to do in life? What would you advise them to be the main thrust of their life? What kind of things should they be doing in order to find fulfilment?

Fine. So **do** them. Start living them yourself **now**. You have an indication of how your life should be lived in order for it to be satisfying and meaningful.

Extinguish your candle and be grateful to have moved a little further on in your self-cultivation.

Self-cultivation is a perfecting of the Spirit through the integration of the physical body, the mind and the Soul, with the Spirit and the establishment of the composite Self which is the totality of your being. When we set out to perfect something we are not making it faultless but bringing it to a fuller development and completion. That is the opportunity we have through Shamanics – bringing ourselves to a greater fullness through the quality of life we live on Earth.

Let us now understand more of the nature of the Spirit.

The Ego is the little self that pretends to be the only self and speaks so loudly that the still, small voice of the Greater Self, whose whisperings come from within the Soul, are rarely heard – unless we learn to listen.

10. The Reality of the Spirit

THE WORDS 'SOUL' AND 'SPIRIT' are often used as synonyms in theological, metaphysical and philosophical writings, but they are not identical, for the Soul was brought into being by the Spirit! So let us now understand a little about the Spirit and what it is.

The Spirit is the original being of an individual before it takes form. Spirit is an essence that builds forms out of its own substance – out of Spirit! Life belongs to the Spirit, not to the form. Only the form 'dies' – or, rather, is transmuted – because *change* is the nature of form as matter is in a process of reverting to primary energy. This is why Spirit has never been discovered by materialistic science. Science examines *form*, and the form is merely a combination of externals, and externals are only details of the form itself. Externals have to do only with the *appearance*, not the *reality*. The appearance changes and the form may disappear, but the Spirit remains because the **life is in the Spirit** and flows from within its own inexhaustible Source.

Your Spirit, then, is your *true* Reality – the *Real* **You**!

Spirit substance cannot be seen because it is vibrating faster than the speed of light. It appears not to be there. We might liken it to a spoked wheel. When the wheel is at rest we can see all the spokes clearly and count their number. But when the wheel is revolved beyond a certain speed the spokes 'disappear'. All we can see is the rim and the hub with nothing to connect them and hold them together. **Spirit is what connects and holds things together by its great Bonding Power!**

So where does this unseen Bonding Power come from? What is its origin?

According to the oral traditions of some Native American shamans, the origin of all things was called the Great Mystery, because it could not be named. Chinese shamans called it the Tao. The Great Mystery, Tao, or whatever we choose to call that which is Nameless, was such an abundance that it overflowed with its own great magnitude in order to share the essence of its own Being, which Native Americans called Great Spirit. That outpouring, that essence, is Love. That is why in the Christian tradition, God is defined as a great Spirit (John 4:24) and as Love (1 John 4:16). Not *has* love, *feels* love, or *shows* love, but **is** Love itself. Since individuated Spirit is derived from a greater source, it follows that we are derived from Love – from the very Spirit substance which Itself **is** Love! Regretfully, the word 'love' has today been given connotations which deprive it of much of its true meaning. Love is a word frequently used as a synonym for 'sex' and meaning 'sexual gratification'. The word has thus been defiled to mean 'lust'! We limit Love when we regard it as just sensual pleasure, an emotional feeling, or even as a *quality* of life. Like light, which has mass (the Sun) as well as radiance, Love has substance, too. That 'substance' is the substance of Spirit. The substance of Love is what the greater Spirit is composed of. So Love is what you *are* at the very core of your being. **Love is what your Spirit is made of because your Spirit emanates from the Source of Love!**

Love – *true* Love – is a sharing of the very essence of itself with another and with others. It is a wilful and complete *merging* that puts no conditions on itself. It is a *bonding* that adheres and holds together as a unity of complementary opposites and even of different kinds. It is that which *creates* bonds, so it is itself a great **bonding** force. So Love is not something you can actually *give* to another, neither can it be *got*. Love **is**, for it has a reality of its own. It is a spiritual reality because it is the *nature* of pure Spirit. Love, then, is the true nature of *your* Spirit. It is within you, whether you recognize it or not. It is what generates the light of your Soul for it is the very movement of life-energy within your Soul. When you are in love, you are experiencing being *immersed* in the essence that is at the very core of your being. You are *experiencing* **Spirit**!

Spirit works *from* the inside and *on* the inside, and it feeds on the substance of its own being. So the food of the Spirit is Love, also. What, then, is a so-called 'evil' spirit? An evil spirit

is a Spirit lacking the life-energy of Love. It is malnourished –
deprived of the substance that comprises its very essence: a
Spirit that has chosen to *deny* Love and to deprive others of it.
'Evil' spirits are often depicted by writers and artists of horror
fantasy as wizened creatures – a depiction drawn from their
own subconscious and unconscious depths – as if deprived of
nourishment. And that is so. They lack the nourishment of
Love, and by isolating themselves from its essence, have set
themselves on a devolutionary path which has its own distorted
sense of creativity. The word 'evil' is 'live' spelt backwards –
an indication, perhaps, of a reversal of natural progression, for
an 'evil' spirit is one that through persistent choosing for and
unto itself has moved into Chaos, disorder and devolution
rather than harmony and evolution, and by so doing has
brought into existence energies which separate and disconnect
beings from the rest of the Universe and put them into opposition, which is a *denial* of Love. Such spirits are malevolent
and destructive.

Malevolent spirits should not be confused with so-called 'lost
Souls'. A 'lost' Soul is a person who has lost contact with the
divine essence within and, therefore, sees no meaning or purpose in life because contact with that inner reality – which is
Love – has been lost. But it can be regained.

The Love that is of the Spirit is *unconditional*. It exudes total
freedom to the loved one – *you*! Freedom to be what you are.
Freedom to accept. Freedom to reject. Freedom to *choose*. Freedom for you to choose to contribute to the well-being of the
Whole and thus express your very essence in a harmonious
way, and freedom to choose to put self first and foremost and
to satisfy the Ego, even at the expense of others. Freedom to
determine your own destiny, for destiny is fashioned from the
consequences of choosings.

A reason why selfish people are in a continuous state of
craving for satisfaction is that they are suffering from a chronic
state of emptiness because they are lacking in the vitality of the
Love of the Spirit. Vitality is defined as the ability to sustain
life and to perform its functions. So, in a spiritual context,
vitality is the ability to sustain Love and to perform bonding
deeds. A 'lost' Soul, therefore, is one who has lost the ability
to sustain and project Love!

Spirit brought the Soul into being. The Soul brought into

being the physical body. The formation of the physical body enabled the human mind to be created in the image of the Soul and as an extension of the Spirit. The mind is by nature the servant of the Spirit because it is an 'extension' of the Spirit. That is the natural order.

If we consider the different levels of awareness I have touched upon in this book, and examine them from the perception of our existence as multi-dimensional beings and their relationship with the powers of the Elements, we gain a further insight into the Spirit and a wider understanding of ourselves.

Soul awareness is related to the Element of **Fire** because the Soul is our body of Light. It is from the Dimension of the Soul that we receive enlightenment, illumination and radiance (warmth – pure feeling).

Mind awareness is related to the Element of **Air** for the Dimension of the Mind is where movement of thought takes place. It is in the Dimension of the Mind that we receive impressions, generate ideas and concepts, and form opinions.

Physical awareness is related to the Element of **Water** because the one constant factor of physical matter is change. It is in the physical dimension that sensations provide us with an awareness of matter so we can experience for ourselves physical reality.

Spirit awareness is related to the Element of **Earth** because Earth is inertia and stillness, and 'grounds' and harmonizes.

Soul, Mind and Body – like Fire, Air and Water – are all 'active' factors in the totality of our being. Spirit, like Earth, is a 'passive' factor. The implication of this is that none of us can be truly spiritual without being Earthly – without being *practical*. Without being *mortal*! In other words, Earth experience is essential for the cultivation of the Spirit! Soul, Body, Mind and Spirit come together when we take our first breath at birth, but it is not until around puberty that a fuller integration takes place and we become responsible for our own actions. Although throughout this book I have so far referred to Body, Mind, Soul and Spirit, energy and form, matter and non-matter, visible and invisible, separately, they are not really 'separate', but aspects of the one Whole functioning in particular ways. They have been dealt with separately in order that they may be examined and considered. It is the same with what I have called different 'realities'. There is only one total Reality,

but it is perceived in a complexity of ways. It is that one Total Reality that is the Real. What makes it complex is that it is perceived in a myriad of ways, each of which may be mistaken for the *only* Reality.

So Body, Mind, Soul and Spirit are not separate from but an integral part of a single composite Being, each functioning in a different layer of Reality, each a different way of experiencing multi-dimensional Reality.

One of the greatest falsehoods perpetuated on mankind is contained in the conditioned belief that the physical and material are inferior to the spiritual – that the physical body, like Nature, the physical environment and the Earth itself, is there to be conquered and overcome, subjected, controlled and manipulated. The reality is that the spiritual is understood through the physical, and that which is material through the spiritual, for the spiritual and the physical are simply two aspects of the one Reality. Spirit is the spark of life. Soul is the light of life. Mind is the patterner of life. Body is the form of life. Each is a complementary feature of the many-faceted Whole.

I have frequently used a many-faceted crystal ball as a tangible means of demonstrating qualities of the Spirit, and also as an effective meditation tool for accessing an understanding of the way Spirit functions. The facets can be perceived as the 'eyes' of the Spirit, whose vision is in all directions and all dimensions through the different 'bodies' that constitute us as multi-dimensional beings. They also enable the Spirit to be self-reflective regarding its own response to the input it receives through the different layers or dimensions, and those reflections provide it with further means of experience. The facets may also be seen to represent the myriad of potentials that lie dormant within, awaiting only to be recognized and awakened into sparkling life.

As I mentioned in Chapter 9, a candle flame has been used in religious and mystical ceremonies throughout the ages as a symbol of the Spirit, because both are associated with light and with flame. The flame may be likened to the substance of the Soul. The Spirit itself is within the 'Light' of the Soul, so it is the heart of a candle flame that is symbolic of the Spirit. Contemplation on a single candle flame can help to trigger enlightenment about your own individuated Spirit.

You will need for this Experience a candle and candle-holder,

matches, your rattle, and a notebook and pen. It is best to undertake the following Experience in a darkened room.

Experience 27: Emanations of the Spirit

Place the candle in its holder on a table or flat surface immediately in front of you. Make sure you are seated comfortably.

Rattle around yourself for a few minutes to prepare your 'space' sonically and to relax and prepare you.

Light the candle and stare into the flame. Just be aware of the candle flame itself. Its appearance. Its texture. Its activity. Don't attempt to compose thoughts about it. Just allow it to **be**, and experience its existence.

After a while, half close your eyes until you are aware of beams of light stabbing outwards from the flame in all directions. Some upwards. Some to your left. Others to your right. Some coming directly towards you. Some seemingly *into* you.

Scan all those radiant beams. Put a number on how many you are seeing. Close your eyes a little more and watch those fibres of light change and fresh rays appear.

Identify with just one of the fibres of light coming directly into you and linking you directly with the candle flame. Consider its individuality. Consider its uniqueness as an emanation of that one candle flame – a radiance from that single source. It is *there*. Perceive its existence as an energy-expression of the candle flame itself.

Liken your Spirit to it. Your Spirit as an emanation from a greater Source. As a thought, perhaps, in the mind of the Great Spirit? **You**, enabled to have your own independent expression. Meditate on this for a while. Make a note of what inspirations come to you.

Return your gaze to the candle flame. This time, regard the flame as *your* Spirit – the *Real* **You**. Half close your eyes again to generate those fibres of light and choose one to identify with. Now liken it to an emanation from the Source that is your Spirit. Consider that single beam – that emanation – as the *physical* 'you', the 'you' that is identified with your physical body. Meditate on this.

Then select another fibre of light. Regard this as another emanation from the 'flame' that is your Spirit 'source'. Identify this with your Mental Body. Meditate on this for a while.

Again, choose another beam radiating from the candle flame. Allow this to represent your Soul Body as another emanation of your Spirit. Meditate on that.

Finally, consider that each ray of light, each 'body' is but an emanation of the one Spirit. Not *separate* from it, but an expression of it.

Write an account of any realizations that come to you. Extinguish the candle, take a few deep breaths, stretch your limbs, and make yourself a hot drink before resuming your normal activities.

The life you are living in this physical dimension of existence is being impressed upon your Spirit. But that impression is not just a sequence of events strung out in a line since your birth, or a collection of personal reminiscences and sentimentalities, for the way we live our lives is more relevant to the Spirit than what we do. The issue is how we direct and make use of the energies at our disposal, and it is this that cultivates the Spirit and enables it to further its own contribution to the Whole from whence it came, or puts it on a devolutionary cycle.

The individual Spirit has intelligence inherent within it because it came into existence from a Source which is Intelligence itself. It *inherited* free will – the freedom to effect causes and to self-determine. *Your* Spirit – the Spirit that is **You** – *chose* to undergo experience here on Earth now as part of its own process of self-determination and cultivation. That is *why* you are here. That is *how* you came to be where you are now at this point in Time.

The Soul was generated by the Spirit so that the 'I' could become self-aware – an '**I am**'; aware of its own individuality as an expression of the Source from which it emerged, which Itself is Spirit. The Soul Self is thus the summation of the experience that has been obtained from all past lives as well as the one being lived now. In the kahuna tradition it was referred to as *Aumakua* – the 'parental' Self, the 'higher' Self of the Soul. In some shamanic traditions this same Soul Self was referred to as 'the One Who Knows'. Knows what? Knows the 'I' that is the Spirit within. Spirit is the 'I' that emerged from the Circle of Infinity, from the 'Nothingness' of the Source, from the Zero that begets all numbers – from the greater Spirit.

Spirit has alive-ness – that is, awareness of its own individual existence, because Life is in the Spirit and the Spirit *is* Life, and has its own identity, its own unique energy-expression. It also has intelligence – that is, a capacity to register activity, to generate activity, to respond to activity, and to make valid *choices* regarding activity. The *Real* **You**, then, is an inner 'I' – an Inner Eye. The Watcher Within that dwells in the inner sanctum of the Soul.

When individuated Spirit enters the Soul dimension a binding pattern is created to maintain a Soul body from the substance of that dimension. By associating itself with the auras of male and female human beings to whom it is attracted, provision of a physical body that is appropriate for the Spirit is made possible. Hence a belief among some indigenous peoples that family descendants are a guarantee of future incarnations! Soul and Spirit, however, are independent of physical parents. The physical body activates the mind through the pattern given to it by the Soul. Spirituality is thus not a focusing on theological concepts, religious ritualism or textual literalism, but an integrating of all aspects of the total, composite being so that thoughts, actions and feelings become congruent.

We come into physical reality to learn to experience the process of exchanging and interchanging our essential energies with others and with the Universe. Every organ of the physical body is not just a 'component' of a living 'machine' but is itself a transforming process to link us with the physical Universe in our own individual way, for we are none of us 'separate' from the Universe. Any perception of separateness is itself an illusion.

Every aspect of your composite being is thus important. Each is required to be developed in relation to the others and not in isolation from them, so they may function together in total harmony. Body, Mind, Soul and Spirit are each indivisibly connected:

The physical body is a reflection of the Mind.
The Mind is a mirror of the Soul.
The Soul is the Light of the Spirit.
The Spirit is the Life within them all.

Native American shamans expressed the truth of this succinctly in the saying, 'Walk your talk!' Do as you *think*, as you *feel*, as you **are**.

Taoist shamans represented the Soul as a golden lotus flower with a Sun-like radiance that surrounded the Spirit within – the Jewel in the Lotus. As petals of a flower are an expression of the qualities of the essence of the plant itself, so the petals of the symbolic lotus indicate the same qualities, or energies, that combine together in the Soul to form an expression of the Spirit's essence. So the Spirit expresses its essence through the Soul.

The Soul is connected to the Spirit by a fine silver thread from which are suspended pearl-like 'seeds' – like a necklace of pearls. Each seed – each pearl – has locked within it the potential of what it can become. Each contains a design that is different from all others and which complements the Spirit's own uniqueness as an expression of its Original Source. The Spirit has its own 'sound', which is a combination of all the individual 'notes' of each seed. Each seed is an expression of the Spirit in a particular dimension. So each seed vitalizes a 'body' – a facet of the total composite being in a dimension of its multi-dimensional existence.

This is the wonder of **You**!

The Gift of Love

Emerging as only a bud of energy
We are given a single gift
The gift of Love.

Weathering timeless journeys and countless lives
Our roots are strengthened by a single light source
The Light of Love.

Sharing, caring, giving and receiving
Our energy is cultivated into a finer essence
The Pure Essence of Love.

Blossoming to open our hearts
And reveal the brilliance and depth of our love
We have but a single purpose
The Gift of Love.

Reproduced by kind permission of
Michael R. Warwick,
Walnut Creek, California, USA

11. Your Different 'Selves'

CHRISTIAN MISSIONARIES IN HAWAII EARLY in the nineteenth century rejected the understanding of kahuna shamans that humans are composite beings comprising a number of different intelligences – 'selves' or 'spirits' – each functioning on a different layer of existence from the others. The missionaries themselves appeared to have been oblivious to a similarity with the Christian doctrine they themselves preached regarding a trinity of gods who comprised the One God – a dogma they were unable to explain yet demanded should be believed! The kahuna understanding, on the other hand, could not only be explained but could be experienced! This, however, did not prevent the understanding from being condemned as heresy and attributed to demonism; and the kahunas themselves – as with shamans of other cultures – were persecuted and virtually wiped out for perpetuating a teaching that differed from the one imposed by religious dogmatism.

It was not until after the bitter controversy that raged as a result of the publication of Charles Darwin's theory – that living beings have evolved through a long process of natural selection – that a more tolerant attitude towards different perceptions of reality began to prevail at the close of the century. Darwin, a British naturalist, concluded that living creatures, including man, had evolved over great expanses of time; but this claim conflicted with the Christian fundamentalist interpretation of the biblical account of Creation in just seven days, and the appearance of the first man, Adam, a mere 4000 years before the beginning of the Christian era. A furtherance in the release of human minds from the dogmatic conditioning of the

past came as a result of the work of Sigmund Freud (1856–1939), the Austrian pioneer of psychoanalysis, and Swiss psychiatrist Carl Jung (1875–1961). Their concept of different levels of the mind – conscious, subconscious and unconscious – not only established that there are different aspects of one total human mind, but brought modern science and philosophical thought a step nearer to coming into harmony with an ancient wisdom that predated the times of religious bigotry and intolerance. It took two world wars and the subsequent upheavals in the structure of Western society to bring about the greater freedom of thought and activity that is all too often taken for granted today, as if it has always existed.

Like shamans of other cultures during the times of religious persecution, the kahunas kept their ancient wisdom alive through their oral traditions, some of which was 'hidden' within the allegories of their myths, legends and chants. Some also was contained in the form of picture-writing on clothes made of *tapa* – a parchment-like material made from the bark of trees – in which every line, stroke, curve or symbol had an esoteric meaning. The Hawaiian word *tapa* originally meant 'an enclosure made with wood'; it later became also the word for clothing because traditional dress material was made from tree bark which had patterns put onto it, so the relationship was continued since tree bark has grain patterns on it that are impressed from *within*. The Hawaiians understood that we 'clothe' our own Spirit with the patterns we impress upon it through the process of living our lives on Earth, and that we humans 'grow' organically, too, as a tree does. The physical wearing of a dress of *tapa* and its display of unique patterns was but a similarity with the Spirit which 'wears' the patterns that Earth-life experience has impressed upon it.

As was the case with other indigenous peoples, the tree was a basic symbol for shamanic understanding. The trunk and lower branches indicated the conscious 'self' functioning in 'ordinary' reality. The roots were likened to a subconscious 'self' which functioned beneath the surface of normal awareness, and the deeper roots to an intelligence operating in the realm of the unconscious. The upper branches and leaves indicated a superconscious 'self' with god-like creative qualities existing at a level 'above' that of ordinary reality. The sap which rose up from the roots to the very summit of the tree

was symbolic of the Life Force – the Mana or Chi that feeds every layer and level of one's existence. One tree, one human being, but many layers or levels, each with its own function for the well-being of the whole, each with its own awareness of reality at that level, each serving and supporting one another in the totality of the individual existence.

Before we examine the kahuna understanding of the 'selves' in some detail, let us gather a little more insight into ourselves through a *thoughtful* Experience.

Experience 28: How Many Persons Are You?

Go to your usual Quiet Place where you can be relaxed and undisturbed for a while. You will need a candle and its stand, and a notebook and pen.

Light the candle and regard this action as a 'switch', symbolic of a transition from mundane to shamanic activity.

Consider: You have, perhaps, never realized that you are not the same person to everyone you meet. Each may perceive a different 'you' from the one you think you are, and a different 'you' from the one others see.

Although you are a single entity, you fulfil many roles and are a different person to different people whilst remaining the same 'you'.

For instance, to your parents you are a son or daughter. You may also be a husband, wife or partner; a sister or brother; a nephew, niece, cousin, aunt or uncle . . . There is also the 'you' who is a lover, friend, companion or colleague. Another who is an employee, a boss, or unemployed. Or the 'you' who is a teacher, student, apprentice, nurse, housewife, salesperson, or whatever your work role is. And so the list goes on . . .

Examine aspects of your life and list the many roles you play: who you are to the many people with whom your life brings you in contact.

When you are fairly confident that you have exhausted them all, add up your 'score'. Is it possible that there are some that may have eluded you? So the list you have is the minimum number of individuals you are to the people you are in touch with in your ordinary, everyday life.

Consider all these different people you are. Recognize your tremendous versatility.

Coming into a realization that there are four 'selves' in the totality of your being is not now so incredible after all.

As you snuff out your candle flame, regard this action as an 'off' switch from shamanic to 'ordinary' activity.

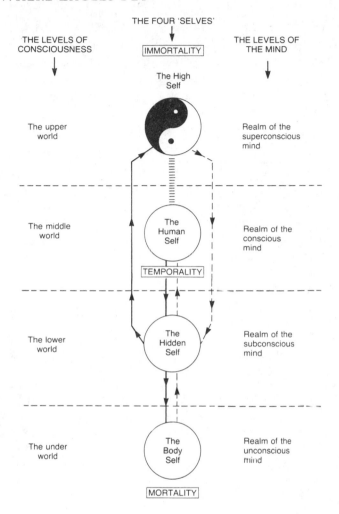

Figure 33. The four 'Selves' in relation to levels of awareness and the mind

THE EGO-SELF – *A-UHANE*

The 'self' we are most familiar with – indeed, for the vast majority of people, the *only* 'self' that is known – is the Ego-self, or what the kahunas called *A-Uhane* (pronounced Ow-oo-hah-nee). *A-U* means 'I' or 'self' or 'spirit'. *Hane* means 'to give life and spirit' and 'to talk'. So *A-Uhane* is the 'I' – the spirit – that talks! But the voice of this 'talking' self is not the voice of the Spirit that is at the Source of your being – your greater

Spirit. Your Ego tells you what it wants to satisfy its own insatiable needs. It reminds you constantly of inadequacies, limitations and constraints, and it leads you into making comparisons and judgements. The voice of your Spirit is still and, perhaps, rarely heard above the constant chatter of the Ego. The Ego-self is the 'little' self that pretends to be the 'greater' Self and speaks so loudly that the still, small voice of the greater Self, whose whisperings come from within, is rarely heard. It is not difficult to identify with the Ego-self because it is the self of your everyday physical and mental activity. It is that aspect of your total being that expresses itself through personality, and is concerned with making decisions in the process of practical, everyday reality. It is the 'self' whose birthday you keep. It is the 'you' that attended certain schools, was educated to a particular level, engaged itself in particular work, and has certain qualities and assets. It has likes and dislikes, dreams and aspirations, hopes and fears. It is the 'self' you project most of the time.

Although the Ego-self resides within the physical body, it functions in the mental body and is the motivating force behind the conscious mind and our illusory sense of self-identity: illusory in that it limits its awareness to externals – to what *appears* to be – and keeps the mind fixed on what is physical as if the material is the *only* reality. Ego locks us into the limitations of lateral thinking; and by perceiving things only through the Ego, we have a narrow perspective of Reality and one that confines us to the physical dimension and prevents us from experiencing any real depth to our lives.

An understanding of the Ego can help us to better comprehend the nature of this 'talking spirit' that conditions our human nature. 'Ego' is a term used in psychoanalysis to describe an aspect of the mind that is closely in touch with external reality – with what is happening in the immediate surroundings – and it functions rationally. Psychoanalysis is a therapy derived from the modern science of psychology. The word 'psychology' is, however, a misnomer for this area of study. It is a word derived from two Greek words – *psyche*, which means 'Soul', and *logos*, which means 'wisdom'. So the word 'psychology' means literally 'the study of the wisdom of the Soul'. Yet psychology is a study not of the Soul but of the mind and human behaviour. It is concerned with the motivating factors

behind the conscious mind and the sense of self-identity that exists in the mind. In other words, the *mental* 'self' – the Ego-self that is conditioned by the concepts and beliefs impressed upon it by society and by cultural, family, parental, religious and other pressures, and which responds to external influences by attempting to reconcile them in accordance with what seems to be in its own self-interest.

The seat of consciousness of this mental 'self' – this Ego-self, which reasons, analyses, speculates, considers, forms beliefs, holds opinions and makes judgements and comparisons – seems to be at a point behind the forehead and between the eyes on a level with the bridge of the nose. This centre of awareness, where the 'you' that thinks seems to *be*, is 'located' where information is received from the two hemispheres of the brain. In the physical realm, information is conveyed in the physical body in the form of electrical and chemical impulses, and this information is conveyed to the mind as experience of sensation. Information from the Mental Realm is conveyed to the physical body as thoughts and ideas. The left lobe of the brain deals with verbal skills and the logical, reasoning aspect of your nature. Because of its conditioning, through the input of information coming into it, this side of the brain is usually more dominant than the right hemisphere. Meditation and some other mental techniques are ways of quietening the internal chattering of thoughts that flow through the left lobe of the brain so the Ego-self can listen to the activity in the right lobe, which goes on comparatively unnoticed in many people and deals with the intuitive side of our nature.

The left lobe governs the right side of the physical body, which is related to what might be described as 'masculine', Yang, or active attributes. For instance, primitive peoples regard the right hand which holds a tool, implement or weapon, as the 'doing' or 'attacking' hand and it is thus associated with the body's masculine or Yang polarity. The left hand is regarded as more passive and defensive and the hand used for 'receiving', and is thus related to the body's feminine or Yin polarity.

Left-brain activity is linear and logical, so things are perceived in straight lines: past, present and future; beginning, middle and end. It is the side that wants to take things apart and break them down to specifics so they can be examined as

separates. It is the side which expresses the Will. Right-brain activity is concerned with putting things together and perceiving them as a unified whole. The right lobe governs the left side of the body and the intuitive, creative, receptive, nurturing side of our nature. It is the side that designs patterns from what is received in order for the Will to be exerted and action taken.

Will-power – or, rather, the Will's power – is an ability to focus on the directing of energy along a predetermined route and for a specific purpose. The Will is what *drives* the energy along that route. Malfunctioning occurs because we have been conditioned to connect the Will with the mind rather than the Spirit. The Will is thus exercised in accordance with what the Ego-self *thinks* it *wants* rather than with what the Spirit *needs* for the well-being of the whole.

When the A-Uhane is enabled to come into conscious contact with the other intelligences of our total being – with our *other* 'selves' – the capacity of both sides of the brain becomes enhanced. The right brain functions receptively, senses intuitively and produces creatively, whilst the left brain organizes, structures and initiates those creative patterns into action and form. When the two hemispheres function as a partnership and complement each other in this way, information from each is integrated into the whole and potential is enhanced.

To experience conscious awareness of the 'selves' that constitute our entire being and to connect with our own multi-dimensional reality, we need to break through the Ego-energies that keep us confined and limited to a conditioned view of Reality.

THE HIDDEN SELF – *UNIHIPILI*

The second 'self' functions silently and discreetly 'beneath the surface' of conscious activity so its actions are not so obvious. Kahuna shamans called this second intelligence *A-Unihipili* (pronounced Ow-oo-nee-hip-ee-lee), which means 'the I – or self, or spirit – that *clings*'. It clings like a shadow to the A-Uhane Ego-self. It is a subservient intelligence with a trusting nature and an inherent willingness to obey. It responds to what it regards as an instruction or command, provided that instruction conforms to the memory-pattern of beliefs and attitudes

imposed upon it by the A-Uhane Ego-self. It will either not respond to any requirement that conflicts with what has been previously programmed into it, or it will signal incompatability in some disharmonious way.

The equivalent of the Unihipili is referred to in some traditions as 'the Child Within' because of its child-like, though not child-ish, attitude. Like a child, it cannot discern between beliefs and actuality, between fantasy and fact, real and unreal. Tell a child about Santa Claus distributing gifts to children world-wide at Christmas and it does not have the cynicism to check out the story. They will believe you because you are an adult and a figure of authority and wisdom. Similarly, your Unihipili accepts your beliefs – whether mundane, religious or superstitious – as facts and will act accordingly because A-Uhane, your Ego-self, is not only its authority but its 'god', because it exists in a dimension beyond its own!

In childhood, behaviour conditioning is largely by parents and teachers and the growing influence of television. In adolescence it is by social and sporting figures that are made objects of 'hero' worship and idolization. In adulthood it is by the 'gods' that claim devotion; and today these are mostly secular ones such as money, property, careers, automobiles, and the material possessions into which the Ego-self chooses to channel its energies.

The hidden subconscious self thus has little reasoning power, but it does have memory, and it learns skills through repetition or command. It experiences emotion because emotion is a flow of energy activated by thought and by association and when experienced induces action. But although it is influenced by the power of emotion, the language of Unihipili is primarily imagery and impressions, not words.

In some shamanic traditions, Unihipili is referred to as 'the Animal-self' because it has qualities and characteristics that are observable in some animals; and it responds to certain situations instinctively, as animals do, and not logically. Indeed, I understand that some shamans regard this silent, servant self as the person's principal power animal!

What is a power animal? A power animal is *not* an external entity that can somehow take possession of you. You possess it, for it is an internal energy-pattern that has attributes similar to the animal species it characterizes. In order to comprehend

that fully, let us examine the title 'power animal'. The word 'power' has a number of meanings. It can be defined as 'an energizing force' – like nuclear power. Power can also mean 'to have control over' or 'to exert mastery'. Another meaning is 'authority to govern'. There is a further definition, however: 'the ability to perform work'. This is the definition that applies to power animals and to Shamanics. Power – shamanic power – is an ability to perform specific work! Now let us examine the word 'animal'. According to dictionary definitions, an animal is 'an intelligent creature that possesses life, sensation, and the power of voluntary motion'. So now we have arrived at a definition of a power animal: 'A power animal is an energy-pattern – or energy-system – that appears in animal form and possesses sensation and the power of voluntary movement to carry out its inherent ability to perform the specific work it *characterizes*'. **A power animal is the very energy-pattern of an ability or abilities that the animal form characterizes!**

According to shamanic understanding, we each have a number of power animals, for they are patterns of natural abilities and potentials that are inherent within us. A principal power animal is one that has *prominence*. Unihipili reflects something of its nature not only through the expression of deep-rooted, subconscious behaviour tendencies, but also, to an extent, in our human physical features. For instance, in jest it is sometimes suggested that people who have a close attachment to a domestic pet take on something of the physical features of the animal they adore. Likewise, this seems to be so with a principal power animal that Unihipili may reflect. We can thus know something about a person's Unihipili by recognizing the 'animal' that is 'hidden' in their physical features. The penetrating, staring eyes of Eagle. A Hawk-like facial expression. The calm, absent-mindedness of Owl. The long, pointed nose of Wolf. The hair-line of Badger. The over-size ears of Elephant. The close-set eyes of Weasel. And so on.

Once an animal characteristic is recognized, study the behaviour pattern of that animal species and you will come to an understanding of the way the underlying Unihipili behaves and responds to human-life situations.

Unihipili uses that aspect of the mind that is below the level of waking consciousness. As I defined earlier, the mind is a process, not an object, so we might say that Unihipili uses a

process that is hidden beneath the surface of awareness and which is not logical and analytical, but literal and factual. In other words, it takes the Ego-self literally and exactly. It processes speech and words and verbalized thoughts and converts them into imagery patterns and stores them in its memory bank. Since it cannot discern between what is *believed* and what is *actual* – fact from fantasy, actuality from imagination – everything that is fed into it is compatible with information it has already accepted. So it remembers past conditioning – all your inhibitions, taboos, prohibitions, restrictions and limitations. It refuses to accept new input that does not 'compute' with this memory data. Your Unihipili has been conditioned by the way it has functioned since your infancy. It has been conditioned by your habits – your repetitive actions, whether good for you or otherwise. It has been conditioned by the firm expectations of your Ego-self of what is and what is not possible, by your fixed attitudes, values, judgements, ideas and beliefs. It has accepted what you deep down have accepted. It rejects what you deep down have rejected, and distrusts what you deep down distrust. For Unihipili is the deep down 'you', hidden away yet apparent.

Unihipili is the self that performs all skills that are based on a sequential pattern of actions, such as writing, for instance, or driving a vehicle; each action triggering the next. Ritual was once a means of communicating directly with Unihipili in order to obtain a desired result. Ritual was a way of teaching Unihipili what was required to be achieved; and since Unihipili is your servant self it would act upon the instruction which was symbolically given in the ritual. Unihipili is the genie in Aladdin's lamp! The intention was inserted in the sequence of ritualistic actions, energized by desire, and directed by the Will. In the course of time, and through ignorance of the essential purpose of ritual, many mistook the ritual for an end in itself – the menu for the meal. Ritual performed through custom and tradition as a series of actions and given a veneer of spirituality has no power to achieve anything because it contains no 'message' and lacks energizing force. It is powerless and meaningless, so Unihipili ignores it!

The nature of your Unihipili is in accordance with a Universal Law: 'Maximum efficiency with minimum effort', so it performs its work as your servant self, simply, silently and effortlessly.

Although Unihipili occupies the same physical body as the A-Uhane, it functions in the Energic Body of shadowy substance which I described in Chapter 2. It is a partner spirit in the total **You**, evolving with you, as dependant on you for its development as you are on it. Come to recognize it. Accept it as an integral co-worker. Come to love it as the Child that is *within* you – a Child that *is* you. A way of establishing constant contact with this Child Within is to give it an identity – a name. Not any old name, or even a 'pet' one, but a name that is deserving of respect. Since many people appear to find it difficult to choose a name which does not have other associations, and after considerable experience with students of Shamanics, I now advocate use of the Hawaiian word Unihipili as a name. This is why I have so frequently referred to this 'hidden' self by that name in these pages. The word Unihipili has a pleasant ring about it – a musical sound – and is a name that cannot be confused with any other.

I have explained that ritual was a principal method of communicating with the Unihipili because the language of Unihipili is not words but imagery. This is partly why symbols are relevant for they, too, are part of the subtle language of the 'hidden' self. But to be effective, ritual needs to be more than a sequence of actions, however meaningful. It has to be fuelled in order that it may be projected to where it can be decoded and its message understood by Unihipili. That 'fuel' is *feeling*. The actions are a way of communicating what it is that is desired. In other words, they carry a *message*. The message must be *clear*. It is what Unihipili is required to **do**. And that message must be energized by being fired with genuine *feeling*. Indeed, the message must be *experienced* and not just thought about with clarity of mind, although that, too, is important. It should be felt as deeply as a physical *sensation*.

All shamanic rituals are thus ways of communicating a clear message to Unihipili, and rituals that 'work' do so only because the message gets through and is then acted upon. Rituals that don't 'work' are ineffective because no message gets through that can be acted upon, or if it does it is contrary to what is acceptable through past 'programming' of Unihipili. In computer terminology, the message does not compute and is therefore rejected. Effective rituals that contain repetitive actions do so because a repetitive signal is often required by the Unihipili

in order for the authenticity of the message to be confirmed. Unihipili is itself a protective censor that deals with a vast volume of information and screens out that which it evaluates as not being required to be acted upon or which does not conform to what has been previously programmed as acceptable.

Some of the Experiences given in this book, and in Chapter 8 particularly, contain simple ritualistic or repetitive actions which are designed to impart the intention of your message to your Unihipili. You can, of course, design your own by making use of the guidelines and examples given in these pages.

Unihipili is the means of access to our other 'selves' – to the Body Self which is the biological intelligence of the physical body, and the High Self or 'greater' Self that functions through the Soul. However, Unihipili is not a mediator or arbiter, but rather a guide and protector – one who both guides the way and protects it. Unihipili is the link between the mental and the physical (mind and matter) and also between the physical and the spiritual (matter and Spirit, body and Soul). Unihipili is thus the key that opens the way to other realities, to other levels of our multi-dimensional existence; and that also unlocks the door to understanding, enabling the mind to connect with the Spirit.

THE BODY SELF

Although kahuna shamans regarded the Unihipili as also the biological intelligence of the physical body, some shamans of other cultures acted on an understanding that there was, in addition, an instinctive intelligence, which I shall call the Body Self. The Body Self functions at unconscious levels of activity to control, maintain, repair and renew the physical body which is *its* body. Your Body Self regulates your heartbeat, governs body temperature, supervises the functions of digestion, the storage of energy, hormone production, and the dispersal and elimination of waste products. It governs also your body's internal communications network and its self-repair system.

It is the Body Self that performs healing. Medicines, drugs, remedies, treatments, therapies and surgery are only *aids* to healing. It is the spirit intelligence of the human body that

actually performs the healing work. A shamanist makes no claim to be a 'healer' because he or she knows that true healing takes place within the one being healed. All another person can do is assist that inner process. A shamanist is a catalyst through whom regenerating change may take place to restore the person to an inner state of wholeness. Shamanic 'healing' is performed through co-operating with a person's Body Self to ascertain the cause of the disharmony in the way the life is being lived and to discover what needs to be learnt – perhaps a willingness to make adjustments to certain aspects of the life style which have been instrumental in bringing about the condition.

From a shamanic perspective, there are two principal causes of sickness. First, something inside that should not be there. Second, something inside that should be there but is missing. The first is an *intrusion* – misplaced energy that has entered in and which does not belong there. The second is *dissipation* – loss of vital energy. Intrusion can come about through the fear, stress, anxiety and vulnerability caused by living habits that are weakening to the energy-system and throw it out of balance – and through psychic attack. The form of shamanic work used to rectify this is called *abstraction*. Dissipation, or loss of vital power, is rectified when energy is restored. That form of shamanic work is called *retrieval*.

One of the prime causes of illness is a sense of separation – of alone-ness, incompleteness. Shamanic 'healing' is essentially a process of reviving a sense of 'belonging'. This is why, in tribal groups, healing was frequently performed by a shaman with the active participation of members of the family and friends, and sometimes the whole community. As I explained in Chapter 9, a part of the purpose of this was to re-establish a sense of 'belonging' through collective empathy and support. Shamanic healing does not depend on so-called psychic powers, mediumistic skills, or a need to exercise 'faith'. But it does require an ability to connect with and respond to the intelligence of the Body Self of the one seeking help.

The Body Self is the physical body's caretaker, protector, guardian and defender. It reacts to fear – which is an emotion that produces hormones triggered by Unihipili to release adrenalin – because it is primarily concerned with physical survival. It wants to stay alive because it is a *mortal* self! It dies

when life leaves the body. It never sleeps for it is in a constant state of awareness, and it functions instinctively. Its language is electro-chemical impulses. Its province is the physical realm. It is related to the unconscious aspect of the mind.

The Body Self knows what is beneficial and what is harmful in the nourishment, sustenance, maintenance and repair of the human body. After all, it is the intelligence that keeps it alive and in existence. The reason we don't know anything of what it *knows* is that we never *ask*. It is not that we don't know *how*. We don't even know we *can*! We are in ignorance about ourselves. The Body Self can tell you what foods are good to eat and what foods may have an adverse effect on the body. It knows better than any dietician or nutritionist the foods best suited to your body to maintain it in harmony and balance. All you need to do is *ask*!

It is the Ego-self – the Mind-self – that chooses the food you eat. So what you eat is what appeals to and satisfies your mind rather than what nourishes your body. The food looks good, smells good and tastes good, so the Ego-self *thinks* it must be good. But it may not be so to the body itself. By a dialogue with your Body Self through Unihipili, you will be able to determine what food is best for you to eat. If you are concerned about your physical condition, or have a weight problem, your own body knows what is beneficial for it to consume in order to restore it to good health or attain the correct body weight that will enable it to function at its most efficient level. Dialogue with your Body Self is a more accurate method of determining body needs than a dietary plan which, after all, has been devised in accordance with certain general principles and theories thought out by someone else's Ego-self!

The Pendulum as a Shamanic Tool

An effective way of communicating with the Body Self through Unihipili is with a pendulum. A pendulum, as a shamanic tool, provides Unihipili with a device that enables it to communicate its awareness of the Body Self to your conscious self (A-Uhane). It does this by means of energy impulses like a binary code, because the Body Self's language is not words or imagery but electrical and chemical impulses: 0–1; positive, neutral and

Figure 34. Using a pendulum. The cord of the pendulum should be held between the thumb and forefinger about 7–10 centimetres (3–4 inches) from the weight, which should be suspended just above a clear surface.

negative. Or put another way – 'Yes', 'Don't Know' or 'Maybe', and 'No'. Provided, then, that you are able to phrase your questions objectively and in such a way as to require 'Yes', 'No', 'Don't Know' or 'Maybe' answers, you can carry out a meaningful conversation!

A pendulum consists of a small weight suspended on a thread, cord or chain. The weight can be a wooden bob, a small crystal, or material that balances when suspended. The thread, cord or chain is held between the thumb and forefinger about 7–10 centimetres (3–4 inches) above the weight. The pendulum will swing either backwards and forwards or from side to side, or revolve clockwise or anti-clockwise. These movements can be related to the four responses of 'Yes', 'No', 'Don't Know' and 'Maybe'. How do you establish which is which? You must establish this for yourself. What is a correct sequence for some people may not be so for others. Shamanic work is very personal, so you need to establish what is the correct code for *you*.

Obtain a pendulum for yourself that appeals to you and follow the instructions given in the following Experience to prepare it as a communication device.

Experience 29: Preparing Your Communication Device

Take your pendulum with you to your indoor Quiet Place and sit comfortably beside a table or piece of furniture that provides you with a flat, solid surface. Hold the thread of the pendulum between the thumb and forefinger of your right hand (left, if you are left-handed) and about 7–10 centimetres (3–4 inches) above the bob. Rest your elbow on a solid surface so the bob is suspended freely just above the surface but firmly supported. Now, in your mind, 'connect' with your Body Self through your Unihipili simply by the intention to do so. Your clear intention is to make conscious contact, so be aware of that connectedness taking place as a result of that intention. This is an important and vital preliminary.

When the pendulum is perfectly still, allow your mind to be relaxed and put the question: 'Which is the direction for "Yes"?' Don't attempt to will the pendulum to move. Simply allow your mind to be passive and allow movement to happen. When the pendulum does begin to move, allow it to develop its own direction of movement. Is it a circular, clockwise rotation? Or anti-clockwise? Is it a perpendicular oscillation, or a horizontal motion? Make a mental note of the direction of movement.

Repeat the procedure for the next question: 'What is the direction for "Maybe"?' Allow the pendulum to respond. Then ask 'What is the direction for "No"?' Finally, ask: 'What is the direction for "Don't Know"?'

Should there be any discrepancy in the responses, go through the entire procedure again until there is no confusion. For instance, if the answer to the first question is a vertical oscillation like a nod of the head, seek confirmation as follows: 'If a vertical movement means "Yes", swing backwards and forwards to confirm this.' After you have received a response you can check the other responses similarly.

The movements you have experienced and the code you have established have nothing to do with the occult. They are generated from inside yourself, not outside, and form an aspect of your being that functions beneath the level of conscious awareness. Through the sensitivity of the pendulum to high-frequency impulses transmitted through your nervous system, and the code you have established with an inner intelligence, a dialogue is now possible. The next stage is to learn to formulate questions that will elicit clear answers.

Your Body Self is the intelligence that governs, maintains and sustains your physical body so it knows your body's needs

and what is beneficial for it, or otherwise. For instance, some foods though good in themselves may not be beneficial for everyone, or a combination of items, although beneficial individually, may have an adverse affect on the body. Conversing with your Body Self through Unihipili by using the pendulum, is a way of checking the suitability or freshness of any food at that particular time.

Experience 30: Testing What Food is Good For You

Hold your pendulum over any item of food and ask first, 'Is this good food?', or, in the case of fruit and vegetables, 'Is this food fresh?' If the answer is 'Yes,' go on to ask, 'Is this food good for me now?'

Some food may not be good for you because it is too highly refined, contains unsuitable additives, too much fat, sugar or salt, or for some other reason. In indicating that any item of food, though good in itself, is not beneficial for you now, the Body Self may be indicating that it may not combine well with other foods, or the body does not require it at this time. It may be quite suitable at another time, so a 'No' should not be interpreted as meaning that you should never eat that particular item.

This simple technique can be extended to apply to menus in a cookery book or dietary plan. In this way, if you are concerned about your weight, you may be able to devise a diet that is uniquely yours and one that is entirely suitable for your body and its metabolism.

You can, of course, put other questions to seek information about yourself, but keep them to simple things. Don't include questions of a prophetic nature. The Body Self and Unihipili do not predict the future. You can, however, obtain guidance about whether a certain activity or action would be helpful to you or likely to cause problems of some kind. So you have here a means of discovering the things in your life that are beneficial to you and your body and bring harmony, and those that might have an adverse effect.

THE GREATER SELF – *AUMAKUA*

There is another 'self' – another intelligence – in your composite being, and one that is the more evolved aspect of your totality. It is the greater 'self' of the Soul. This greater 'self' has

been given many names. Some mystical traditions have referred to it as 'the higher consciousness' because it appears to
have superconscious abilities, or 'the immortal self' because it
is understood to survive death, and even 'the divine self' because it has attributes associated with divinity. In my previous
writings I have called it the 'High Self' because it is the 'self'
we aspire to in our composite being and the self that *inspires*
us.

This 'Higher' Self functions in the Soul body. Its seat of
consciousness in relation to the physical body is above the
head. The halos and solar discs portrayed in religious paintings
and works of art are symbolic representations of it. Its dimension of existence is that of the Soul whose 'substance' is spiritual Light. This 'High' Self created your physical body for it
was in being before your physical existence and will continue
to survive beyond your physical death.

Kahuna shamans called this greater Self *Aumakua* (pronounced Ay-oo-mah-hoo-ah). *Au* means 'I', 'self' or 'spirit';
makua means 'parents' or 'parental', and can also mean
'Father'. So Aumakua means the 'I-parents' or the 'I-Father' –
the 'Our Father' of the spirits or intelligences that comprise the
composite being. Let us examine the name further. *Ma* means
'to flow through', *ku* means 'likeness' and *kua* means 'yoke' or
'that which holds together'. It can also mean 'generates' or
'generations', as with children. So a human being is formed in
the likeness of Aumakua who determined its incarnation
through a relationship that might be likened to that of parent
and child. That is what is meant in some sacred writings where
it says that man was formed in the image of God – in the
likeness of Aumakua.

Interestingly, the Hawaiian word for 'kingdom' is *au puni*.
Au means 'I' and *puni* means 'place'. So 'Our Father's kingdom'
is 'the Place of I'. It is the place where the 'I' is in the Realm of
the Soul 'above' which in religious terminology is called
'Heaven'.

The definition 'I-Parents' indicates that Aumakua is a duality
– a parental *pair* with both a masculine and feminine aspect –
whose emphasis is on eternal values rather than temporal
material and mental considerations. It was thus the *Father*
aspect that produced a seed pattern of information in the Soul
dimension that determined your form, and the *Mother* aspect

that provided the substance with which the form was to be manifested. This principle underlies all that is in physical existence and was represented by Taoist shamans in the form of the Tai Chi symbol.

Like all ancient symbols, the Tai Chi has many facets of understanding. It represents the Great Unity of the integration of the Yin and Yang and the principle of complementary opposites. It also indicates life motion, and is the name given to an ancient art of gentle meditative movement. It may also be understood as the potential that is becoming manifest. Taoist shamans also regarded it as a symbol for the greater Self.

The Chinese ideogram for the word 'I' is a combination of the symbols for the Sun and the Moon and their alternating and complementary qualities. A combination of the Yang and Yin. The thrustful masculine aspect produces the seed pattern for everything and the receptive, nurturing feminine aspect produces the substance in accordance with a Cosmic Law, 'Everything is born of Woman'. The merging of the masculine and feminine – Yang and Yin – is what perpetuates life and creates new forms in which Spirit can find expression and experience itself.

Aumakua – your Soul's 'self' – has greater wisdom than your Ego-self (A-Uhane) because it has gained the experience of many lifetimes. From the Soul dimension it has an overview of your human life-situation at any time. It sees clearly in all directions – past, present and future – and can perceive where all the bits and pieces of your life fit together like a jigsaw puzzle. Your future is not something that is pre-ordained. The future is a crystallization of what is brought into being by choices and actions in the past and by the thoughts and actions of the present, and the greater Self is able in the Soul dimension to perceive patterns that are in the process of formation before they come into manifestation. Answered prayer is the result of changes made in those patterns before they manifest into physical reality.

COMMUNICATING WITH THE SOUL

Your greater Self makes no demands on you, enforces no action even when you are making mistakes, because your development can take place only through learning from the consequences of your own choices, decisions and actions, and those of others whose lives have an effect on yours, too. But, like a loving parent, Aumakua is always *there* to give guidance when called upon to do so, ever supportive, never interfering, wanting only what is in *your* best interests and for your ultimate well-being, because it loves you unconditionally and totally *in spite of yourself*. All you are required to do in response is to recognize it and by so doing bring this 'Higher' Self 'down' into your daily life.

What today is sometimes called 'channelling' – bringing some superior knowledge and wisdom into the consciousness through direct access to some 'higher' source – is, in some cases, *not* mediumistic. It is simply a personal dialogue between an individual and his or her greater Self. Many channelling experiences are thus conversations with an aspect of the channeller's own multi-dimensional being – with his or her own greater Self that exists in another dimension. The greater Self does not take possession of the physical body and mind to manipulate the vocal chords in order to give a message, as is the case with mediums who are left unaware of what is happening during the process. The channeller or shamanist retains full control of his or her free will and is conscious during the entirety of the experience, though in an altered state of awareness.

Shamanic 'journeys' into an altered state of awareness through 'travelling' on a drumming sound and with the intention of coming into conscious contact with the greater Self, are gentle, safe and controlled, because just as the drumming will induce an altered state of awareness from ordinary to non-ordinary reality, so also will it return the individual from non-ordinary to ordinary reality at the conclusion of the experience.

To contact the greater Self in this way, the shamanist transfers the awareness to what is usually referred to as 'the Upper World', which in myths and legends is located in the sky 'above the clouds' because it is a 'higher' or 'heavenly' realm. There the 'higher' Self may appear as a Teacher. It is not,

however, a projection *outside*, but rather a going *inside* to an *inner* plane. It is only *in relation* to the physical body that the Greater Self is in a spatial location *above* the head, but in another dimension.

Meeting a Teacher on the inner planes in this way can only be described as an ecstatic experience and one that is entirely personal. Such an experience is expressed in both words and music by my wife, Beryl, in her symphonic work *Powers of Love*, which is available on music cassette (see Resources). Through the inner Teacher it is possible to tap into a repository of experience and wisdom that is encapsulated within the Soul.

Conscious contact with the ecology of Soul through a shamanic journey is thus possible without the use of hallucinogenic drugs. Whilst certain drugs can induce an altered state of mind and result in an ecstatic 'high', the effects are the result only of chemical changes in the brain and can be addictive and destructive. Drugs are a false substitute and not a way of making contact with the higher nature. Quite the reverse.

It is possible to get through to the Soul and obtain the support of its superior powers through another shamanic technique – telepathic dialogue. In a religious context this is called prayer, although what are often presented as prayers are no more than words, sometimes not even comprehended by the person who speaks or reads them. Jesus, a master shaman, labelled them 'vain repetitions' which are futile and ineffective. Effective prayers are energy-patterns with a potent message, and their true purpose is to involve a 'higher' intelligence in an act of creativity. A reason most religious prayers go unanswered is that they never get through to the 'higher' intelligence – but, of course, that is understandable if the one who does the praying does not know what, who and where that Intelligence is! Ineffective prayers have no clear intention or lack the power to project them into another dimension. They have no life – no Chi. On the other hand, telepathic communication with the Soul is a spontaneous undertaking in which the Ego-self, Body Self, Unihipili and Aumakua are all involved in partnership together.

Let us examine how this kind of communication can take place. First, there is a need to go beyond the limitations that your own conditioning may have imposed upon you and recognize that you are inherently linked with a creative Intelligence

that exists outside of Time and Space. Second, you must want to be in communication with this Intelligence because, although it is concerned with your ultimate well-being and ready to help and guide you, it can respond directly only if it is invited to do so. The greater Self will not intervene in your life unless you invite it. It can be approached only through a child-like attitude of trust and innocence ('innocence' in its meaning of lacking doubt and cynicism). That is, with the spirit of Unihipili! Unihipili, the Child Within, can lead you into the presence of your 'parental' Self so your life may be more fulfilling, more effective, more creative. The channel that connects your physical body via the Energic Body to your Soul body is accessed through Unihipili, just as the unconscious aspect of the mind is reached only through the subconscious. Unihipili thus guards the entrance to the Soul. That is one of its functional responsibilities. So, whatever you intend to communicate to your Soul must be intelligible to your Unihipili. **Child-like simplicity, child-like trust and child-like expectancy are thus prerequisites for shamanic prayer.**

Whilst any approach to the Greater Self needs to be respectful, it should not be submissive. You are not its clone, robot or slave. The relationship is a close and loving one. Only human beings whose Egos require them to assert power over others demand subservience, and have to devise high-sounding words and elevated titles, not always comprehensible, to ensure that it is carried out. We need to free ourselves from the encumbrance and humbug of such conditioning and come to realize that it is the quality of what is being communicated that is important. So let us share an Experience of no-nonsense shamanic dialogue.

Experience 31: Shamanic Dialogue

Go to your indoor Quiet Place or to a power spot outdoors where you can be comfortable and completely at ease for a time and unlikely to be disturbed. Take a notebook and pen with you.

Discard any preconceptions about *who* you are to talk to. There is no need to visualize an image of a person or a deity. Whatever pictures or images you have seen are but *ideas* in the minds of those who created them. They represent only an activity of someone else's Ego, not a Reality, and are a projection of the very conditioning that

has been blocking access to superconscious experience all your life! Whilst any approach to this greater Self requires respect, it is not one of awe but of a loving relationship.

It is vital that you have the *intention* clear at the outset. And this is to bring about a change – in a situation in which you appear to be 'trapped', in the likely outcome of a chain of events that is already in motion, or in a relationship or matter of concern – that will be in accordance with your Soul's purpose and in harmony with your Spirit.

Ask Unihipili to open the way to Aumakua. Visualize a door being opened, or a curtain being gently pulled aside.

Addressing your Soul 'self' as Aumakua identifies it respectfully as both Mentor and Lover, and you – A-Uhane – as the Loved One, and establishes recognition of the true relationship. It involves both a giving and a receiving – a mutual exchange of energies – out of loving concern and respect for one another and the value of that relationship to each other. This is a far cry from the 'unworthy servant' and 'humble slave' approach penned in a bygone age in the forlorn hope that some great Personage outside of Creation would be touched by such patronage.

Aumakua is a beautiful-sounding name. Try using it as you would the name of someone with whom you have a loving relationship and who is precious to you. Be natural. Talk from the heart rather than from the head. Tell Aumakua you love Him/Her and you have a matter you wish to share. Then describe your problem in a heartfelt way. Tell it as it is. Ask for help and guidance in bringing about a beneficent outcome.

Write in your notebook the gist of what you have said. Then sit quietly and receptively. Don't try to work out an answer in your mind. There is no need to think it through and attempt to reason out an answer. Just be attentive and wait patiently for a response.

This may not come in the form of words. It may be that your attention is directed to something that is taking place in your circle of awareness. The movement of a curtain at an open window, perhaps. The rustle of leaves in the breeze. The activities of an insect. A particular design or formation. A colour. Or it may be just a feeling within yourself. An impression that springs into your mind.

Whatever it is, put it into words and describe it in your notebook. If it appears to be symbolic, don't attempt to interpret it. You are merely recording an activity that has come suddenly and unexpectedly into your awareness, not attempting to explain it.

Then talk to Aumakua about what you have just experienced. If it is something you do not understand, ask Aumakua to explain. Write your questioning in your notebook, and wait for a response. Again,

don't try to exercise your imagination or attempt to fabricate an answer. Just be receptive, alert and patient.

When a response comes, make a note of it, too. If it needs clarification, *ask*. Again, write down what you have asked and await a further response. A response will come in any number of ways, so be alert. What is it that you are being shown? What is it that is being indicated?

Continue in this way, writing down your questions, for this helps to get the attention of Unihipili and focuses the intent.

In waiting for a response you will learn to listen to the silence. An answer will come out of the stillness. Sometimes the answer may be to wait – wait to be *shown*. Then the answer may come unexpectedly through synchronicity – a seeming 'coincidence', chance encounter or sudden 'happening'.

Shamanic dialogue will bring into your life answers to many perplexities as well as to the situations for which you seek help.

Answered prayer is not attained by positive thinking or through some kind of divine intervention, but by the power of creation. It comes about through the four 'selves' of the composite being cooperating together in an act of creativity.

Shamanic divination

Another way of communicating with the greater Self is through divination. Shamanic divination is a very ancient art, but it is not fortune-telling, superstition or mind-reading. The word 'divination' is defined in most dictionaries as meaning 'divine guidance'. It is thus a way of consulting a 'higher' intelligence that has superior wisdom. Shamanic divination is a way of consulting the superior wisdom of the greater Self of the querant. Actually, divination is not about the future, but the present. Since most problems encountered in our lives are self-inflicted – that is, inflicted by the Ego-self, which is hardly likely to arrive at a solution through its reasoning powers – divination is a means of obtaining a new perspective by seeing beyond the limitations imposed on the situation by the Ego-self and, through subsequent actions, reshaping the likely outcome.

Shamanic divination is telepathic and intuitive rather than imaginative and analytical, because it is essentially an activity of the Spirit. As I have stressed before, the Soul Self cannot be reached directly by the Ego-self through the use of reason and

the intellect. That way leads only to an abyss which blocks access to higher levels of awareness. This is why so many so-called 'spiritual' paths require subjection to blind belief, for the means of 'knowing' is beyond the reach of the intellect.

Because divination is subjective and also highly personal, a shamanist develops his or her own way of making use of a particular method. A general principle is that the shamanist contacts his or her own greater Self and asks to be connected to the greater Self of the querant. This, however, can only be achieved if the Soul 'selves' of both persons are in agreement.

Another fundamental principle of Shamanics is that the space occupied by every living being is sacred – that is, set apart for that being – and it should, therefore, be respected. A shaman-ist will not wilfully intrude on the space of another person without permission or approval, and this is even more import-ant when working at levels of higher vibrations.

There are a number of divination systems available today which can function effectively to enable information to be brought through from a higher consciousness. The ones out-lined here are listed in alphabetical order and not in a sequence of relative merit, importance or, indeed, of my own personal preference:

I-CHING: The *I Ching* (Book of Changes) originated in ancient China thousands of years ago and is probably the oldest known oracular system. It is based upon the patterns of change that govern every aspect of life, and is a means of providing an enquirer with advice on how best to deal with a problem in order to attain a harmonious outcome. The *I-Ching* requires the casting of sticks, coins or cards in order for a hexagram to be constructed to encapsulate within its pattern both the problem and its solution. If approached with an open mind and sincer-ity of purpose, the *I Ching* will connect the enquirer to a higher level of consciousness where practical wisdom is applied to the resolution of a matter of concern.

RUNES: Runes are more than angular symbols with 'hidden' meanings. They were a primary tool of shamans of Northern and Central Europe. Runes are patterns of energy potencies that function in both 'outer' and 'inner' ecologies to convey an understanding that what appears to be happening 'outside'

oneself is but a reflection of what is taking place 'within'. Runes are an aid to personal development and the cultivation of the Spirit.

As with other divination systems, Runes have been associated with the occult and sinister forces not only through religious bigotry but also because of their use by sorcerers and others who have sought to assume power over others, and they have been depreciated by use as a means of fortune-telling.

Divination, as practised by runic shamans, does not depend on an ability to interpret a rune cast in accordance with meanings given to the Runes by others; rather, it is the ability to experience the flow of energies being indicated through a combination of runic potencies and the telepathic message they contain.

SACRED PATH CARDS: These have been designed in recent years by Jamie Sams, whose beautiful Native American name is *Hancooka Olowampi*, which means 'Midnight Song'. The cards incorporate the ancient wisdom of several American Indian tribes and are thus a synthesis of Native American spirituality. They work effectively for those who are familiar with Medicine Wheel principles and have an affinity with Native American cosmology. The guidance obtained through use of the powerful imagery of the cards enables the enquirer to recognize the steps of his or her own personal development and obtain an insight into a matter of current concern and the lesson it holds.

TAROT: Although Tarot cards are associated with medieval mysticism they have a considerably older origin, for analogies have been found with the Hebrew Kabbalah, Chaldean 'mystery' schools, and the spiritual traditions of ancient Egypt. Used as a means of exploring the wisdom of the Soul, the Tarot is a far cry from its popularized use today in attempts to predict the future. There are many different Tarot decks available offering a wide variety of designs and connotations. The pictures on the cards portray an artist's interpretation of the spiritual forces and principles involved, but it is not the pictures themselves that are of the most importance to the shamanist, nor the symbolic philosophies they are intended to convey. It is how the pictures and symbols affect the shamanist *personally* after he or she has made the link with the High Self of the querant.

PENDULUM: In addition to its use described earlier, the pendulum may also be employed in conversing directly with the Soul and obtaining 'Yes' and 'No' answers to specific and precise questions. This method, however, is only effective when the user's Soul Self is integrated within the body and immediate connection is possible.

INTEGRATING THE FOUR 'SELVES'

Your Soul's perspective is different from that of your Ego-self and its experience of physical reality is obtained only through your physical senses. It perceives itself as not separate from but part of a greater Whole, yet retaining individual identity and unique expression. Your Soul's 'Self' thus has a greater understanding of the Ultimate Source. It is also the most 'permanent' aspect of your total being. It was in existence before your physical body and it will continue to survive after the death of your physical body. Only the physical form through which it finds expression and through which it experiences matter – the physical body – is changed.

The Body Self is the intelligence that controls the physical body. The Hidden Self (Unihipili) is the intelligence that controls the Energic Body. The Ego-self (A-Uhane) is the intelligence that controls the Mental body. The greater Self (Aumakua) is the intelligence that controls the Soul body. Unihipili is the connecting link between the Body Self and A-Uhane and between A-Uhane and Aumakua. The Spirit is the Original Being – the divine spark, the 'I', or essence that is aware of its own alive-ness in every dimension of existence – and is thus a self-aware 'I Am' that enables the Ultimate Source to experience Itself! When we are enabled to bring our Greater Self into active participation in our everyday living, our relationship with 'divinity' is changed from an *idea* in the mind – a mental image of a supernatural being existing in some nebulous 'Heavenly' location – to the down-to-earth practical reality of the 'right here' and the 'right now'.

In connecting directly with the Powers of Nature – with Water, Wind and Earth; with Sun, Moon and Stars; with tree, flora and stone – we bring those energies directly into ourselves and they support the process of our personal growth,

our evolutionary development towards higher states of consciousness and more sophisticated levels of perception, and the
cultivation of the Spirit. Shamanics thus connects us with the
Universe whose substance is energies, and with all aspects of
ourselves. It helps to release us from the need to control,
exploit and manipulate, for in connecting us with our own
Source we can become empowered with a strength that comes
only from within. With that inner strength we are enabled to
see through negative habits, release our uptightness, and relax
the hypertension we have imposed upon ourselves.

Mastering the challenges of our human experience, getting
rid of past conditioning, and aligning the Ego-self with the
higher purpose of the Soul, not only brings about an integration of all the 'selves' – a unity of 'spirits' with the One Spirit
– but intensifies and expands the Light of the Soul.

When, in the ancient 'mystery schools', a neophyte was
advised to 'Know Thyself', what was implanted was far more
than a deeper knowledge of the nature of the Ego-self. What
was being indicated was the need to come into a recognition
of the total composite being and to harmonize the 'selves' of
the different levels and 'bodies' into an integrated working
partnership that would bring about the fulfilment of the true
purpose of life – the Soul's purpose – and the reason for
incarnating.

The Great Mystery

Your Source and mine
Was before the Heavens and Earth were.
Before the Mind was
And the forms that Mind can shape.
Beyond Space and Time
Yet, paradoxically, within it all.
Ever present.
Present everywhere.
Inexhaustible and infinite
Is the Source from which you and I emerged
Each to become an 'I'
An individuated essence of the Source Itself
To provide the Source with another eye
To perceive Itself
And experience the wonder
Of being another unique expression of Itself
This is the wonder
Of you being you
And me being me

Kenneth Meadows
January 1993

12. The Path of Love and Harmony

LAO TZU, THE CHINESE SAGE who lived around the fifth century BC and imparted much wisdom of ancient shamanism, meant something different from goodness and moral excellence when he wrote about a 'Way of Virtue' in his classic work *Tao Te Ching*, which is revered by many today alongside the sacred writings of other cultures. He was not referring to the kind of virtue which is associated with morality, nor is the title of this collection of writings about the ethics of human behaviour. The virtue being referred to is a quality that entails a transformation of the mind and allows a person's true spiritual nature to find expression in practical, everyday living. Lao Tzu was imparting in his writings the essence of what, some 2500 years ago, was considered at that time to be *ancient* wisdom and expressing it in the ideograms of Chinese writing in a way that was relevant and meaningful for people on the threshold of a new Age. The ancient wisdom that was being related was that of the Taoist shamans, whose knowledge and understanding, though universal, had been passed on orally through a select few up until Lao Tzu's time. What he did was to reclaim it for the benefit of future generations.

THE EGO AND CONDITIONING

What Lao Tzu was stressing was that virtue is a manifestation of a human being's true spiritual nature in the way the life is being lived. The colloquialism, 'Virtue has its own reward', truly means that the reward is a direct experience of living in

a virtuous way – not that which is received from some external authority after death! When the Ego is encouraged to fulfil its natural role as a *supporter*, intended to *serve* the total being, rather than the *master*, and the Spirit is encouraged to take pre-eminence, virtuous qualities are enabled to find manifestation in the realm of physical existence. However, when the Ego is allowed to be in *control*, it clamours for exclusive rights to existence. It absorbs our full attention and when fed on flattery and encouraged by greed, keeps us confined to the limitations of the physical and mental realms which *it* conditions.

The transformation of the mind is a de-conditioning process. It is the mind becoming free of its conditioning. Conditioning is fundamentally a form of energy. *Conditioned* energies are primarily *Ego*-energies. The Ego, in being assigned responsibility for making choices and deciding actions, invariably chooses that which keeps it in control and isolated from any other aspect of our composite being. It seeks to satisfy *itself*, expand *itself*, extend *itself*, elevate *itself*, and cause us to believe that *it* is the totality of our being.

In relation to our total, composite being, the Ego is an adversary. Not an Adversary that is an external entity, but one which is an *inner* power that prevents us from experiencing our essential whole-ness and keeps us in a state of separation. It is the Ego-self that prevents us from experiencing not just our closeness to Nature but our actual *one-ness* with it. It is the Ego-self that puts up barriers to our understanding because the Ego-self seeks precedence over our natural Spirit-ual Self. Rather than be the *servant* of the Spirit, it wants to be the *master*, and attempts either to obscure the Spirit by leading us through its logic into assuming the Spirit does not exist, or to put itself in the *place* of the Spirit and thus become the *determiner*. It can even delude us by masquerading *as* the Spirit: the adversary, by deceit, seemingly the divine! The ultimate role-reversal. By assuming the role of Master rather than servant, the Ego-self feeds on vanity and works against the composite being when it should be manifesting virtue by allowing the Spirit to find expression through it. That is its true purpose – to serve the Spirit and by so doing develop virtue. That is the *natural* way. That is what Lao Tzu was referring to in his writings. That is the hidden truth contained in the myths, legends and folk

stories of all cultures and traditions. That is the hidden truth contained in all sacred writings!

Our 'conditioned' senses tell us we are separate, when the reality is that we are a part of a greater Whole. Our conditioned senses tell us our physical body is 'solid', when the reality is that this fleshy body is made up of atoms which are composed mostly of 'empty' space. Our conditioned senses tell us we are standing still when the reality is that the ground beneath our feet is on a planet that is rotating at more than 530 kilometres an hour (nearly 300 mph) and hurtling through space at an incredible speed as the Earth makes its yearly journey round the Sun. Our conditioned senses tell us we have but one body, when the reality its that we have several, each composed of a different 'substance'. Our conditioned energies are like grit or water that has got into the engine oil of an automobile, preventing it from functioning efficiently and effectively as it has been designed to do.

Conditioning blocks the ability to express the essence that is within us and alters the Spirit energy-expression, changing what we are and have the potential to become. We are thus prevented from manifesting the most creative aspects of ourselves and so our lives remain largely unfulfilled. Our spiritual essence is the very source and basis of our power – our 'medicine'. Multi-dimensional development brings about a recognition of what that spiritual essence is and so enables us as individuals to grow into a greater fullness of our potential. Personal development, in this context, is not simply a matter of improving the personality, for the personality is not '*you*' but something you possess as a means of expressing your own unique identity. It is a 'face' the *real* **You** 'wears' in order to show itself to the physical world. In many native traditions the human skull was not regarded as a sinister object as it often is today. It was a respected and revered symbol that indicated a reality existing behind facial appearance, which is just a 'mask' the real individual has put on!

The Ego-self is thus an adverse influence underlying our thoughts and emotions and which actually enslaves us from within, keeping us in a continual cycle of restriction and fear and preventing us from coming into an understanding of who and what we are, why we are here, and what our essential purpose is. It makes comparisons based upon superficial

appearances and puts responsibility on external influences by blaming others for what it considers it lacks itself. In times of adversity and disaster the Ego-self will even shift responsibility onto an external deity, blaming It for allowing such events to take place.

The Ego-self generates negative energies that are the cause of much misery, unhappiness and discontent in the world. Present-day medical science assigns this adverse influence to the subconscious. In psychotherapy the approach is to bring negative and destructive subconscious energies under control by suppression and distraction – by the use of drugs and by positive thinking. Religion counters this adverse influence by the exercise of faith, which is regarded as a spiritual quality synonymous with belief. But faith itself is not a spiritual quality at all, but simply another way of using the *mind*. Religious faith shifts responsibility away from the individual and places it upon an external authority – a personal deity. Faith is a combination of the energies of belief and trust and is not a virtue in itself but a power that can be used either for benevolent and harmonious purposes or for harmful effects. In other words, faith needs wisdom to guide it. History abounds with examples of faith that has resulted in the persecution and destruction of those who were unwilling to participate in its blind side. Only those who are blind are required to believe. There is no need to believe in the Sun and the Moon and the Earth, or the mountains, hills and valleys, or the lakes and the rivers, or the grass beneath your feet. They are *there*. You are aware of them because there is light that enables you to see them. Only a blind person needs to exercise belief that there is such a thing as light! So belief can even *hamper* spiritual understanding because it can prevent the intelligence from giving direction to its action and become itself a 'conditioned' energy along with all the rest.

Conditioned energy cannot continue in a state of suspension. It has to go somewhere, and that 'somewhere' is often part of the physical body where it accumulates and manifests ultimately as a physical condition. It is an accumulation of these conditioned energies that accelerates the ageing process, that produces stiffness and inflexibility in the limbs, that causes imbalance in the vital organs resulting in heart problems, kidney troubles, lung complaints, and so on. It is the depositing of

conditioned energies in the physical body that is the real cause of many debilitating and even life-threatening illnesses, and is at the root of psychological and emotional disorders that result in so much unhappiness and sorrow in people's lives.

DISPERSING CONDITIONED ENERGIES

This acquired conditioning can only be dispersed when we act from a position of strength from our own energy-source. That is one of the benefits of Shamanics for it helps us to deal *directly* with such energies by generating Chi – that subtle, inner power that enlivens, enhances and meshes in perfect harmony with the positive energies of the body, mind and Spirit. There are four major sources of Chi – Air, Sun, Water and Earth.

Chi from *Air* is absorbed through the breathing and revitalizes and stimulates.

Chi from the Sun (*Fire*) invigorates and is expansive.

Chi from *Water* that is charged with solar energy is potently soothing and healing.

Chi from *Earth* is absorbed through the soles of the feet and from the food we eat, which itself originates from the Earth.

Trees and plants absorb Chi from the Air, Sun, Water and Earth, and exude it in great quantities. This is why such great benefit can be obtained from spending time among trees. How do we generate Chi for ourselves? Firstly, by motive and intent. The very *intention* to generate energies of harmony into the body brings the first influx of Chi. But we must first make a decision to choose to set ourselves in the direction of Love and Harmony and to eliminate the conditioned energies that have accumulated in the body. The more strongly the intention is made and the more deeply it is felt, the greater will be the flow of Chi to flush out negativity, get rid of conditioning, and replace them with harmony.

Fundamental to Shamanics is an understanding that Nature is a powerful *support* for those who choose Love and Harmony. Indeed, it is disconnection from Nature that in modern times has brought about an increase in stress, anxiety and fear in people's lives. In connecting directly with the energies of Nature – with Water, Wind and Earth; with Sun, Moon and Stars; with trees, flora and stone – we bring those energies

directly into our bodies and they support the process of connecting with the innermost You inside. The Medicine Wheel is a device that helps to connect us with that supportiveness and serves as another way of dealing with conditioning.

The Fetish

Many indigenous peoples had a powerful way of dispersing conditioned energies. It was through the use of a *fetish* – a technique much misunderstood and maligned through bigotry, ignorance and superstition. A fetish is simply an object that is fashioned from natural materials and given human or animal form. Its purpose is to serve as a focus for conditioned energies during its making and be symbolic of those energies as it is ceremonially burned in a fire ritual. It has no power in itself. The burning symbolizes the transmutation of those conditioned energies into positive qualities which can arise from their ashes.

A purpose of a fire ritual is to convey a clear message to the subconscious (Unihipili) through the use of powerful symbols. In this case, conditioning that has been recognized as having caused pain, grief, suffering, distress, limitation and deprivation, is given form through the fetish and ceremonially burned to indicate its banishment and transmutation. **It is a way of pushing aside the Ego in order that the Spirit may shine through; for in order for the Spirit to increase, the Ego must decrease.**

The materials for making a fetish are best gathered during meditative walks that are undertaken with the intention of gathering items to serve as reminders of particular traits, conditions, situations and events that have left a conditioning that you want to banish. Twigs, cones, acorns, grasses, leaves, flowers, berries, feathers, tufts of animal hair or fur, for instance. A short length of fallen branch may serve as a 'spine' around which the body and features can be formed. In collecting such material, take care not to harm any tree or plant or cause any damage to the environment. It is an important principle of Shamanics that Nature is respected and the natural environment protected.

The Medicine Wheel mandala is used as a means of

connecting with and identifying the specific conditioning so that it might be dealt with effectively through the fashioning of the fetish and its ultimate demise by fire. 'Working' the Directions in the following Experience may be completed in a single day or spread over two or more days if necessary.

Experience 32: Banishing Conditioning

Go on a meditative walk in a woodland location. Take with you a small pocket compass and pouch or bag for the materials you will be collecting. This whole Experience needs to be approached in a relaxed and unhurried manner, so it is best not to set a pre-arranged time limit. Just let it 'happen'.

Look first for something suitable for the backbone for your fetish. A small length cut from a fallen branch makes a good, firm spine. Once you have obtained the spine you can begin the directional work.

Let us begin in the **East**, which on the Medicine Wheel is associated with the illumination that activates the miraculous energizing power that bursts forth at the dawn of each new day. In the yearly cycle, East represents the freshness of Springtime which starts with the Spring Equinox and with growth that involves rapid change. It embraces the pioneering energy that is involved in new projects and the invigoration that comes with the initiation of every new beginning. In the lifetime cycle, it represents the period of childhood and rapid learning.

On your meditative walk towards the East, recall your own childhood and recognize what negative conditioning you may have received through your parents, teachers, and people who had an influence on your upbringing. Were you disadvantaged in any way – and how? What things have you blamed on your parents, either because of what they did at some time or what they failed to do? What experiences during your formative years which have influenced you adversely can you identify as being the fault of a parent, teacher, or someone else who had a strong influence during your childhood? Choose a word or words to describe that conditioning. Then be on the look-out for anything in your surroundings that can be identified with it in some way; that can serve to symbolize that aspect of your life. It may be in the shape of a twig on the ground, or in the texture of a leaf or a cluster of grasses. It may be in the colour of a flower, the prickliness of holly or the threatening stab of the thorn on a rosebush. Make a collection of whatever items are meaningful to you to serve as representatives of those aspects of your childhood that

may have had an adverse effect and from whose hold you now wish to be released.

The next stage is to take a meditative walk towards the **South**, for we are going to traverse the Medicine Wheel in a circular direction, Sunwise.

South on the Medicine Wheel is associated with the period of daytime when the Sun is at its strongest, so we can liken it to the performance of work and the prime time for exerting our energies, developing our strengths, and obtaining reward for our endeavours. In the yearly cycle, South is associated with Summer, the season that begins with the Summer Solstice, and the period of blossoming. In the lifetime cycle it represents the years of young adulthood when the pattern of life is being established. It is the time of bringing plans and ambitions to fruition, of forging partnerships, of marriage and the raising of children.

Consider during your walk southwards the dreams you have had regarding your work, personal relationships and living conditions. What has frustrated any of your aspirations and prevented your plans from bearing fruit? What is it that has caused difficulties in personal relationships and prevented them from flowering in accordance with your expectations? Consider what has caused obstructiveness and emotional upsets.

Again, look for items in Nature to collect for your fetish that can serve to represent what you have now identified as having contributed to the negative conditioning in your life.

Next go to the **West** which, on the Medicine Wheel, is associated with the maturity that develops from the acquisition of inner strength gained through personal experience. West indicates the evening period in the daily cycle, and Autumn in the yearly cycle, beginning with the Autumn Equinox – a time for enjoying the benefits of one's labours. In the lifetime cycle it represents the time of consolidation.

West emphasizes the material and physical aspects of life. So on your walk westwards your thoughts should be on those things that have hampered you materially and may have limited you physically, preventing you from making changes in your life. Consider what conditions, circumstances and things you are still hanging onto which have long served their purpose and are now hindering you. Identify those conditions that lock you into an inertia which is actually sapping you physically.

Look for items for your fetish that will represent the conditioning you have now recognized in the West.

Now to the **North**. This direction on the Medicine Wheel is associated with clarity of thinking, with clear vision of what lies ahead, and with the wisdom derived from practical experience. It is related to

night-time and the period of rest and refreshment in the daily cycle. In the yearly cycle it is the period of Winter, beginning with the Winter Solstice; and in the lifetime cycle it is the retirement period and time of renewal.

North is related to the realm of thought and ideas, to the intellect, and to the rules and regulations by which we make conditions for ourselves. North is where we can examine more carefully our own mental conditioning and discover in what areas we have put limitations on ourselves. Consider what limitations you are experiencing that have been self-imposed through ideas that you can now see clearly as having been false. What has prevented you from perceiving things for what they are? Identify that conditioning and look around for materials in nature to represent them on your fetish.

Finally, to the **Centre**. The Centre is best 'worked' at your indoor Quiet Place, for the Centre is where you can consider carefully all you have gathered from the Four Directions and bring them together in the shaping, fashioning and completion of your fetish.

At the centre of all your conditioning are your *fears*. Recognize that whatever your fears may be, they are mostly *imaginary*. Imaginary fears may be defined as acute and often emotionally painful concerns about something that has not yet happened. Though very powerful, they are a factor of *mental* conditioning. Real fears are life-threatening for they are about actual physical survival. Imaginary fears exist in the mind and take on a reality of their own which is debilitating. They can grip us in a state of near helplessness and desperation.

The first step in banishing those fears is to recognize them for what they are.

Fear of not being liked?
Fear of upsetting someone?
Fear of telling the truth?
Fear of being alone?
Fear of loss of income?
Fear of redundancy?

Just recall those fears. Recognize them. Identify them. You now have the power to banish them because you have the courage to face them. That power is within you, for within you is an inexhaustible Source – the power of the Spirit which has seen you through many, many traumas and enabled you to face many, many fears. Yet you are still here. Alive. A true survivor! So just work those fears you have identified into the fashioning of your fetish. Let the fetish absorb your worries. Work them out of your life and into your fetish!

Forgive whoever may have wronged you. That does not mean

condoning what harmful action they may have performed, but forgive them – because forgiveness releases any hold or power that person or persons may still have over you. Forgiveness also applies to what someone may have neglected to do. Whatever it is – forgive. Let it go and let it be.

Then forgive *yourself*. That is sometimes even more difficult than forgiving others. Let go of the shackles that have bound you. You didn't know then what you know now. This is the time of your renewal. This is the time of your revealing so that you can become what you truly *are*. This is *your* Revealing Time.

You are going to watch those fears be consumed before you – transmuted into opportunities to provide you with new strengths, and therefore not to be dreaded because they no longer have any power over you. You will now have power over them.

The fetish can be made as beautiful or as ugly as you see fit, and as elaborate or as simple as you want it to be. It is not for showing to others. Its meaning and relevance is entirely personal to you who have fashioned it. It represents the whole of the conditioning you have recognized in yourself and which you now wish to banish from your life so that new strengths can arise from the ashes when it is consumed by the flame that will symbolize to you the fire of the Spirit.

When your fetish is completed, the next stage in this Experience is its burning. This can be done in a private ceremony at home if you have an open fireplace. If not, it should be performed outdoors, in a secluded and safe part of your garden, perhaps, or in some other place where you will not be drawing attention to yourself.

All that is needed is a few sheets of newspaper rolled into balls or strips and a few dry twigs or sticks which, when lit, will produce sufficient flame and burn long enough to consume your fetish when it is thrown onto the blaze.

Consider carefully as you watch your fetish burning. Sense that all the conditioning that you have identified within yourself is being transmuted because you have willingly been prepared to give it up. In watching the fetish burn you are watching that conditioning vanish before your very eyes through this symbolic action.

THE POWER OF LOVE

Deconditioning releases us from the need to manipulate and exploit in order to be in control, and helps us to become connected with an intrinsic power which itself cannot be grasped

and manipulated – the power of Love, which is not external as is commonly *supposed* for it can be found only *within*. This is true Love – not physical desire or emotional self-indulgence that masquerade as Love and seek only the gratification of physical senses. These are but parodies of Love, a *false* love that actually deprives the Spirit of its integrity – that is, its true nature and constitution – so that it cannot be cultivated. True Love is not external and can only be found within because it is at the very Source. The nature of *true* Love is the creative energy within you and the Universe! It is the *bonding* power that enables the magnetic force between electrons and protons to be sustained and so hold matter together! It is what empowers gravitational pull and keeps Earth, planets and stars in their precise tracks and orbits within the Universe. So true Love is no indulgence of the physical senses for the purpose of self-satisfaction – which at best is but a conditional exchange of energies – but is an unconditional giving of itself, merging totally with the loved one. You, as a Spirit, came into existence as a result of a total merging of the Yin and Yang aspects of the Universe. We are children of God by *origin*, not by adoption through some religious initiation. That is the truth of our own original being. In other words, we originate out of Love and can fulfil ourselves only *through* Love. Love is thus the fundamental nature of the Source, for it is what that Source **is**. Love is a total giving of itself. For instance, if you had no money and no possessions, what would there be for you to give to a loved one? Nothing, except you! The giving of yourself. The giving of oneself is the only expression of Love that is *real*. Yet we human beings rarely give of ourselves. We give money. We give gifts. We give things that may 'belong' to us and that we even treasure, so the giving is a 'sacrifice', but most of us stop at the very giving of *ourselves* – our own being-ness – our 'selves'! And how frequently do we set conditions on our giving? Love sets no conditions. Love is *unconditional*. It sets no conditions on the behaviour of the loved one. The loved one is free to be who they are. It was 'original' Love that imparted to us our own individuality, with the freedom of our own 'space', and the freedom also to determine for ourselves our own destiny – to become the result of our own choosings, to fashion ourselves according to what we want to *be*. So we each have the power of Love within us.

DIMENSIONS OF EXISTENCE

Within us is to be found also the entrance to other dimensions of existence, for only by going within can we begin to experience our own multi-dimensional nature and that of the Universe. As physical beings we live in three dimensions which enable us to experience the 'solidity' of material things because they have length, breadth, and height or depth. The First Dimension is that of length or distance. It has neither width nor height. It is an infinite line which has no start or finish except that which is arbitrarily placed within it as a beginning and ending. The Second Dimension has width as well as length, but no depth or height. It is sometimes called a plane. You experience two-dimensional reality by looking at yourself in a mirror, and by observing a shadow. A mirror-image is a two-dimensional reflection of a three-dimensional body. A shadow, also, is a two-dimensional image. Your reflection and your shadow cannot reproduce the fullness of your three-dimensional reality. Further, your reflection and your shadow lack independent motion. Neither can move unless the third-dimensional 'you' moves. The Third Dimension is height or depth, which together with length and width produces an appearance of solidity. Thus we are able to perceive ourselves and what is in physical existence around us as 'solid' beings and objects.

But there is a fourth factor that enables us to perceive what is around us as a segment of Time. Indeed, we might regard Time as a Fourth Dimension. In this Dimension of Time we perceive only what is happening in the present. We cannot know the future and we cannot go back and change the past. Only our *reaction* to what has happened in the past can be changed. Were it possible to move beyond the Dimension of Time and into another dimension – a Fifth Dimension – we would be enabled to see ourselves 'all at once' without any separation into past, present and future. We would see the whole shape of our lives, including all the lives we have ever been, as a totality!

Each of our many lives is like a jewel on a necklace that is being made up of an undetermined number of gems. The 'string' of the necklace is the Life-line or, more appropriately, the *lives*-line, from which each life in turn has arisen and to

which each is attached as an individuated expression of the one Source, or Spirit, each reflecting a facet inherent in the Whole.

So we each experience a succession of lifetimes, in each of which experiences are gathered and potential is developed. None of these lifetimes actually ceases to exist at death, but is merely involved in a transformational process of change. Immortality itself is a natural process. It is a continual process of change in which energies are transformed. Each life lives on to become an inner 'guide' in the succeeding lifetime. So we are each our own ancestors, and those ancestors are inherent within our energy-system for each has contributed to what we are now and has helped to bring us to where we are now. Nature helps us to understand this. When water vaporizes and becomes invisible it is not extinct but in a state of suspension, and it re-appears when conditions are suitable for it to do so. It is the same with death. Death is not extinction but part of a creative cycle of Life itself. The Spirit withdraws its life from physical reality only to re-appear in the visible world when conditions are right for it to do so to further its own *cultivation*. It takes on another physical body – another set of 'clothes' – and may wear a different personality 'mask'. Another jewel on the necklace. Another expression of the 'You' who will always be 'You'. Each lifetime may also be likened to a piece of coloured glass in a great stained-glass window that curls and revolves like a spiralling Catherine Wheel. Each life – however great or humble – and each personality 'face' that is put on, is no greater and no less than any other. Each is a part of the beauty of the whole. Any disadvantage, impediment or handicap in this lifetime is not an infliction because of some misdeed in a previous incarnation. Nor is inheritance or class some sort of 'reward' for past-life achievement. Such ideas were fashioned as a tool of fear to exercise control over people.

Before the Cosmic Law of Cause and Effect – karma – was placed within a religious context, it was understood to be the experiences the Spirit *chooses* in order to further its own development, and sometimes that of others, also. In other words, karma is the lessons we – from the perspective of the Soul – have chosen to teach ourselves and, perhaps, to benefit others! Many who are born with a handicap are full of love and compassion and contribute beneficial qualities through their own lives that cannot be measured or evaluated in material terms.

And many born in humble circumstances have, through their own energy, drive and creativity, risen to positions that have benefited masses of people, and by so doing have demonstrated a lesson for us all.

If the essence of past lives is inherent within us, then it must be possible to obtain access to those potencies. Past-life recall is a technique employed by shamanists that enables connection to be made with the essence of a previous life that has a direct relevance to the life now being lived. This 'connection' is possible because the essence of a past life is stored within the Soul and is therefore part of what we are now. Such a connection can help us to cope better with the challenges and conflicts that face us and to develop an inherent talent or 'natural' skill, because the essence of that energy is already 'there'. The technique employed by shamanists does not involve hypnosis, trance regression or mediumship, nor is its purpose to uncover traumatic incidents or harrowing experiences as explanations for current misfortunes. The technique is based upon a sensitivity to subtle essences inherited from the past and stored in the Soul, and therefore accessible. This information comes into the conscious awareness of both the shamanist who is performing the work and the individual for whom it is being done, and it is achieved in an atmosphere that is positive and uplifting. As with Life-energy restoral, it is not a technique that can, or should, be learned from the pages of a book.

The Fifth Dimension is within. It is an Inner Reality of wondrous enormity which, once entered, enables us to perceive that our Universe of Space and Time is but an outer expression – a physical manifestation – of an inner and greater Reality. So outer and inner – visible and invisible – are not separate, but integrated. Understanding of the 'outer' physical reality is obtained only through experience of the 'inner' Reality which brought it into being and continues its creative activity.

The Sixth Dimension is actually a moral dimension where it is possible to perceive both the 'inside' and the 'outside'. It might also be described as 'the Dimension of Choice'. From this understanding it follows that our own inner and outer realities are not separate either, and that our experiences in the 'outside' world of 'ordinary' reality are expressions of our own 'inside' world. What is happening in one affects also the other.

The final Experience of this book is, therefore, within.

On the Medicine Wheel the Centre is where all energies can be brought into balance and harmony. The *within* is where the 'inner' and 'outer' may be brought into *unison*. It is where what you learn about yourself at different levels, or in different dimensions of yourself, may be absorbed at the Source, which is within. It is *within* that you are 'connected' with All That Is. It is *within* that is your 'Place of Potentials'. It is *within* where your empowerment lies. It is *within* that you may connect with your Inexhaustible Source.

The emphasis at the Centre is on the wholeness of multi-dimensional being – on becoming and being whole. The emphasis on the Within is on the reality of the 'I' at the very core of your being – the reality of your Spirit!

This Experience should be conducted in your indoor Quiet Place. You will need a candle, candle-holder, matches, rattle, smudge-stick and smudge pot, notebook and pen. Make sure you will not be disturbed for the next half hour.

Experience 33: Contacting the Source Within

Light your candle. Remember, this serves as a signal for switching from mundane to shamanic activity. The flame is also symbolic of the Spirit contained within the Soul, the wick is symbolic of the mind, and the wax of the candle itself of the flesh of the physical body.

Contemplate on that symbolism for a while.

Now light your smudge-stick or smudge mix and smudge yourself and your surroundings. Remember, smudging is an act of cleansing and purification which disperses negativities and attracts harmonious and beneficial vibrations. Breathe in the aroma of the smudge smoke so you are aware of that cleansing taking place inside as well as outside.

When you have finished, stub the smudge-stick into a smudge pot or container and ensure that it will not continue smouldering and cause distraction.

Sit comfortably, pick up your rattle, and rattle around yourself as you learned to do earlier in this book. The intention is to connect with your Soul Self and bring it into conscious awareness and integrate it with your other 'selves'. Be open and receptive to whatever teaching may come to you. Rattle above your head, in front of you and to the sides, with your eyes closed so that your awareness is in the rattling. Don't hurry this in any way. Allow it to take as long as it takes. You will know intuitively when it is time to stop.

When you have finished, put the rattle down and make notes of any teaching that came to you during the rattling.

Now sit comfortably and concentrate on the candle flame – the symbol of your own Spirit and the Light within you. Place your hands, palms down, on your navel – which is the centre of your physical body – and allow your awareness be in your own Centre within.

You are now going to unify all aspects of yourself, including any essence of yourself that may have inadvertently become 'lost', or which you may have given away or had taken from you at any level.

Speak aloud the following words, and put real feeling into what you are saying:

> I call back into myself
> Any of my essence
> That I may have inadvertently or willingly
> Given away, or had taken from me
> At any time, and in any place
> In any dimension of my being.
> I call it back into myself *now*.
> That I may be Whole
> Fully restored
> Fully balanced
> Fully harmonized
> Fully empowered
> Unified, and fully my *Self*.
> I call it back into myself *now*!

Now be silent and still and await a response which will bring you enlightenment about your Unified Self.

Make notes of your experience.

Now to affirm the truths about yourself which you have acquired during the practical work of 'working' the Medicine Wheel.

Stand up, face each of the cardinal directions in turn, and repeat aloud four times, and with feeling and emphasis, the relevant Affirmation.

First, *North*, where you connected with *Air*:
'I am a greater being than I *think* I am.'

Next, *West*, where you connected with *Earth*:
'I am here to manifest what I *am*.'

Now *East*, where you connected with *Fire*:
'I have a light within to *show* me the way.'

Then *South*, where you connected with *Water*:
'I am what I have *chosen* to be.'

Finally, bring your awareness to your *Centre* and *Within* and make this Affirmation: 'I choose now, and from this time forth, to be true to my *Spirit*, which is my real self.'

Stay still and await a response. Make notes of that response.

Sit down again and read through all the notes you have made during this session and consider carefully their meaning and relevance.

Extinguish the candle flame which, remember, serves as a switch – from shamanic activity back to ordinary, everyday activity.

THE POWER OF CHOICE

The Experience you have just undergone may now help you to comprehend the greatest difference between human life and any other life form on Earth, be it animal, mineral or plant. Although the physical forms are so very different, all are composed and shaped from the same basic materials of the Earth. So what is the essential difference? Many would say the mind. But is the human mind that can create works of art and invent such wonderful machines as automobiles, airplanes, computers, television, radio, space craft and ships, any greater than, say, the mind of a plant that can produce a beautiful flower and its own unique perfume?

The essential difference between human, animal, plant and mineral life is one of *choice*. We humans have free will – an unfettered ability to *choose*. Minerals, which have their being in the ground, have no option but to react in the particular way they do. Trees and plants grow and blossom without the exercise of choice. Animals, though appearing to make choices under particular circumstances, act primarily on instinct. The only beings on Earth with the freedom and power of choice are humans. And it is important for us to recognize the tremendous power that is inherent in that ability to make choices.

Your Spirit is experiencing physical existence in order to fulfil both a general and a specific purpose. The general purpose is to thrive and endure – that is, to grow into an awareness of the innermost 'You' and the totality of one's being, and to

continue to experience alive-ness. The specific purpose is the Soul's reason for your present incarnation, for which you are in possession of certain attributes and potentials that are intended to be awakened from their dormancy and employed as learning experiences to further your growth and development and to cultivate the Spirit. That specific purpose is also to allow the essence of your energy-expression to radiate itself in harmony with other beings.

You have a mission in life – a reason for being where you are at this time in human history. Everything that happens in your life is a learning experience – an adventure in growing into a greater awareness of what you are and of what you can become. So life on Earth is an experience of *receiving* new growth. And it is a lesson in *giving* so that others may grow because of you.

We are each required to give of *ourselves* – to give of what we *are*, not of possessions – and to learn that grabbing what others have in order to obtain it for ourselves only deprives us of something more valuable.

The power to choose is the ability to determine the direction of your life and to create your own destiny – your own future. It is an ability with enormous responsibility. Responsibility may be defined as 'being accountable for one's actions', but it is more than that. It is an ability to *respond* to one's *choices*, to the consequences of one's own choice-decisions and actions. We are each responsible for how we use the power we have – how we use and apply our own 'Medicine' – whether we mentally accept responsibility or not.

You alone live *your* life. No one else can live it for you, much as anyone may try. Ultimately you are responsible for what you have made of it and what you have done with it. That 'Day of Judgement' takes place at Soul level. Human life on Earth – our Earth 'Walk' – is a learning experience. Its purpose is to learn through the experience of living what it is that needs to be learned. It is living the learning. Earth life is a school to many, a university to some, a workshop to others. We are each of us 'students'. A single lifetime may be compared to a term at school, or a semester at college. But everyone is not in the same group or at the same level or grade. We are not all progressing or falling back (evolving or devolving) at the same rate. We are at different stages of development. However,

everything that happens in each of our lives is an experience in receiving and giving: *receiving* what is necessary for new growth, and *giving* so that others may grow because of us. We can, of course, choose to *misuse* the opportunity and turn receiving into *taking* and giving into *getting*, but that way not only harms others but creates obstacles in our own path of destiny.

THE WAY WITH HEART

Shamanics is a practical Way of coming into an awareness of our multi-dimensional reality, and, through that understanding, cultivating and refining the Spirit that is within. A 'Way' or a 'Path' must not be mistaken for a mystical method or a mental and physical discipline often assigned to it. A 'Way' is a direction of travel: it does not entail the resistance of alluring temptations or the maintenance of a set of 'beliefs' along a route littered with obstacles that must be overcome. That is a false 'Way'. Shamanics is the 'Way with Heart' – the Path of Love and Harmony. Not the Way *of* the Heart, but the Way *with* Heart. For it does not mean that the heart should rule the mind. People who wear their hearts on their sleeves are often victims of their emotions and easily vulnerable. When the mind rules the heart it is the Ego and personal vanity that are most often served. On the 'Way with Heart' the mind and the heart are joined together in harmonic unity to bring about a greater creative expression that will resonate for the benefit of others also. It is a matter of balance, and the Path of Love and Harmony is a way of balance. On that Path the focus of attention is not on a destination but on the Way or 'journey' itself; not on believing but on do-ing and be-ing. The Path of Love and Harmony is the Way of directing your mind to what it is you want to be in your heart – an expression of your true essence in the ordinary things of everyday life – and by so doing, experiencing the extra-ordinary. A fundamental purpose of our existence is to enable our Spirit essence to shine through in the way we live our lives.

The truth about who you are, what you are, and what is your essential Spirit-energy-expression, is within you – and that is so for all of us. It is known in the heart, but we have been 'disconnected' or it has been obscured by past conditioning. It

is comprehended first by the *heart* before understanding is imparted to the *mind*, because it is essentially spiritual rather than mental. Only by making connections with different aspects of ourselves in different dimensions can realization and recognition take place. Recognition that the 'I' that is within you is what enables you to be aware of your own existence. Realization that the 'I' that is within you is not the same awareness as the 'I' that is within me and within others, but shares the same '*alive*-ness' because the same Life Force that is in us is the life of the Universe also.

You are the Universe experiencing being *you* – looking out on itself through your eyes. Through your 'I's'! And I am the Universe experiencing itself through my 'I' – my 'I's'. So it is with everyone and with everything. Each of us is a perception point of awareness enabling the Universe to expand awareness of itself!

We come into these dimensions of Space and Time to experience ways of transforming energy, for the human body is a unique and highly sophisticated vehicle for exchanging energy with the body of the Universe. Your physical body and mine are thus not separate from the Universe, but part of it. Such a realization liberates us from the limiting conditioning that sees each of us as separate beings in an impersonal and hostile Universe, dependant on some beneficent deity who is regarded as an external designer of Nature, like an inventor of a machine. It is not even that we are a *part* of Creation, separate from the Source, or even part of the *Experience*. We *are* the Experience! We are each responsible not only for our own development, or lack of it, but also for supporting the growth and cultivation of other living beings in the sustenance of the harmony of the Whole.

So, no longer is there a need to philosophize and speculate on such questions as 'Does God exist?' because *you* exist. You *know* you exist because you are self-aware. And you are self-aware because you are a Spirit and only Spirit can generate *awareness*. And Spirit cannot cease to exist because it is non-material and not conditioned by either Time or Space. You – the physical you – have direct access to that True Reality because it is within you. It is the source of you – the physical you – which is an expression of It. That is your True Reality.

In the Reality of what *is*, energies we put into action either

come back to us empowered and enriched to renew and energize us for our further development and evolution, or they pull us towards Chaos and confusion on a downwards path of devolution.

The True Reality cannot be contained in a building or in the pages of a book. It cannot be 'owned' by an organization, nor are there individuals who are closer to it than others. What some people call 'God' is a presence that can be found only through an inner search, and then *experienced* directly as the Source from which we came and also as the Source of what we *are*.

So-called 'primitive' peoples have, perhaps, come closer to an understanding of the True Reality than the conditioned minds of great intellects. For instance, Aborigine legends suggest that the Sun, Moon and Stars were each fashioned from the dreams and actions of Creative Ancestors – beings who existed in a time before Time began. According to this understanding, the Earth and its environment; the seas and continents; lakes, rivers and mountains; trees and plants; creatures that swim, crawl, run or fly; and human beings, were each created in accordance with the 'dreamings' of these Original Beings, and are manifestations of those Dreamtimes. Again, according to the legends, these Original Beings became the potencies within that which had been brought into manifestation so they could experience for themselves any part of the Creation they had helped the Creative Source to bring about.

What such legends were imparting was an understanding that everything in physical reality – including you and me – is a perception of the Creative Source's consciousness, and every form – including ours – is an imprint which mirrors a facet of Itself. Everything has been brought into manifestation through a combination of primary universal energies integrated into unique patterns.

A similar understanding is contained within the mythology and oral traditions of other cultures which also are built around racial or tribal 'memories' of an earlier wisdom. What they are telling us is that we each have our own individual identity within a Greater Body; we each share a common purpose in sustaining that Greater Body, and we each have an individual mission within that Greater Body. The common purpose is to discover what we are, who we are, and why we are as we are –

and what potentials we possess for expression. Our individual mission is to discover our own uniqueness and not only to develop the potentials we have, but to find ways of giving them expression that will be in harmony with the Whole. When I write about meaning and purpose in life, I am not inferring that there is some heavenly bureaucracy that determines the course of our individual lives; rather, that meaning and purpose are actually within each of us. But each of us must discover this for ourselves. A 'teacher' can give only helpful *indications*. We must each make the discovery ourselves and give expression to that meaning when we have found it.

The Wonder at the very core of each of us is that we are not simply a part of a progressive Creation that is still going on, but that Creation is within us and *with* us. We are absorbed in it and permeated by it and are thus imbued with an ability to be *co-creators*!

Free to create beauty and harmony out of loving concern.

Free also to create ugliness and despair out of self-interest.

When we create for harmony and beauty we have the support of Nature and every living form, for they are our 'relatives' – all with origins in the One Ultimate Source.

When we create for self-interest, Nature is subdued and exploited and living creatures are treated as 'objects' to be taken and 'used' to satisfy the lusts of self-will. This ultimately leads to Chaos. Actually, it is not a choice between Love and Harmony and self-interest. It is a choice between serving our True Self – our greater Self – or our Ego-self. When we act out of self-interest and Nature is subdued and exploited to serve the wants and wastefulness of a consumer-oriented society with little or no regard for its effects on the Whole, and living creatures are regarded as 'there' for the taking to satisfy human needs, then Nature no longer supports us.

The world we are surrounded by is the result of what we humans have done collectively with the powers of co-creation. We have each of us contributed – by word and deed, lethargy and ignorance – in making it what it is. The world 'out there' is the one we have created. Where have we all gone *wrong*? We have mistaken the appearance for the Real, accepted a substitute for Reality. What most of us regard as the *Real* world is actually a *substitute* world of cultural and historical conditioning. It has been created by the thought processes and belief

systems that actually *deny* us our power to be what we are, and hold us in the grip of a continuous cycle of restriction and insecurity, and in a fear that locks us into a dependence on *them*.

The *Real* is the primary reality of the Universe. It is the way the Universe **is**. It is how the Universe works from the *inside*!

No longer is it necessary for you and I to continue the search for the mystery of who and what we are. It was here within us all the time. We just looked everywhere else but there. It is this recognition that since ancient times has been called enlightenment.

The ancient Chinese ideogram for 'enlightenment' can be pronounced *Wu Li* (Woo Lee). *Wu* can mean energy and matter. *Li* can mean an organic pattern, like the grain in wood. So Wu Li can mean 'patterns of organic energy'. It also has another meaning: 'My Way' or 'My Heart'. This is interesting because to the Native American, life was regarded as a 'dance' – an expression of patterns of energy. The salutation 'Dance in Beauty' might be interpreted, 'Let the patterns of energy expressed by the way you live your life be ones of beauty', for then others would be touched by beauty. Enlightenment, then, is a realization that your life should be an expression of how your Soul wants you to move your patterns of energy – in a natural way so they resonate in harmony with your Spirit. That is what was meant when the Medicine Wheel was described by Native Americans as 'the Way with Heart'. It is a way of bringing all your Life-energies into harmony with the Spirit that is within you – bringing that which is the You within you to experience life through your eyes, your ears, your touch, your taste and your smell. Through your mind. Through your Soul. Through your Heart!

To the kahuna shamans of Hawaii, to know the Way was to know the One that is within us and to bring it into the Heart. That was the Taoist Way of Virtue also. And the Way of the Rainbow Bridge of the ancient Northern peoples. The Dreamtime Path of the Aborigines. The Peaceful Way.

To be peaceful means more than just an avoidance of conflict in the physical world. It means following a way of living that is in harmony with Nature and is respectful of all life forms. Peace is not just a condition that exists outside ourselves. It comes from within our own being and is a condition of

thinking and acting. It is a way of life which begins in the heart and recognizes a divine Light that shines within. It is this Light that can reveal to us every aspect of our multi-dimensional being and shine out to enable us to recognize the beauty that is in others and to acknowledge the place of each in the overall scheme of things.

This essence honours all teachings, all teachers, all ways, all paths, all 'medicines' that are imparted in Love and work towards Harmony, for the purpose of helping struggling humanity to find the Inner Light within. To find the Beauty Way – the beautiful way – the natural Way of Love and Harmony. The Way with Heart. The Way with Heart which leads us closer to the Sun. Closer to the Source. Where Eagles fly.

The Commission given to me by Medicine Chief Silver Bear

Make a lantern,
Lit from the Red Indian fire
And whose light shines clear
For the way you've come
To be seen and marked,
And the way ahead to hold no fear
For others who come after you
To walk with an assurance,
Seeing by light from a torch you have left.
For those who walk this Path
Should not be left to grope in the dark
When light can make them aware
That the Path is beautiful
And the steps they take
Can be a choreography of beauty, too.
For this Path is the Beauty Way, the beautiful way,
Where all who will may Dance in Beauty
Around their own hearth fire
What they need to light the Way
Is a lantern that is bright.
So make one.
Lit from the torch you have been given.
The eight-rayed Torch,
The Flame Within
That illuminates the Eight Directions
And the Eight Dimensions.
Make one.
Be a Sun, Grandfather.

(This book is the fourth component of that Lantern)

Fifty Shamanic Meditations

Written and compiled by Kenneth Meadows

Adversity is not the punishment of an angry deity, but an interplay of energies that provides opportunity for growth in a new direction.

At the moment of its emerging, a seedling contains the complete pattern for its entire growth – perhaps into a great and magnificent tree. So it is with us. Except that we have the power to choose, and therefore have control of our own development.

Be wary of leaders who keep their followers in a state of continual dependence.

By the choices we make, changes are brought into our lives.

Celebrate each day as it comes to you as if it is the only one in your entire existence.

Compassion comes through a recognition that all living creatures are our 'relatives'.

Creativity is not the making of something through a quality of the mind. It is a spontaneous movement of Spirit energy within the Soul, like the revolving of the Earth round the Sun which creates night and day.

Deceitful people are those who look only for ways of taking advantage of you.

Detachment does not mean retreating from the world to escape its responsibilities. It is being *in* the world but not *of* it.

Determination is the power that gives momentum to desire.

Everything that can be understood is already within us.

Experience is the ultimate teacher, for then belief in the words of another is no longer necessary. You know it for yourself.

Find the Centre and you are in touch with the Whole.

Follow your heart, for what you feel is nearer the truth than what you think.

Forgiveness is a power that lets in Light from the Soul and can remove any darkness that is clouding your life. It is a preliminary 'give-ness' – a giving which opens the way to a special kind of receiving.

God, the Great Spirit, or whatever name we give to our Original Source, finds expression not in miracles but in the simple things of our everyday activities.

Gratitude is the recognition of the preciousness of ordinary things.

Happiness is unattainable alone for it can only be shared.

Information needs to be internalized before it can be of practical value.

Innocence is not that which is separate from moral wrong, for innocence is not divisive. An innocent child lives for the moment. The past is forgotten and the future does not exist. Only the moment has importance. That is innocence.

Joy is the gladness that springs from the wonder of being alive to enjoy the moment.

Knowledge is the effect of learning.

Knowledge that is of the greatest value is that which reveals the things that have kept us in the comfort of ignorance and stirs us with the challenge of pursuing it further.

Let not those who would deprive you of your freedom to choose, have power over you.

Look to a Way that is not a route to a destination but rather the journey itself, for you cannot become what it is you aspire to unless you can be it where you are now.

Love sets no conditions on itself nor seeks something in exchange for itself, and by giving of its entirety does not deplete but expands itself.

Maturity comes through mortality. That is why your Spirit requires you to be human, so it, too, may develop its fullness.

Movement without purpose is meaningless.

Natural is being what you truly are and not what others might suppose you to be.

Not to be aware of your own Inner Light is to live in darkness.

Omnipotence is to experience the one-ness not only of all life but of all your lives.

Once you remove the attachments that hold you fixed and stagnant, your life can begin to flow again and your circumstances are then free to change.

Past, present and future are but a constantly moving moment which embraces the whole of Time.

Philosophers are seekers who think about what they find and so remain thinkers. Believers are seekers who believe what they are told and so become followers. But the purpose of seeking is to live what is found so that one can become a know-er.

Quite simply, Spirit is a state of being.

Rainbows are a demonstration of all colours combining together into a wholeness, and illustrate that separateness is an illusion. A rainbow indicates that all paths that are harmonious are ways to wholeness, all races are part of a greater unity, and all paths that create beauty are deserving of respect.

Recognize that Spirit is the purest form of energy and the essence of that energy is Love. Why, then, is there so much misery, despair and unhappiness in the world? Because humankind has allowed the mind to be controlled by the Ego and the Ego has been allowed to supersede the Spirit.

Soul's purpose in your life is what you have the potential to accomplish.

Spirit is obscured when the Ego is allowed to get in the way.

Take anything to its extreme and you lead it to its destruction.

The most joyful sounds are heard not with the ears but with the

Spirit. Only by finding the solitude of our own personal Quiet Place can we experience the sound of the silence.

The Spirit has substance and has no form, but it can wear a multitude of faces.

To love Nature is to love your Real Self, for Nature itself is an expression of the essence of what you are.

Truth wears many masks in order to teach us not to mistake appearances for the reality.

Understand this: the talents, skills and potentials with which you are endowed are tools for the fashioning and manifesting of your creative energies for the good of all and the harm of none, and so strengthen and cultivate your Spirit. Misused to serve only the Ego, they deprive others, harm some, and weaken the Spirit.

Value a teacher who leads you to the True Teacher within where the answers you seek are to be found, for such are rare.

When a weapon is held in the hand it begs to be used, for that is the intention of its makers.

Words are only symbols to enable communication to take place between mind and mind and enable us to comprehend the illusory world of 'appearances'. But words are imperfect and subject to interpretation and misunderstanding. Only communication between Spirit and Spirit makes it possible to experience the 'Real' world together.

You alone have the power to make something of yourself simply by choosing to do so.

YEHWAH is the 'I Am That I Am' whose name means: 'I Am Absolute Love and That Absolute Love is What I Am.'

Zero is the Nothing that precedes creation, out of which an infinity of numbers and combinations is possible, and to which everything returns, for it shares itself with all that can be numbered and contains within it everything in existence. An apt symbol for Great Mystery.

Glossary

Affirmation: A declaration of the determination of the inner power of the Spirit.

Alpha: A level of brainwave activity when the mind and physical body are in a relaxed state.

Ancestors: The Ancestors are not only our predecessors but also our own past lives which are present with us in our genes. Thus the cells of the physical body contain 'echoes' of our personal, family, national, and racial past, and have an influence on the way we perceive reality.

Archetype: A universal symbol of an energy-pattern that indicates how certain forces or influences are operating. An archetype is presented usually in human or animal form.

Aumakua: The parental Father/Mother 'guardian' Intelligence. The noblest aspect of one's total being, sometimes referred to as the High Self because it has superior wisdom and resides in the 'higher' dimension of the Soul.

Aura: A cocoon-like fibrous energy-field in which a life form is immersed.

Awareness: Being alert to what goes on outside and inside yourself. Awareness is a registering of activity and is a function of the Spirit.

Balance: A state of steadiness and equilibrium. An equal and harmonious relationship.

Belief system: A religion or philosophy of not knowing, which rests upon faith in the word or authority of another.

Buffalo: A natural symbol of the Universe to the Native American

because historically the buffalo provided food, material for clothing, shelter, utensils, tools and weapons, and thus represented the totality of all that was manifested.

Causal healing: Causal healing centres around an understanding that an illness or adverse physical condition is essentially an energy imbalance, and that the cause of that imbalance not only lies beyond its physical manifestation but has a fundamental purpose. In other words, because the physical body is manifesting a state of disharmony, it wants also to communicate what has caused it to react in this way in order that harmony may be restored. The shamanist, functioning as a catalyst rather than a therapist, endeavours to discover the cause of an imbalance through direct contact with the body Intelligence.

Centred: A state of calm receptivity and equilibrium in which attention is no longer directed towards meeting the expectations of others. A condition of being yourself.

Chakra: A Sanskrit word meaning 'wheel' or 'disc'. A chakra is a wheel-like spiralling power centre located in the Energic Body. It serves as a 'gateway' between different levels or planes of existence and between different states of awareness, and receives, assimilates and distributes subtle energies that are pulled into its whirlpool.

Chaos: An unorganized and disorderly state in which random laws condition existence and in which untransformed energy moves freely and without direction in a disruptive fashion.

Chi: An activating essence that energizes all living beings and provides a state of 'aliveness' and wholeness.

Clairvoyance: An ability to perceive energy-fields that are beyond the range of normal sight.

Consecration: An act of setting aside for specific use. It involves cleansing, purification, dedication and empowerment.

Cosmology: A system of comprehending the geography of non-ordinary reality.

Cosmos: The organized intelligence of the Universe, functioning in accordance with natural and Cosmic laws, and thus law-abiding.

Death: A transition from one state of being to another in a continuous cycle of change.

Divination: A means of observing energy-patterns that are in the process of moving into physical manifestation.

Drumming: A sonic method of enabling the awareness to transfer from ordinary reality into a non-ordinary state.

Earth Medicine: A system of personality profiling and self-realization based upon Medicine Wheel principles and an understanding that Earth forces and Nature's energies prevalent at the time of birth influence the way we are to perceive life and present ourselves to the world. Earth Medicine might also be called Nature's 'Horoscope'.

Earthing: A method of ensuring that awareness is fully restored to ordinary reality after any form of shamanic or meditative work. Earthing serves as an 'off' switch from non-ordinary activity, ensuring that one is fully grounded.

Ego: One's sense of self-existence. A mental concept of self-identity. The personality 'I'.

Ego-self: The self-aware intelligence that functions in the physical and mental planes. That aspect of the human being Hawaiian shamans called *A-Uhane* – the 'spirit that talks'.

Elements: Expressions of the Great Spirit that are coming into manifestation to form physical reality. Powers that generate the movement of energies and the nature of that movement. Each Element has abstract qualities which can be comprehended in human terms by relating them to characteristics found in tangible earth, fire, water and air.

Emotion: A flow of energy from subconscious levels stimulated by thought and which is experienced as feelings.

Energy: The driving force that activates every function. Its power is in its ability to perform work.

Enlightenment: Empowerment to 'see in the dark' – that is, to perceive what is hidden from others.

Evil: Utilization of misdirected, misplaced or malignant energies contrary to the power of Love and in opposition to natural development.

Feather: A feather is symbolic of the human aura because it gives out impulses of high frequency energy, and its fibres are arranged in a structure that is similar to the threads of energy that comprise the aura. Feathers are used by shamans and shamanists as a tool to align auric fibres. The feather is also symbolic of a message or messenger and may also be used as a badge of office.

Fixation: A fixed belief which the subconscious mind has accepted as a result of past conditioning, and usually accompanied by a feeling

of guilt or shame. However much will power is exerted by the Ego-self in the area of the fixation, the subconscious 'self' – *Unihipili* – will refuse to obey unless the fixation is removed.

Free will: Liberty to learn by experience and to self-determine – that is, to have freedom of direction in determining one's own destiny.

Frequency: The vibratory rate of an energy-field or entity.

Gentleness: A power that causes no disturbance.

Gods/Goddesses: Higher intelligences that function principally through the mind. Celestial forces of great power that are personified by humans.

Harmony: A dynamic interchange of energies that resonate together in unison within one's own being and in relationship with others, to create a beneficial condition. Harmony is the creator of beauty in all dimensions of existence.

Hidden Self: The intelligence that functions at a subconscious level to perform and carry out what is required at a conscious level. It is sometimes referred to as 'the Child Within' because it has the nature of an obedient child. It is 'hidden' because it carries out its functions silently and 'secretly'. See also *Unihipili*.

High Self: The 'greater' Self – a higher aspect of one's composite being. The 'parental' spirit known as *Aumakua* to Hawaiian shamans. See also Soul Self.

Human Self: The conscious intelligence of a human being that functions through the five physical senses and the mind. It is the 'self' that is identified with human personality – the 'spirit' known as *A-Uhane* to Hawaiian shamans. See also Ego-self.

Imagination: An ability to allow pictures to form in the mind that stimulate the senses.

Inner light: The Spirit within that emanates from the centre of the Soul and is an individuation of the Great Spirit.

Inner space: A dimension of non-ordinary reality where Time is not constant.

Innocence: Complete impartiality and objectivity. The reverse of opinion and judgement.

Intention: A clear and precise instruction to the subconscious Hidden Self (*Unihipili*) to provide a route along which energy may flow to bring about a desired result. The energy is generated by motive (see Motive) and directed by the Will.

Intuition: A sudden 'knowing' that transcends the reasoning mind. Teaching from within.

Kahuna: A Hawaiian word meaning priest, teacher or expert, but when 'decoded' indicates a highly-skilled shaman who acts as a catalyst.

Karma: Life experiences revealed in one's destiny. Karma is a law of action and change in which repetitive conditions and circumstances indicate areas of life that are not working harmoniously, or which need to be experienced to further the individual's spiritual evolution.

Love: An unconditional, all-embracing expression of the Spirit which creates Harmony. Love is the substance of the Spirit, and the bonding force which holds together everything in existence.

Lower world: The reality experienced at subconscious levels of awareness.

Magik: A technique for bringing desired changes into physical manifestation. A process of crafting and shaping one's life. Not to be confused with the magic of the clever illusionist and of superstition, or with the magick of the ceremonial occultist or sorcerer.

Mana: A vital force that is the pure energy of creation. See also *Chi*.

Mandala: A universal circular symbol which, as well as being an expression of the wholeness contained within the totality of life, represents the Self and the Source.

Medicine: Inherent power that imparts strength and understanding and restores wholeness.

Medicine Wheel: A multi-functioning and multi-dimensional symbolic device for making connections and finding direction. A means of coming into harmony with the forces of Nature and with ourselves.

Mind: An intangible receptacle in which information is processed. Thoughts are the movement of energy-patterns within the reality of the mind and which can be shaped and fashioned to manifest in physical reality. In shamanic understanding, the mind should serve the Spirit.

Motive: The choice of direction in which energy is generated to flow.

Nagua: The hidden or unseen realm of the Spirit. The 'unknown'. That which transcends Time and Space.

Path: A route the awareness may take within and between dimensions, or a channel along which information may be carried by the consciousness.

Power spot: A place which emits energy that has a beneficial effect on the person or persons there. A personal power spot is an indoor or outdoor place which has a harmonious atmosphere in which personal empowerment may be attained.

Problems: The effect of negative choices which work against our natural being and alienate us from another aspect of ourselves. Negative choices are made when we isolate a part of ourselves from the totality of our being by thinking and acting as if we exist only in physical reality.

Real: The Real is the way the Universe *is*. What most of us perceive as 'the real world' is a secondary one that is imbued with negative energies created by the thought processes of historical, cultural and social conditioning and belief systems.

Relaxation: A letting go of physical tensions and mental and emotional stress and a slowing down of the energy-system so that attunement is possible with subconscious activity.

Ritual: A method of converting thoughts into symbolic actions in order to impress the subconscious 'self' (*Unihipili*) to act on the intention.

Runes: Angular patterns of energy potencies within Nature and within ourselves.

Science: A systematic study and formulated knowledge of phenomena, with principles regulating its pursuit.

Self-interest: Self-willed energy characterized by a dedication to its own needs and unconcern for others. The essence of self-interest is separateness.

Sexuality: Expression of polarized life-energies inherent in all life forms and especially significant to humans. Sexuality is a process of bonding. It is concerned with continuance – with doing that brings joy.

Shaman: One who perceives what others cannot see, who understands that everything experiences its own awareness of 'aliveness', and who is able to explore dimensions other than physical reality.

Shamanic perspective: An understanding of the holistic and holographic nature of the Universe, and the application of that understanding to everyday life experiences.

Shamanics: A personal development process which incorporates the essence of universal shamanism – the ancient wisdom of the visionaries and 'Wise Ones' of many cultures and traditions – into a Science

of Living for modern times that is the most natural and practical of all metaphysical systems. A way of experienced and revealed knowledge that is motivated by the Spirit, enabling individuals to relate to Nature and come into harmony with the totality of their own being and so find meaning, purpose and fulfilment in their own lives.

Shamanism: The practice of the principles and techniques of shamans, which involves working with the powers of Nature that exist both inside and outside the individual as both manifest forms and unmanifest potentials. Learning by direct personal experience.

Shamanist: A person who applies the principles and teachings of Shamanics in furtherance of his or her own personal development and in service to others.

Sitting place: Your Earth Medicine birthplace on the Medicine Wheel, or the direction from which you are perceiving reality.

Skull: An ancient symbol of the seat of consciousness and of the existence of other realms of conscious awareness that lie behind the material, fleshly world of appearances.

Smudging: The use of smoke to clear away negative vibrations and to attract beneficial energies to oneself and others.

Soul: The body of Light-energy which enables the individuated Spirit within to express itself and gain experience at conscious, subconscious and superconscious levels. The vehicle of the Spirit and of Life-energy. A life-expression system which retains the essence of relevant life experience. The Soul retains what the individuated Spirit has accomplished with the Life Force.

Soul Self: The intelligence or 'spirit' of the Soul – the most perfected aspect of a total being – whose knowledge and wisdom is a summation of experience gained through many lifetimes. Hawaiian shamans called it *Aumakua*.

Spirit: The intelligent essence that animates a life form but which usually cannot be seen, though its presence is experienced. That which *is*. The intelligence 'within' that is aware of its own being-ness and alive-ness. Spirit is experienced as awareness of being.

Spiritual: The non-physical essential nature of a life form. The invisible reality behind physical appearance.

Spirituality: A quality of being rather than an activity of belief. Guided power. Being guided in one's actions by the Spirit within. Influence by principles rather than conditioning by rules and beliefs.

Stalking: The pursuit of and approach to energy-patterns required to fulfil shamanic work.

Substance: That through which energy may flow in order to perform its work.

Symbol: A means of exchanging energy between different planes of reality. Symbols are links between the objective and the subjective, between one level of consciousness and another.

Telepathy: Transference of thought by mental action.

Theta: A level of brainwave activity that is just above the unconscious.

Thought Form: A thought pattern which, through persistence, has stability and duration and takes on form by use of mental substance in the realm of the mind.

Timelessness: A state of no movement. Stillness. The Eternal Now.

Tonal: The known. The physical realm of mundane, everyday activity. The things you are aware of and which may be causing difficulties. Tonal problems are problems of everyday life. In the Tonal the Spirit experiences mortality and is conditioned by Time.

Totem: A symbolic sensor that serves as a link between levels of existence, and serves as an aid to comprehending non-physical powers and formative forces. Since a totem expresses the qualities inherent in the living entity it represents, it is thus easier to relate to and is a more effective learning aid than a geometric symbol or glyph.

Tracking: Following the signs that lead to where shamanic work may be performed.

Tree: A life form which has its expression in one place and lacks the freedom of mobility. In general terms, trees are guardians of the environment and of the entrances to other dimensions.

Truth: That which is effective. Truth is what works. What is often dogmatically asserted as Absolute Truth is but information.

Unconditional: Free of conditioning. Without the imposition of restriction, preference, expectation or distinction. Not being limited by the imposition of conditions.

Under-world: The non-ordinary reality of unconscious existence. The reality of the unconscious mind. The realm of activity of the intelligence of the physical body – the Body Self.

Unihipili: A Hawaiian word meaning the silent 'spirit' or servant 'self'. The subconscious.

Upper World: The non-ordinary reality of superconscious existence. The reality of the Soul. The realm of experience of the Soul Self – *Aumakua*.

Virtue: A positive attribute which supports the total being. A restoration to one's original nature.

Wakan-Tanka: The greater Spirit in manifestation, which Itself is evolving. The Great Everything.

Wheel: A hoop or circular container in which interrelated energies flow in circular, cyclical and spiralling movements.

Yang: The masculine, active, positive, conceptual force in all that manifests. Represented in some ancient cultures as the God-power behind Nature.

Yin: The feminine, passive, receptive, nurturing force in all that manifests. Represented in some cultures as the Goddess-power behind Nature.

Recommended Reading

AMERINDIAN

Andrews, Lynn V. *Teachings Around the Medicine Wheel*, Harper & Row, 1990.

Andrews, Ted. *Animal-Speak*, Llewellyn, 1994.

Eastman, Charles Alexander. *The Soul of the Indian*, University of Nebraska Press, 1980.

Ross, Dr A.C. *Mitakuye Oyasin* (We Are All Related), Bear, 1989.

Steiger, Brad. *Indian Medicine Power*, Para Research, 1984.

Sun Bear and Wabun. *The Medicine Wheel*, Prentice-Hall, 1980.

AUSTRALIAN ABORIGINES

Cowan, James. *The Mysteries of the Dream-Time*, Prism Unity, 1989.

Lawlor, Robert. *Voices of the First Day*, Inner Traditions, 1991.

KAHUNA

Bray, David Kaonohiokala and Low, Douglas. *The Kahuna Religion of Hawaii*, Borderline Sciences, 1960.

Hoffman, Enid. *Huna – a Beginner's Guide*. Whitford Press, 1987.

King, Serge Kahali. *Urban Shaman*, Simon & Schuster, 1990.

Long, Max Freedom. *The Secret Science Behind Miracles*, De Vorss & Co, 1988.

Melville, Leinani. *Children of the Rainbow*, Theosophical Publishing House, 1990.

Nau, Dr Erika S. *Huna Self-Awareness*, Samuel Weiser Inc., 1992.

TAOISM

Capra, Fritjof. *The Tao of Physics*, Flamingo, 1976.

Chang, Dr Stephen T. *The Great Tao*, Tao Publishing, 1985.

Kwok, Man-ho; Palmer, Martin and Ramsay, Jay (translators). *The Illustrated Tao Te Ching*, Element Books, 1993.

Hua-Ching, Ni. *The Complete Works of Lao-Tzu*. Shrine of the Eternal Breath of Tao, 1979.

Hua-Ching, Ni. *Tao, the Subtle Universal Law and the Integral Way*, Shrine of the Eternal Breath of Tao, 1979.

Legge, James. *The Texts of Tao*, Dover Publications, 1962.

Wing, R.L. *The Tao of Power*, Aquarian Press, 1986.

Zukav, Gary. *The Dancing Wu Li Masters*, Rider, 1979.

SHAMANISM

Alan, Fred. *The Eagle's Quest*, Mandala, 1991.

Cahill, Sedonia and Halpen, Joshua. *The Ceremonial Circle*, Mandala, 1991.

Doore, Gary. *Shaman's Path*, Shambhala, 1988.

Earley, J. *Inner Journeys*, Samuel Weiser Inc., 1990.

Eliade, Mircea. *Shamanism*, Princeton University Press, 1972.

Meadows, Kenneth. *Earth Medicine*, Element Books, 1989.

Meadows, Kenneth. *The Medicine Way*, Element Books, 1990.

Meadows, Kenneth. *Shamanic Experience*, Element Books, 1991.

Scott, Gini Graham. *Shamans and Personal Mastery*, Paragon House, 1991.

Summer Rain, Mary. *Spirit Song*, Donning Company, 1985.

Walsh, Roger N. *The Spirit of Shamanism*, Mandala, 1990.

Ywahou, Dhymani. *Voices of Our Ancestors*, Shambhala, 1987.

MISCELLANEOUS

A–Z of the Human Body. Reader's Digest Assn, 1987.

Crawford, E. A. *Chinese Elemental Astrology*, Piatkus, 1992.

Levine, Barbara Hoberman. *Your Body Believes Every Word You Say*, Aslan Publishing, 1991.

Rowett, H.G.Q. *Basic Anatomy and Physiology*, John Murray, 1959 and 1973.

Resources

Kenneth Meadows' *Shamanic Experience Drumming Tape*, mentioned in this book, provides a drumming sequence to induce a state of awareness in which shamanic consciousness may be experienced. This 60-minute audio-cassette includes narrated instruction and guidance.

Beryl Meadows' unique musical work, *Powers of Love*, is a musical journey of the Soul to other dimensions of experience, and contains much shamanic teaching in the lyrics. Its gentle melodies and sweeping orchestrations make pleasant listening for all musical tastes, and its inspirational theme has touched the hearts of all who have listened to it.

Both cassettes are available by mail order for £10 each (or foreign currency equivalent), including postage and packing, from:

Peridot Publishing
27 Old Gloucester Street
London WC1N 3XX
England

For information on seminars, workshops and tuition in Shamanics write to:

The Faculty of Shamanics
PO Box 300
Potters Bar
Hertfordshire EN6 4LE
England

A *Power-for-Life Kit* containing a beautifully-crafted multi-faceted crystal sphere, a pendulum, a crystal pyramid in a silk-lined container and a booklet of simple instructions written by Kenneth Meadows, to bring power into your life, is available (price £47 plus £1-50p postage and packing) from:

Crystal Balls Ltd.
PO Box 3232
London NW7 9LZ
England

Further information on Chi Dynamics is available from:

Gaye Wright
Creative Life Company
PO Box 227
Lutwyche
Queensland 4030
Australia

The author appreciates receiving letters from readers, especially those relating the benefits derived from practising the techniques imparted in this book. Although he cannot guarantee to answer every letter, please do enclose a stamped addressed envelope. Write to:

Kenneth Meadows
BM Box 8602,
London WC1N 3XX, England.

Index